AUTHOR'S NOTE

'The time has come,' the Walrus said,
 'To talk of many things:
Of shoes – and ships – and sealing-wax –
 Of cabbages and – kings – '
LEWIS CARROLL

THE title of *The Time Has Come . . .* is not altogether in-
appropriate in view of the fact that:

I spent four years of my youth in a *ship* and later, in others,
voyaged in Arctic Waters and the South Seas.

I have many times taken off my *shoes*, in order to admire
the magnificent interiors of most of the finest mosques in the
world.

During the three years that I was a member of the Joint
Planning Staff of the War Cabinet I sent and received
scores of top-secret documents in envelopes fastened down
with red *sealing wax*.

After the war, as a part-time occupation to assist food
supplies, I ran an amateur's market garden, and grew even
cabbages.

For a part of my life I was the wine-merchant to three
kings.

DRINK AND INK

An enthusiastic welcome was given by critics and readers to the first two volumes of Dennis Wheatley's memoirs. Reviewing the first volume in the *Daily Telegraph* David Holloway said: 'Mr Wheatley still writes with astonishing vigour'; and in his notice of the second volume, *Officer and Temporary Gentleman*, Graham Lord wrote in the *Sunday Express*: 'Dennis Wheatley had style. . . . It was a style of joyous exuberance in life that suffuses with lively fun almost every page of this vivid, entertaining and sometimes hilarious book.'

In this third and final volume of his memoirs Mr Wheatley covers the years 1919 to 1977. Returning to civilian life after service on the Western Front, he rejoined the family business and rapidly increased his knowledge of the vintner's trade. But like many of his generation he missed no opportunity to compensate for the 'missing years of youth' by playing a full part in the glittering whirl of the Twenties. Then a crisis in his personal affairs obliged him to look for a new career. So he began to write, and from the publication of his first novel, *The Forbidden Territory*, which was reprinted seven times in seven weeks, established his great reputation as an author. And with the coming of the Second World War, the already famous best-selling novelist was quick to look for new ways in which he could again serve his country. Following the war he resumed his successful writing career and continued to lead a varied and active life at home and abroad until his death at the age of 80 in November 1977.

Dennis Wheatley portrays these years in fascinating detail. He writes of travels to foreign lands, reveals much of the mystique of the publishing world, and also tells the story of how lasting romance came into his life. Like its warmly received predecessors, *Drink and Ink* makes compelling reading from first to last, combining personal recollection with shrewd observation of the wider world scene.

BY DENNIS WHEATLEY

NOVELS

Duke de Richleau:
The Prisoner in the Mask
The Second Seal
Vendetta in Spain
Three Inquisitive People
Forbidden Territory
†The Devil Rides Out
The Golden Spaniard
†Strange Conflict
Codeword – Golden Fleece
Dangerous Inheritance
†Gateway to Hell

Gregory Sallust:
Contraband
The Scarlet Impostor
Faked Passports
The Black Baroness
V for Vengeance
Come into My Parlour
Traitors' Gate
†They Used Dark Forces
Black August
The Island Where Time Stands Still
The White Witch of the South Seas

Julian Day:
The Quest of Julian Day
The Sword of Fate
Bill for the Use of a Body

Roger Brook:
The Launching of Roger Brook
The Shadow of Tyburn Tree
The Rising Storm
The Man Who Killed the King
The Dark Secret of Josephine
The Rape of Venice
The Sultan's Daughter
The Wanton Princess
Evil in a Mask
The Ravishing of Lady Mary Ware
†The Irish Witch*
Desperate Measures*

†To the Devil – a Daughter
†The Satanist

The Eunuch of Stamboul
The Secret War
The Fabulous Valley
Sixty Days to Live
Such Power is Dangerous
Uncharted Seas
The Man Who Missed the War
†The Haunting of Toby Jugg
Star of Ill-Omen
They Found Atlantis
†The Ka of Gifford Hillary
Curtain of Fear
Mayhem in Greece
Unholy Crusade
The Strange Story of Linda Lee*

SHORT STORIES

Mediterranean Nights

Gunmen, Gallants and Ghosts

HISTORICAL

'Old Rowley': A Private Life of Charles II (*Illustrated by Frank C. Papé*)
Red Eagle (*The Story of the Russian Revolution*)

AUTOBIOGRAPHICAL

Stranger than Fiction* (*War Papers for the Joint Planning Staff*)

Saturdays with Bricks*

MEMOIRS: THE TIME HAS COME . . .

The Young Man Said 1897–1914*
Officer and Temporary Gentleman 1914–1919*
Drink and Ink 1919–1977*

SATANISM

The Devil and All His Works*

All these books, with the exception of those
marked*, are available in The Lymington Edition
†Black magic stories

Wine merchant and author

THE TIME HAS COME...

The Memoirs of
Dennis Wheatley

Drink and Ink

1919–1977

HUTCHINSON OF LONDON

Hutchinson & Co (Publishers) Ltd
3 Fitzroy Square, London wip 6jd

London Melbourne Sydney Auckland
Wellington Johannesburg and agencies
throughout the world

First published 1979
© Dennis Wheatley Ltd 1979

Set in Monotype Baskerville

Printed in Great Britain by
The Anchor Press Ltd and bound by
Wm Brendon & Son Ltd
both of Tiptree, Essex

isbn 0 09 136680 1

I dedicate these memoirs
to

My father, my grandfathers and
to my great friend in the First
World War, Gordon Eric Gordon-Tombe,
who, between them, made me what I am.

PUBLISHER'S NOTE

Drink and Ink brings to a close Dennis Wheatley's memoirs, which have the overall title of *The Time Has Come* . . . . The present volume covers the years 1919 to 1977 and completes the autobiography which he began with *The Young Man Said* and continued in *Officer and Temporary Gentleman*.

The millions of readers who grieved to learn of his death in November 1977 will however be glad to know that one further book by Dennis Wheatley remains to be published. This will deal with the years 1941 to 1944 when, recommissioned in the RAFVR, he filled a specially created post on the Joint Planning Staff of the War Cabinet. As this book, *Secrets of the War Cabinet*, is concerned with the strategy and conduct of the war seen from an unusual standpoint and not with Dennis Wheatley's personal life, it will be published separately from the sequence of his memoirs.

In the meantime, the directors of Dennis Wheatley Ltd join the publishers in expressing their thanks to Anthony Lejeune for his help with the preparation of *Drink and Ink*.

CONTENTS

ILLUSTRATIONS

PART ONE

Drink

MAYFAIR 1919 AND MY FIRST
SEA VOYAGE

On 1 January, 1919, I went back to work at 26 South Audley Street in the office I had left four years and four months before to become a 2nd Lieutenant in the 2/1st City of London Royal Field Artillery (T).

Technically I was still a soldier as, having got myself boarded fit on 13 November, I had hastened to London to participate in the Armistice rejoicings. After a fortnight's leave I was liable to be sent abroad again on active service. But I took that risk and pulled it off. No order reached me to report anywhere or notice that I was discharged; so I remained on leave, spent a merry Christmas with my mother, father, sister and a group of their friends at the Grand Hotel, Brighton; then my father decided that in the New Year I should put off my uniform and again become a wine merchant.

I had little claim to style myself one; for my experience consisted only of spending the last nine months of 1913 in the cellars of Julius Kayser at Traben-Trarbach on the Moselle and the six months that followed in my father's business, either helping in the cellars or selling single bottles to ready-money customers.

Herr Julius adopted me as one of his family and could not have been kinder, but he never invited me to a tasting; so all I learnt in Germany was from spending my mornings bottling, corking, capsuling and labelling wines. I do not recall ever having discussed wines with my father either. I do not think he was really interested. He had had a hard youth, had been driven by his own father to sell, sell, sell and that remained his principal interest for the remainder of his life.

He was the second oldest of four sons, each of whom my grandfather Wheatley established in a separate business, then retired at an early age to Westgate. My father was put in charge of the wine merchant's, the others were poulterers and grocers. As our office was in the very heart of Mayfair it had great potentialities but for many years it had been an uphill fight. The majority of the nobility who, in those days, occupied the great houses that then formed Grosvenor and Berkeley Squares and the streets adjacent to them, had for generations bought their wines from Justerini and Brooks, Berry Brothers, Christophers and a few others who had been established for well over a century.

The one advantage we had over these aristocrats of the Trade was that we also supplied beers and mineral waters, which they despised. We stocked over forty different varieties and, as the wealthy early in this century often took cures at Vichy, Contrexéville, Evian and other spas, there was a considerable demand for their waters in London. We were, too, the biggest suppliers of both Schweppes soft drinks and Bulmer's ciders.

This gave us the 'in' to many big houses and, as at that time the ordering of all drinks was often left to competent stewards, more and more of them could be persuaded to have Wheatley and Son send in a few cases of wines or spirits. In this way my father gradually built up a business which, while still not comparable with the best of the old-established firms, became a prosperous concern and one on which the principal wine shippers called regularly.

During the war Mayfair had not perceptibly changed. The square mile bounded by Park Lane, Oxford Street, Bond Street and Piccadilly consisted almost entirely of the great houses of the rich, and Embassies. With very few exceptions the only shops were in North and South Audley Streets, Mount Street and Shepherd's Market. The latter was Mayfair's red light district; the commodious flats above the others were mostly the London homes of young men about town.

Our premises stood on the corner next to the Grosvenor Chapel, separated from it by a useful cul-de-sac leading to

the small public garden at the far end of which lies Farm
Street Church. The office was long and narrow, the shop
occupying the corner and, further in, three rooms for inter-
viewing special customers and writing up ledgers. On the
board floor of the shop fresh sawdust was scattered every
morning and the whole place was panelled with hideous
pitch-pine; but this was largely obscured by shelves of
bottles.

My father no longer worked there. At that time the
northern end of the National Provincial Bank, almost opposite to us, was a shop. My father's ambition led him to take
a lease of it and make it into a well-furnished private office
where he expected to receive his most important customers.
But the venture was a failure. Hardly anyone except members
of the Trade, seeking orders, ever went there. Our old
customers continued to come to No. 26; so he spent most
of his days with a solitary assistant making out accounts,
which he always did himself as we did not employ a
typist. This proved a bore as we often needed the ledger and
it frequently had to be fetched from the other side of the
street.

Prices of wines had gone up very little. From a list I see
that Graves and Italian Vermouth were 3/– per bottle,
Sherry and Port 5/–, but spirits were much more expensive
than in pre-war days: Gin 9/–, Whisky 12/–, Hennessey's
XXX 17/6, Crème de Menthe 13/6 and Benedictine 18/6.

We were still living out at Streatham and I continued to
see a lot of beautiful Barbara Symonds, with whom my long
affair seemed to be going well. My principal friends were
Cyril Moat – nicknamed Tanko – who had been my companion while convalescing at Staines for several months in
the summer of 1918 and Cecil Cross, a pre-war friend who
had survived the war in the Westminster Dragoons.

I say 'principal' because I saw much more of them than
I did the most intimate of all my friends. This was Gordon
Eric Gordon-Tombe. We had shared a hut at Luton for over
half a year before I was sent to France in August 1917. He
had a great sense of humour, was completely immoral and
immensely knowledgeable. He weaned me from reading

trash to books by the finest authors of all nations, and to books about ancient civilizations and the occult.

Gordon Eric was also a crook of the first order. He never robbed people, but swindled insurance companies and the government out of considerable sums. In the latter years of the war he had a job in the Air Ministry, and a friend of his, an Australian named 'Bill' Dyer, remained on there for a year or more. When the war ended thousands of claims came in from engineering firms, large and small, for work on machine parts uncompleted and no longer required. Dyer's job was to vet these claims and okay them for settlement. Gordon Eric conceived the plan of starting a number of small-part suppliers in London and various other cities. This entailed, of course, opening and operating bank accounts, printing stationery, putting in telephones and a girl – one of Gordon Eric's mistresses – to staff the almost empty office behind thick window curtains. From each of them Gordon Eric sent to the Air Ministry a claim for several hundred pounds as compensation for work that had not even been started. Dyer promptly okayed it, the cheque went through the bank, Gordon Eric drew the cash and a few weeks later the firm closed down leaving no forwarding address. It entailed extraordinary organizing ability and brought the two conspirators many thousand pounds.

When Gordon Eric had been in the Air Ministry his job had been to inspect progress in factories, mainly in the Midlands and the North. He was frequently entertained by their owners and in Huddersfield by a wealthy manufacturer whom we always referred to as ''Undreds an' 'Undreds', who had a very lovely wife, much younger than himself. An affair developed between her and Gordon Eric. After the war she took a large flat in Knightsbridge where Gordon Eric lived with her for considerable periods. She was very charming, always beautifully dressed and became a great friend of mine.

Neither I nor his mistress-in-chief knew anything of his nefarious activities until after his death. While playing the role of the Joyful Hedonist, enjoying every pleasure that came his way, he created a succession of cul-de-sacs which prevented any of his associates, girl friends or men, learning anything about the others.

In May 1918 I had been gassed in France and invalided home. Eight months of convalescence had still not cleared my chest of the chlorine gas, so I continued to suffer attacks of bronchitis brought on by foggy days. In the spring my father generously decided to send me on one of the first post-war cruises to the sunshine.

I sailed from Liverpool on 12 March in the ss *Andorinha*. The normal cruise took, I think, about three weeks, but it was prolonged for me by stopping off for a fortnight on Madeira, and by unforeseen delays both in the Bay of Biscay and in Lisbon.

I have crossed the Bay at least fourteen times, but never again did I meet with really bad weather. The poor little *Andorinha* ran into a tempest. For most of the time the decks were a swirl of water as huge waves crashed upon them and nearly everyone was seasick. I managed to hang out, but only because I was put on to the age-old preventative, which is sipping Champagne and chewing dry biscuits.

After twenty-four hours of this frightful buffeting the Captain feared that the ship would capsize. He took the extreme measure of altering his course by ninety degrees and heading straight out into the Atlantic, so that instead of the great waves hitting her sideways on she should face the gale and cut through the wave crests with her bow. For three days we suffered while rushing up mountains of water then plunging down their far sides. No meals could be served; one could not get any rest at all; every cabin was awash, with broken gear and sodden clothes floating about its floor.

At last the tempest eased. I then witnessed a sight that everyone has heard of but, I imagine, few people can have seen. Oil was poured on the troubled waters. Fearing the ship might yet capsize as he turned her back on the course for Lisbon, the Captain had a large barrel of oil poured overboard. The effect was astonishing. Within a few minutes the rough seas for a mile around the ship subsided. The oil, only a fraction of an inch thick, spread out turning the sea into an undulating calm.

In Lisbon it had been intended that we should berth for only one day, in order to unload a small cargo of merchandise. But we arrived to find a revolution in progress. The convicts had been released from the prisons and a general strike had been declared, but there was no fighting and we were allowed to go ashore. A British destroyer flaunting the White Ensign was anchored right in the middle of Lisbon harbour, and woe betide anyone who dared to lay a hand on a British subject or his property. Those were the days.

This pacific revolution did not trouble us in the least. The hotels, shops and night-clubs were open and the people in them most friendly. The Army carried on as though nothing unusual was happening, and we were greatly amused when on 21 March a splendid parade marched through the streets to celebrate the anniversary of the great battle in which our gallant allies had 'saved the Line on the Western Front', when we were well aware that they had fled like rabbits, their General even jumping into his car clad only in his pyjamas in his haste to get away from the attacking Germans.

Our next call was Funchal, the capital of Madeira, a pleasant little town situated on a lovely bay. Half-a-dozen of us passengers landed there for a stay and Mr Reid, who owned the fine hotel on the great headland to the south side of the harbour, opened it up for us.

I had made numerous friends on our voyage out, and particularly during our week in Lisbon, so those of us who stayed off on Madeira were a happy little group. In addition, as a wine merchant I had been furnished with introductions to a number of Madeira shippers, including the Leacocks and the Blandys.

Madeira being a Portuguese possession, it had a Governor of that nationality. This was a much-sought-after post and few men were able to cling on to it for more than six months, because a small fortune could be made in that time by illicit means. Half-way between Reid's and the town lay the little Casino, to which we went most nights. By law, gambling was illegal, but roulette was played there regularly. Every night about nine o'clock a bell would ring, a large baize cloth was thrown over the roulette table and cards swiftly scattered on

it. The Governor would then make his entrance in full
uniform. As we stood up he would salute us politely and cry:

'Good evenings, leddies and gentlemens. I 'opes you 'ave a
good time.'

He would then disappear to collect his rake-off, the baize
cover was removed from the roulette table and the game
went on.

But it was Blandy who was really King of the Island. As
well as great vineyards, he owned extensive farm lands and
the immensely valuable concession to coal all ships that put
into the harbour. His home was a fine mansion on a mountain side, with marvellous views and the only grass tennis
court on Madeira.

One day Blandy took me for a tour of part of his estate.
It was still run on the medieval system that all the peasants
should bring their own grapes to his presses and their corn
to his mills. For pressing or grinding they paid him 10 per
cent of their crop.

In agriculture the peasantry had not changed from Roman
times. Blandy took me to a great barn. It was full of rusting
agricultural machinery. He had had it sent from England to
make their work easier and swifter. But they refused to use it
and insisted on continuing to use man-pushed ploughs.

One episode occurred in Madeira that I shall never forget.
Reid's Hotel stands at the base of the tall promontory which
forms one arm of Funchal Bay. Between it and the cliff are
several hundred yards of lovely gardens. Then, from the cliff
edge, a stairway of a hundred or more steps brings one down
to a platform about fifty by thirty feet in extent which has
been cut out of the rock so that visitors can swim from it.

One morning I went down there on my own. The place
had not been used for years, the two small wooden changing
cabins were a wreck and the whole of the platform was
covered with seaweed. This did not deter me from going in
for a swim. It was a lovely day and the water was pleasantly
warm.

After a while I thought I would swim across the bay to the
lighthouse on its far side. I was a fairly strong swimmer but
the light was so clear that it made distance deceptive. About

a third of the way across I suddenly realized that I could not possibly make it; so I turned back.

It was not until I reached the bathing platform that I found myself in real trouble. It stood about four feet above the average level of the sea; but rollers were coming in from the Atlantic; at times the wave crests broke only a foot or two below the platform wall, at others six or eight feet of it were exposed. Along it at intervals there were iron rings by which bathers could pull themselves out; but from years of neglect they had become overgrown with slimy green weed.

As each wave carried me in I tried to grab one of the rings but either I missed it or the slime caused my fingers to lose their temporary hold on it. Again and again receding waves swept me back twenty or thirty feet until I became breathless.

The hotel was out of sight a quarter of a mile away, there was no one in the garden, the bay had not even a rowing boat crossing it and the beach was deserted. I could have shouted for help with all the power of my lungs but there was not a chance in a thousand of anyone hearing me.

I realized that my only hope was to hold my breath and keep my head, so I began to tread water. Time after time incoming waves lifted and swept me towards the platform. Each time I made a grab at one of the slimy rings. At last, when I was nearly dead-beat, I succeeded in clutching one and keeping a hold on it against the pull of the receding rush of waves. For ten minutes at least I simply hung there until I got my breath back; then, as another wave broke over me, I made a final effort, hoisted myself over the edge of the platform and flopped down on it utterly exhausted – but still with another half-century of life before me.

It was at this time I suffered a most terrible blow. During my absence beautiful, golden-haired, blue-eyed Barbara Symonds had become engaged to my friend Cecil Cross. She had been the love of my life for over four years. There had been many other girls, of course, to whom I had been sexually attracted, but Barbara was my only real idyllic love and I had carried her photograph in a gold locket round my neck on a blue ribbon all the time I was on the Western Front.

I did not blame her because she had never made any pretence of returning my love; but since my return from France I had taken her to many dances and theatres and, although she did not conceal the fact that she went out with other men, we had recently become close enough to raise my hopes.

Cecil was another matter. I regarded his having stolen the girl whom he well knew to be my great love as an act of the basest treachery. But that is another story, and I have already told it in the second volume of these memoirs.

2

THE RELUCTANT REPRESEN-TATIVE, PARIS AND JAMAICA

ON my return to South Audley Street I resumed the jobs I had taken over in the New Year.

From ten until twelve I was supposed to call on the head men-servants of the aristocracy. All these top people below stairs expected not only to receive a commission but also to be visited from time to time. If not looked after, they could remove the custom of their masters by serving a bottle of indifferent wine which was supposed to be a fine one; or chefs could get the butcher changed by sending up steaks that had not been marinaded.

I enjoyed spending half-an-hour beside a blazing fire in their comfortable sitting-rooms, while drinking with them a glass of their masters' excellent wine. But this did not apply to the great majority. In the smaller households the butlers when off duty were a far from pleasant type. They secretly hated their employers and their only interest was racing. To me, some of them were unpleasantly servile and others openly rude.

The result was that, after a time, I gave up calling on any of them except those I liked; and I could not decently do that more than once in three weeks or so. Instead, I spent most mornings in a Lyons Tea Shop reading books, while eking out a couple of cups of coffee.

At midday I returned to the office and spent an hour selling wine and beer at our ready-money counter. Then in the afternoons I either helped in the cellar or worked on the Stock and Day books, of which I had been given charge. So perhaps I did earn the £5 per week which was my salary.

Peace having been declared, 1919 was a year of great

festivities. In an endeavour to put Barbara out of my mind I went to many dances and made love to a number of pretty girls. Having taken up my Freedom of the City shortly after my return from France, I also attended my first Vintners' dinner as a Liveryman. The menu was Mock Turtle Soup, Salmon, Whitebait, Supreme de Volaille, Roast Beef, Asparagus, Ham and Salad, Orange Jelly, Apricot Tart, Croûtes Ivanhoe, Dessert, Coffee.

The highspot was the Peace Celebration on 19 July, when probably the biggest parade ever marched through the streets of London. It started from Albert Gate at 10 a.m. Via Belgrave Square it crossed Vauxhall Bridge, took in Kennington and Lambeth, re-crossed the river over Westminster Bridge, went up Whitehall and along the Mall to salute the King while passing Buckingham Palace; then up Constitution Hill to Hyde Park Corner, where it disbanded at 12.20.

The procession was led by the Commanders of the thirteen Allied Forces, including Marshal Foch and General Pershing. Contingents of troops and bands from each country marched between them. Then came our own Forces led by Admiral Sir David Beatty, followed by many Admirals and detachments representing every activity of the Royal Navy. After them came Field Marshal Sir Douglas Haig, followed by over thirty Generals and scores of contingents from every arm of the Service, including, of course, troops from all parts of the Empire. There were dozens of bands, guns, trench-mortars, the Household Brigade, massed pipers and hundreds of regimental standards. No Triumph can have equalled it since the days of Ancient Rome.

We were particularly lucky, because the narrowest street of all through which the procession had to pass was Pont Street. In it a builder named Smith had his office and he erected a stand in front of it, to which my mother, father and I were invited; as the great men rode by, we were near enough to have touched them with the end of a fishing rod.

Owing to my maternal grandfather's death in 1916, my parents now enjoyed a considerable income. They had a chauffeur-driven Wolseley which took my father and me to the office every morning. The 'Blood Money' paid out after the First World War was at a much higher rate than after the Second; so I put myself down for a Charron-Laycock. It was a powerful three-seater car, costing £515, and would have been great fun. But delivery was not promised for several months. In the summer the agents wrote to tell me that costs had compelled them to put the price up 30 per cent. For me this was fortunate, as it let me out, for, having spent all my 'Blood Money' by then, I could not have found even £500.

My father generously paid for the long novel I had begun in France and finished at Catterick to be typed; and I sent it to Cassells. They rejected it, and I am now very glad they did. The writing was so appalling that it was quite unfit for publication. By then I was far too immersed in collecting books and having affairs with pretty girls even to think of another attempt at writing.

My father was already a Liveryman of the Distillers and early in 1920 he also had me made one. Their dinners were more fun than those of the Vintners because many of my friends in the Trade were Distillers, whereas it was next to impossible to get into the Vintners except by being apprenticed while in one's teens.

My relations with my father, in spite of his generosity towards me, continued to be far from friendly. He disapproved of many of my activities, such as 'squandering' money on books, and particularly of my nights out with Gordon Eric.

Nevertheless, he must have recognized the fact that I had brains and competence, for in November he even proposed that, over a series of years, I should buy him out. Figures were gone into with the accountants and it emerged that I should have to pay him an average of about £3000 a year for seven years. The snag then arose that I had not a penny of my own, so could not guarantee even a part of the payment.

An attempt was made to provide me with capital by breaking my grandfather's Trust. He had left the bulk of his fortune to my mother, then – so I was told but rather doubted it – to my father, and after that to my sister and myself in such proportions as my mother might decide. However, the legacy was 'without powers of anticipation'. This was a precaution against our selling our prospects. The lawyers ruled that this clause debarred me from making use of the Trust; so the deal fell through.

After eighteen months in the business I still knew very little about wine; but I did know what I liked and was evidently blessed with a natural palate, as at professional tastings I have rarely failed to pick two or three of the best out of a dozen or more. In our own office we never had a tasting. My father, perhaps wisely, left it to friends he trusted among the shippers to send him the wines he required.

When customers died we frequently bought what remained of their cellars. This enabled me to drink with my father many of the finest Clarets of the 1870s, '74s and '78s which, after long maturing, had reached their peak by the 1920s. I was often asked by shippers to lunches in their offices in the city, which usually lasted about three hours and were great fun. At the end of the meal we always followed the old custom of each putting a half-crown in the kitty then writing on a slip of paper what we believed to be the shipper and the year of the vintage Port. It amused me to see that often it was a guest with nothing to do with the Trade who guessed right.

I have never been a great lover of Port and much prefer rich brown Sherry. But the trouble is that the only kind one can obtain in the normal way is sickly stuff. Wines of this kind need at least twenty years in bottle to become really palatable, and in Victorian times the rich used to lay them down as they did vintage Port. While Ports throw a crust each year, becoming thinner and paler with time, rich Sherries and Madeiras appear to last almost indefinitely. On several occasions I have drunk Waterloo Sherry laid down in 1815, and many beautiful Madeiras vintaged in early Victorian times.

All my life I have loved fine wine and am fortunate enough to have drunk some of the finest from every wine-producing country in the world. My favourites are the great Hocks, and it puzzles me that in recent years Hocks and Moselles have not greatly increased in price, whereas absurd prices have been paid for first-growth Clarets. In the 1920s a top Schloss Johannisberg or Steinberg Kabinet cost £5 per bottle, whereas few Clarets cost more than £1.

Although I had still not been discharged from the Army, I was sent for and medically boarded, then awarded a pension of £30 per annum. During the winter of 1919/20, my cough was very bad again, so in the spring my father generously sent me on another cruise, this time to the sunshine of Jamaica.

I sailed from Avonmouth on the ss *Camuto*, an Elders and Fyffes banana boat, which carried about sixty passengers. With an eye to enjoying the voyage I arrived on board early and, having had a look at my cabin, settled myself on a chair opposite the gangway down which the other passengers were coming aboard. Presently a group of five arrived, who I learned from the steward were a Mr and Mrs Lester, two pretty daughters and an elderly Colonel who was a friend of theirs. I then arranged for my deckchair to be moved so that it should be next to the group of chairs they had booked. Next morning I made their acquaintance, and it developed rapidly. The elder daughter, Jean, was certainly the prettiest girl in the ship and for the whole of the voyage we delighted in one another's companionship.

They were a county family and I don't think that they had ever before met a tradesman socially, so were much surprised on learning how I earned my living. But my manners were irreproachable, I was a good conversationalist and, after all, had held the King's Commission for over four years; so, after the first shock, pleasant Mrs Lester raised no objection to Jean and me disappearing after dinner into dark corners of the deck for long periods.

Long before we ploughed our way through the bright green weed of the Sargasso Sea to the blue waters of the Caribbean, I had been adopted as one of the family. On my trip to the Canaries I had seen dolphins but never before the great albatrosses and shoals of flying fish which enlivened our run down the long north coast of Puerto Rico. In Kingston, Jamaica's capital, the best hotel was the Myrtle Bank, and I was delighted to learn that the Lesters were all booked in here.

Five out of every six of the people staying at the Hotel were American Naval Officers, and at night the streets of the city could be dangerous. The reason for this was Prohibition. Cuba was then virtually a US colony, so was also dry; so, too, was the Fleet. In consequence, the American Naval C-in-C based the bulk of their fleet on Cuba. It spent two days each week patrolling there and the other five anchored off Jamaica, which was wet – very wet indeed. So wet that lorries ran through the streets every night for the Marines to throw in sailors who were too drunk to stagger any further.

As there was nowhere to go in the evenings we spent them dancing in the hotel, or strolling under a sky brilliant with stars among the palm trees in the big garden. The Negro servants were cheerful and respectful, the drinks cheap, and my affair with lovely Jean Lester continued most happily.

It was then that the Lesters found themselves in some difficulty. I had arranged to stay about three weeks, then return in the ss *Patuca*. They wished to stay about the same time but had not bothered to book their passage home. When they tried to do so they found to their dismay that no berths in the Elders and Fyffes ships were available for some three months.

As a wine merchant I had been given a number of introductions to rum distillers. I used these, and they took me over their plantations and entertained me most kindly. But it had never occurred to me to use an introduction that had been thrust into my hand at the last moment. It was to the General Manager of the United Fruit Company; and they ran the banana boats.

Hurrying down town I presented my letter to a Mr McCormack. He proved to be a charming little man, and I then made a discovery. Jamaica was undoubtedly a British possession, but it was virtually owned by the United States. Our Governor acted only as a figurehead. McCormack was the boy who counted. His company owned most of the plantations, the railways that ran through the island, half the wharfs in the harbour, most of the hotels and the race course.

I put my problem to the uncrowned King and he could not have proved more friendly. Of course the Lesters should return to England with me on the *Patuca* if they wished. He would see to it that accommodation was found for them. And would I be his guest at his box at the races next Sunday, bringing my friends with me?

It was in Jamaica that for the first time I saw the real tropics, the colourful birds, the tree ferns and the bright blue sea. I made several expeditions on my own. One was by car up to the top of the Blue Mountains. The road up the mountain consisted of simply a rough track along a steep gradient with many hairpin bends. Every time we reached one my Negro driver stopped the car, backed it until it was on the very brink of a precipice, then shoved the wheel round and dashed forward again at full speed. I was terrified.

In due course our party boarded the ss *Patuca* and sailed for home. I afterwards saw tall, slim, dark-haired Jean only twice: once shortly after our return, when she invited me to tea at a flat they had in St John's Wood; then many years later, when I had become an author, she came to hear me speak as Chairman at a Foyle's lunch.

When I had tea with her we discovered that we had no interests in common. Our lives were utterly different. Hers was county society, point-to-points and hunt balls; mine was that of a London suburbanite. Yet for a brief spell the Gods had blessed us with perfect companionship.

3

THE TWENTIES AND A NEW HORIZON

THE twenties were a wonderful decade to live in. By '21 the war was forgotten. We no longer sang, 'The roses are blooming in Picardy' but such songs as, 'She wouldn't do just what I wanted her to, so I sloshed her in the eye'. It was the age of 'The Bright Young People' who, under the benign Luigi's eye, dined and danced at the very exclusive Embassy Club; and who delighted in such jokes as dressing up as workmen and digging up a length of road surface in Piccadilly. I became a member of Ciro's, with its beautiful pillared ball-room and restaurant.

Among the lesser night-clubs was Rector's, a favourite haunt of Gordon Eric's. The dance hall was a big basement underground; so to keep it cool they always had a large block of ice on a table in the middle of the dance floor.

That Christmas we spent at the Grand Hotel with a party of friends: Sir Louis Newton, who had recently been Lord Mayor of London, his son Sidney, his two daughters, a Mr and Mrs Hilton, their daughter and a son named Wally. None of the girls attracted me but Wally was fun and through coming to know him I landed myself in another mess.

He was a leading light in an amateur acting society known as The Nondescript Players, which held rehearsals every Wednesday evening in a hall in South London not far from his home. I had no voice and no particular desire to become one of the chorus in musical plays; but I found that, as far as the men were concerned, the real object was to get merry on rounds of drinks at the local pub; so I let Wally persuade me to join.

The show being put on that year was *Miss Hook of Holland*.

B

After we had inflicted a full dress performance on an audience, I relieved my boredom by celebrating to such an extent that I was even tighter than Wally and two other chaps he was taking home in his car.

I insisted on his stopping at a lamp-post every few hundred yards, got out of the car and, raising my walking-stick, smashed the glass that protected the light. Encouraged by the others and accompanied by their songs and laughter, I had smashed a score or so of lamps when a policeman suddenly leapt out of a dark corner and grabbed me.

Very stupidly, as I might have received a huge sentence, I endeavoured to bribe the bobby to let me go, but he would not take the money and marched me off to the station, while Wally and the others followed slowly in the car.

When questioned by a sergeant my principal concern was to avoid a local scandal, but I knew that, if I gave a false name and the police traced me, I would be in still worse trouble. So I gave my first two names, Dennis Yeats, of 26 South Audley Street, and had to say I was a wine merchant.

Instead of putting me in a cell they let me sit in the office, which was entered by a short passage leading to the front door. From time to time Wally hooted on the horn of his car to let me know that he was waiting there to learn what was happening to me. Suddenly it flashed into my still bemused brain that with a little luck I might escape. When the nearest officer's back was turned I jumped to my feet and made a dash for the short corridor. Within seconds two policemen were after me, and one landed on my back throwing me face down on the floor.

But they were awfully pleasant about it, laughing the matter off as a joke. Then, ten minutes later, having told me that I was to report at the Bromley Magistrate's Court at ten o'clock on the Monday, they let me go and Wally ran me home.

The next day was Sunday. My wartime friend, Bertie Davis, lived not far off on Tulse Hill. He had already built up a good solicitor's practice, so I went to his home and poured out my doleful story.

Bertie proved a true friend. He scrapped his normal work

on the Monday morning to accompany and defend me at Bromley. He made an excellent speech about my war service and general respectability, so I got off lightly.

However, one most unpleasant happening did result from my stupid escapade. The following Sunday we had been asked over to lunch with the Newtons at Bromley. My father, Sir Louis and I were seated round a low table drinking Sherry before the meal. The local newspaper lay on the table opened at an inside page. Suddenly I saw that one column consisted of an account of my arrest and appearance in court for drunkenness. Obviously that ever-smiling but secretly malicious Lord Mayor had left it there to catch my father's eye. Fortunately it didn't, but I sat in torment for twenty minutes. After my father and Lady Newton were both dead, my mother married Sir Louis. I had very good reason to distrust my tortuous-minded new stepfather.

My holiday abroad in 1921 consisted of accompanying my Uncle Dennis to Corsica. We sailed in the Bibby liner, ss *Hertfordshire* from Liverpool round to Marseilles; but from there small steamers sailed for Corsica only once a week, so we had to spend several days in the big French port. My uncle was a rather silent man but good-natured and no prude. One night we went to the Red Light district, adjacent to the Vieux-Port. In the Second World War the Germans almost demolished it, which was rather a pity as it was one of the sights of Europe. The common whores each occupied a small room adjacent to the street. It had a bed and wash-basin at the back, and its door was in two parts like that of a stable. The top half was kept open while the painted lady sat behind the lower half, leaning on it and calling invitations to passers-by, who were mostly sailors. When she had attracted one he simply joined her, they shut the top half of the door and did that which there was to do.

There were also brothels, ranging from cheap to expensive. My uncle and I patronized one of the latter and, surrounded by near-naked beauties, watched a blue film – the only one I have seen in my life.

We also went out to the Château d'If, made famous in *The Count of Monte Cristo*. Afterwards we lunched at a large

Hotel Restaurant on the coast, next to the lovely villa with which the King of Spain provided his French mistress, the beautiful Gaby Deslys. It was some miles outside Marseilles and its cuisine was excellent. Some years later our visit there had most unexpected results. One winter my father and mother planned to spend a few nights in Avignon, Arles and Marseilles before going on to Menton. I suggested that they should stay at this delightful Hotel Restaurant on the shore, instead of in Marseilles itself; so my father wrote and booked rooms there. On their arrival they had a splendid dinner but a disturbed night because strange cries and laughter came through the walls from the adjacent rooms. In the morning my father complained to the manager, who smiled apologetically and said: 'When I received Monsieur's letter I feared there must be some mistake, and when I saw the great pile of luggage with which Monsieur arrived yesterday afternoon I became certain of it.'

He told my father then that the mansion was not a hotel in the ordinary sense but one of the most expensive *maisons de rendezvous* in the South of France, to which rich men took their pretty ladies to dine and spend the night. I need hardly add that, having re-packed, my parents had a car take them to more respectable quarters.

From Marseilles to Ajaccio was an overnight trip. I am told that during the past quarter of a century the island has become a pleasure resort, but in 1921 the number of visitors was very limited and there was only one passably good hotel, made mainly of wood.

Naturally we went to see the house in which Napoleon was born, but the Corsicans are more Italian than French and do not regard him as a national hero. If he is mentioned they make an ugly grimace and say, 'What did he ever do for Corsica?'

From Ajaccio we went to Corte, high up in the mountains in the centre of the island. The little train that took us there passed through many miles of deserted chestnut woods. In them, as in few other countries in Europe, small herds of wild *mouflon* still exist and make good game for the hunter. It was recalling the precipices many hundred feet deep surrounding Corte that later gave me the idea for my first – and perhaps best – published short story, *Vendetta*.

Leaving Corte we went down the far side of the mountains to the port of Bastia, where in May 1794 Nelson transported the guns of his ships to commanding positions on shore and so compelled the town to surrender. It was after this action and during the subsequent capture of Calvi that he lost the sight of his right eye. From there we paid a visit to Monte Carlo, where I made my first appearance in the famous Casino. But I was more intrigued by the shooting of clay pigeons from the terrace than by the mild gamble in which we indulged. During our drives along the coast I acquired a love for the beautiful South of France that in fifty years has never left me.

Back in London I was to find another love, if one can call it that, for it was neither profound nor long. One morning in Bond Street I stopped to look in Asprey's window. Prominently displayed was a figure of Kuan-yin, the Chinese Queen of Heaven. The figure's hand was raised, in the traditional attitude of listening to prayer. I murmured, 'Dear goddess, send me a pretty mistress.'

At that very moment reflected in the glass of the shop window I saw a pretty dark-haired girl walk past me. I turned at once and followed her. I decided to try and pick her up. It did not prove difficult. She had nothing to do that morning and was just out for a stroll.

I walked with her down to Hyde Park. After a while I learned that she was an artist's model and shared a room in a dingy boarding-house with another girl. It so happened that my father and mother were away at Harrogate so, being my own master, I took her out to lunch and spent the afternoon with her, returning to the office only in time to lock up.

During our hours together we had progressed quite a long way and, somewhat hesitantly, she had agreed to spend the next Saturday night with me. For such romps Gordon Eric and I had an admirable arrangement with the porter at Yeoman House, a block of furnished flats in the Haymarket. He was not supposed to let them for less than a week; but one was usually vacant for a while and by letting it to one of us for a night or two he could put the money in his own pocket.

On the Saturday I met the girl again and took her there. She had come from a poor home, but her accent was not common. She was only eighteen, in the first bloom of youthful loveliness, and her slender figure made her perfect for an artist's model. In bed she proved inexperienced but gave herself willingly.

For some weeks we continued our liaison and I was as kind and generous to her as I could be; but, unfortunately, she had nothing but her beautiful body to give. In consequence the affair gradually petered out.

Gordon Eric and I spent many hectic nights at Yeoman House. At times he would produce two of his part-time, broad-minded young mistresses. At other times I would dine with him and his elegant, permanent mistress who, of course, knew nothing of his infidelities, and with whom I formed a lasting friendship. Sometimes the three of us went to the theatre. We always went to each new series of short *grand guignol* plays at the Little Theatre. Some of these playlets were brief comedies, but most were horrors that chilled one to the marrow. Sybil and Russell Thorndike and Lewis Casson were the brilliant leads.

Among my papers I find a Statement of Expected Income for 1921. It totalled £530 10s. od. Not too bad in those days for a young man of twenty-four, particularly as I then paid only 2/3 in the £1 Income Tax.

In spite of my relative affluence, I continued to be perpetually hard up. More than once my father had to pay my debts and in the autumn of 1921 this was occasioned by what I considered an unforgivable act of treachery. The father of the charming, bemonocled Buchan, who secured for me my first commission, was a Director of the National Provincial, and after the war he departed for higher spheres. He was replaced as Manager by his Under-Manager, an unpleasant little blue-nosed Welshman, whose custom it was to come over to our office at eleven o'clock every morning, knowing that he could cadge a whisky and soda off my father. One day he told my father that my account was £10 7s. 4d. over-drawn. To reveal the state of one customer's account to another is, I have always understood, one of the most serious offences a Bank Manager can commit, and I suppose that had I reported the matter to Head Office he would have found himself in very hot water. But I was in no position to do that.

The reason for my sad financial state was the small contributions which were all that Gordon Eric would accept for nights out together, and presents to girls; but mainly expenditure on books and on a number of Globe Wernicke bookcases. I had not yet started collecting first editions but already had sets of Tolstoy, Flaubert, Gautier, Dumas, Oscar Wilde, Walter Pater, Victor Hugo, Gibbon's *Rome*, Grote's *Greece*, *Religions of the East*, Casanova, Stendhal, Burton's *Arabian Nights*, Havelock Ellis's *Sexual Psychology*, Motley, Proust and several hundred odd volumes.

The bank manager's disclosure resulted in a scene and I produced bills for clothes, theatre tickets, and so on, amounting to above £57, which my father paid for me.

That October my dear friend, Hilda Gosling, who through my teens had played the part of a sister to me, got married. She had fallen in love with a print-seller named John Gardner. He was a tall, fine-looking man, but far from well off, so Hilda's mother strongly opposed the match. Her jovial father, having died, could play no part in the matter.

I liked John and felt that, although he had little capital, there was a good chance of his doing well. After the war officers who applied were allowed six months' pay to study for a trade or profession. Although print-selling was not on the recognized list, John persuaded the officer who interviewed him to let him spend six months examining the print collection in the British Museum. For him that was an invaluable experience. In due course, he opened a shop in Buckingham Gate, and made a very good living.

I was best man at John and Hilda's wedding in St Leonard's Church, Streatham, and as a present they gave me a soapstone figure of Chao-Lao, the Chinese god of Wisdom, who

is said to have acquired his great knowledge through having
been carried in his mother's womb for eighty years.

The ceremony was performed by the Rector, Canon
Brook-Jackson. He too became a friend of mine, although he
was twice my age and aware that I never went to church on
Sundays. I think it pleased him to talk to a young man who
was seriously interested in history and was knowledgeable
about ancient religions. He was an enthusiastic collector of
Napoleana, had a big library about the Emperor and owned
a pair of slippers that Napoleon had used while in exile on
St Helena.

By November I had other things to think about besides
lack of money.

Up at Harrogate that year my parents met a Mrs Robinson,
and on their return to London asked her, her youngest
daughter, Nancy, and some other people to a dinner party
on 12 November.

Nancy was a lovely *cendré* blonde with beautiful, blue eyes.
She sat next to me at dinner and I learned that she was about
two years younger than myself. She was extremely vivacious
and amusing; and when we came to the Port and walnuts
stage she insisted on cracking the nuts for me.

The Robinsons lived in Clapham Park, a district that then
consisted of several long roads of large Victorian houses,
each having several acres of garden. Our car had been
ordered to take the Robinsons home, but when the time came
our chauffeur reported some fault in the engine. It was a fine
night and Clapham Park only a mile or so away on the other
side of the London–Brighton road, so I volunteered to escort
the ladies home. On the porch of their house as we said good
night I took Nancy's hand, bowed low over it and kissed it.

Next day I telephoned her and we dined together. Her
letter of thanks warmed my heart. I wrote to her comparing
her to Sheherezade. We dined again. Her second letter began
'Oh Prince of a Thousand charms'. Within a week of meeting
we were engaged to be married.

4

OF LOVE AND MURDER

It had been on a Saturday evening that Nancy and her mother had dined with us. On the Sunday eight days later I ordered our cautious but surly chauffeur to get out the car and drive Nancy and me to Eastbourne, where my parents had gone for a short stay at the Grand Hotel.

They were naturally taken greatly by surprise when I produced Nancy as my fiancée, but had no reason at all to be displeased as she was not only a beauty but an heiress.

Her father, Tom Robinson, already dead, had been a financier, who with two partners put up the capital for Dan Fitte to start the Nugget Polish Co., which later amalgamated with the Chiswick Polish Co. and eventually became a substantial division of Reckitt & Colman. They had also helped finance some of the London race courses such as Kempton and Sandown Park.

By his first marriage he had a son, Tom, who had been killed on the Western Front, and a daughter, Gertie, who was married to another businessman, Gem Spindler, who, in some mysterious way, ran his business in Flushing although he lived in a fine Regency house in Hove. Gem was a small, impeccably dressed, little man. He had a fine library of beautifully bound books, loved fine wine and was so selective that he would eat only the undercut of a sirloin of beef.

By Nancy's mother, Amy, old Tom had had a son, Harry, and five daughters. Harry was a fattish, cheerful, lazy fellow; by profession a solicitor but he rarely bothered to go to his office. Cissie was married to a Colonel in the Royal Army Medical Corps; Ethel had married Hans Wessel, a banker, whose brother-in-law, a Captain von Muller, was ADC to the Crown Prince, and so had had to spend the whole of the war in Germany; Baba was married to an amiable man, Fred Lucas, who started the National Car Parks Co.; Lily was unmarried and still studying at London University – later she became a doctor and married the distinguished obstetrician, Leonard Phillips. Nancy was the last of the hatch.

I was therefore about to acquire a large family of in-laws. They were all most kind to me and it was a new pleasure, because my only sister, Muriel, was seven years younger than myself. The war years, and the fact that she was for a long period at boarding schools, kept us apart, so we never came to know one another really well.

Old Tom Robinson had made a considerable fortune; large enough to make his son Harry a rich man and to settle £500 per annum on each of his daughters after providing lavishly for his wife. She must have had an income of at least £14,000 a year – better than £100,000 a year today.

At the time I met Nancy the Robinsons were in the process of moving. Harry and three of Amy's daughters having married, she had decided to give up the big house in Clapham Park and move to a ten-room flat in Northgate Mansions, overlooking Regent's Park. During the move she occupied a suite at the Great Central Hotel. It was at a family dinner party there on 11 December that our engagement was formally announced. It was agreed that we should get married in the following June.

We were both desperately in love and snatched every moment we could to be together. To my fury my parents dragged me off again with the Newtons and Hiltons on 24 December to spend Christmas at the Sackville, Bexhill. This time, however, instead of making a round of the bars with Wally and Sidney Newton, I spent most of my time thinking about or writing to Nancy.

Unfortunately, I have always lacked an appreciation of fine poetry but, when young, often laboriously wrote doggerel verses for girls with whom I was in love. One which I wrote for Barbara Symonds ran to over ninety verses; but, as she had made it clear that she did not return my love, it was a dreary affair. The following, which I wrote for Nancy, has much more *joie de vivre* in it.

If I were King of Babylon and Tetrarch of Judaea,
The Lord of all Assyria and Mighty in Chaldea,
I'd overthrow the Idols and I'd slay the Sacred Bull
That men might worship Thee instead – my own most beautiful.

Thou should dispense Thy wisdom from out the Justice Seat,
Giving Laws unto the People – they kneeling at Thy feet.
And they should sing Thy praises – Thy Beauty and Thy Worth,
Thy Glory and Thy Splendour should travel o'er the Earth.

I'd build a Temple to Thee there – the Wonder of all Time,
Of Marble Halls with Crystal Lamps set in a Mystic Sign
With Columns made of Jasper and Balconies of Jade,
Of Onyx-panelled Passages, with precious gems inlaid.

From Khorazan and Bokhara I'd bring Thee Carpets rare,
Woven in cunning patterns, wrought in every colour fair.
From far Cathay I'd have the Silks to make Thine own Divan;
For Thee I'd buy the precious stuffs that come by Caravan.

I'd give Thee mighty Nubian Slaves, ebony-skinned and tall,
Who with fair-haired maids from Attica should heed Thy slightest call.
And in the purple Sunset, when the Evening Song was done,
Thy Lord, Thy Slave, Thy Lover, unto his Love would come.

Into the Secret Garden where Fountains play with Wine;
But, Love, I would forget them when my lips were pressed to Thine.
We would walk together, Sweetheart, 'neath the Palm Trees, green and cool;
Then I'd bathe Thy Wondrous Body in the Marble Lotus Pool.

Thy Hair I'd spray with Incense and Thy Hands with Henna dye,
Thy Breasts with Myrrh I'd Perfume, and my head thereon I'd lie.
In the glory of a Southern Night, with Stars like Thine own Eyes,
We'd Love until we Died, mine Own, in Passion-Scented Sighs.
If I was King of Babylon and Tetrarch of Judaea,
The Lord of all Assyria and Mighty in Chaldea.

In return Nancy sent me a painting by herself of me as

'Dennis the Valiant' and a sixteen-page romance called *The Legend of the Lovers Nancia and Denesco*.

Early in January my parents went as usual to the South of France; at the end of the month Amy went with Gertie Spindler to Monte Carlo and would normally have taken Nancy as well, but, after much pleading, it was arranged that Nancy should stay with her sister, Baba Lucas, who lived with her husband at 26 Stanhope Gate.

By March I decided that the time had come for me to set about finding a home. We did not mind where we lived providing that it was within reasonable distance of the West End; so I gave my requirements to every house agent in Kensington, Bayswater, Pimlico, Marylebone, Chelsea and Westminster. Naturally, I received hundreds of replies, the majority of which were quite unsuitable, but, having sifted through the particulars, Nancy and I went to see a score or so of them.

Eventually we settled on a ground floor and basement, 20a Trebovir Road, Earl's Court; a district which in those days had no coloured population. The first floor of the flat consisted of a large sitting-room in front with a bay window and at the back two bedrooms. The basement had a kitchen in front, and a bedroom for a maid under the ground floor hall, with at the back a dining-room and a bathroom. The rooms were all not only reasonably large but fairly lofty.

The tenant, a Mr Henry Winning, agreed to let it to me for £160 per annum, provided I would pay the current quarter's rent from December to March. This I agreed to do and also paid him £70 for the fixtures and fittings.

Nancy and I decided on the decorations, and, having had several estimates, gave the work to John Barker's. But when it was well advanced I met with a most unpleasant surprise. A nasty little man claiming to be the landlord turned up. My agreement with Winning – who had disappeared leaving no address – was worthless, he said; if I wished to retain possession of the flat I must also ante up the last quarter's rent, back to September '21 which was still unpaid.

My father's solicitor found that the autumn quarter had been paid and that the landlord was attempting to put a fast one over on me. Eventually a compromise was arrived at by which I could have the flat for a twenty-one-year lease but this wretched transaction cost me £143 7s. 10d.

Soon after Mrs Robinson's return, in mid March, she went to Margate for a month and whisked Nancy off with her. I am sure she had hoped for a richer son-in-law, or one with better prospects than mine, and she may have thought that, if we were separated for that length of time, one or other of us might have second thoughts about marrying. But this may be doing her a great injustice because, although domineering, she was one of the kindest women I have ever met.

While they were at Margate I went down for the weekend and took the opportunity to face up to a matter that had been giving me some concern.

My parents were Protestants, and so were all the Robinsons with the exception of Baba and Nancy. In their 'teens they and their sisters had all been to a Convent in Clapham Park and, to Amy's annoyance, these two had been converted to Catholicism. Nancy refused to give up her religion, and to obtain permission for mixed marriages was much more difficult than it is in these days. I had to agree that I would receive instruction which might possibly persuade me to become an R C, and to sign a declaration that any children of the marriage should be baptized into that faith. Being much averse from being hectored by Nancy's confessor, I agreed to listen to the arguments of a priest that neither of us knew, and I took the opportunity of calling on the Catholic priest at Margate.

He turned out to be a benign, elderly man who received me in a big library in which there were hundreds of books with old leather bindings that were falling to pieces.

Within five minutes this wise old man said it was clear to him that nothing he could say would persuade me to become a Roman Catholic. We then spent a very happy hour talking about Buddha, Confucius and Lao Tze. I then signed on the dotted line and he gave me my dispensation.

As we were parting he said, 'There is one thing I wish you would do for me, my son. Read Mallock's *Doctrine and Doctrinal Disruption.*

'But,' he added with a twinkle, 'don't read the last chapter.'

On my return to London I bought a copy of the book. It dealt with the Low, Moderate and High Church, showing clearly that none of the Protestant creeds could claim to have been inspired by God.

With this I entirely agreed. Luther, throwing inkpots at devils no one else could see, was obviously a nut. Our Henry VIII broke with the Pope because he was determined to live legally with Ann Boleyn, and what a girl she must have been – reported to have committed incest with her brother, and once to have been surprised in bed with six young men (they had big beds in those days). As for Calvin, had I ever had the chance I would have whipped him till he screamed for the misery his doctrine and those derived from it brought on tens of thousands of people.

Then, of course, I read Mallock's last chapter. It said that, if one wanted to follow the Christian faith, the only creed which has directly inherited divine sanction was the Roman Catholic. But, after all, what proof was there that God the Father ever existed at all?

Reverting to Amy Robinson, no man ever had a better mother-in-law. She was short, plump, rosy-cheeked, with a slightly roman nose and a pile of fine, grey hair. She had a passion for gambling, at the tables, playing bridge and on race horses. When at home she spent a good part of every morning conferring with her confidante and house-keeper, the hugely buxom Carrie, who was beloved by us all, about which horses they should back that day.

Dear Amy loved good living and cheerful company. A night rarely passed when there were not two or more guests at her table. She told me once that, whenever she went abroad and stayed at an hotel where she was not known, on the first night she always sent for the head waiter and gave him the equivalent of a fiver, with a promise of more to come if she was well looked after; most women on their own were mean about tips and, knowing that, waiters usually gave them poor service.

In due course she bought Nancy a splendid *trousseau*, then

asked us if we would prefer a quiet wedding and £500 to start our furnishing with or a big reception with all the trimmings.

We chose the latter and, it proved, wisely. Between them some 500 guests sent us over 300 presents which, when I later had them assessed for insurance, were valued at more than £800.

I then made out a list of anticipated expenses, per annum, which came to £720. As my income was then £880 this left barely £3 a week for holidays, theatres, Christmas and birthday presents, taxis, books, repairs and unforeseen extras of all sorts; so things would not have looked too bright had it not been that Nancy had £500 a year of her own and was as generous as her mother.

In April there occurred an event which temporarily distracted my thoughts from Nancy and gave me great concern. Early on during my engagement I had introduced Nancy to Gordon Eric. I had previously praised him so highly to her that, after our evening with him and his charming 'lady from Huddersfield', she said how pleased she was at finding I was not, as she had thought, entirely subservient to my friend but at times expressed opinions contrary to his and was not in the least dominated by him. Her approval of Gordon Eric enabled me to spend evenings with him without any qualms, although I now refrained from any sexual frolics when in his company.

One day he told me that he needed an alibi for a certain project, then asked me to dine with two girls we knew in a flat. He would join us later and, should the need arise, all three of us would say that he had been there all evening.

With Nancy in mind I was loath to dine alone with the two girls, one of whom had for a short while been my mistress; but, not wishing to let Gordon Eric down, I agreed.

The threesome dinner party went off without incident, then about midnight Gordon Eric joined us. He was in white tie, tails, topper and a special evening overcoat that he had had made for him by Walkers of Albermarle Street; I had had a copy made for myself. It had no pockets (so fitted like a sheath) and silk lapels.

His partner in defrauding the government, an Australian

named Ernest Dyer, had left the Air Ministry some time back and bought a derelict racing stable – The Welcomes, Hayes Lane, Kenley – not far from Purley. It was not until long afterwards that I learned how Gordon Eric had spent his evening. He and Dyer had decided to burn the place down and claim the insurance. Having laid combustibles beneath the floors, Dyer went off to Brighton. Then Gordon Eric, wearing dress clothes so that anyone seeing him would assume he was attending a big dance that was being held in the neighbourhood, went to The Welcomes and set the place alight.

The ingenious plot apparently failed, as the insurance company refused to pay up. A week or two later Gordon Eric again went down to The Welcomes one evening, presumably to find out what had gone wrong.

The following morning Dyer called at my office to ask if I knew where Gordon Eric had got to, as he had failed to keep an appointment down at Kenley the previous evening and had not slept at the flat in Knightsbridge of 'the lady from Huddersfield' which was his normal base when in London. I had met Dyer a few times before. He seemed quite a pleasant chap, although rather a rough diamond. I could not help him.

Shortly afterwards the lady rang up and asked me to come over to see her. I went and found her in a great state of anxiety as Gordon Eric had disappeared without leaving any message and he had not telephoned. The following day she had become quite frantic, and at her request I went to see the Manager of Gordon Eric's bank, which was in Bond Street. It transpired that he had a joint account with Dyer there, and the Manager opened up to me because of an unusual occurrence the day before. The account ran to several thousand pounds. Dyer had come in, drawn out the lot and closed the account. The lady at Knightsbridge then implored me to institute enquiries through a private detective, and also gave me the key of Gordon Eric's safe deposit box at Harrods. In it there was neither any money nor any clue to his disappearance. The head of the detective agency I went to was a very shrewd bird. He asked me many questions that

Father on the Promenade des Anglais, Nice

Mother in the South of France

Nancy Robinson, D.W.'s first wife, 1922

(Below left) *Nancy and D.W. on their honeymoon*
(Below right) *Nancy and D.W. shortly after their marriage*

The Gay Twenties

(Above) *D.W. and Joan on the left. In the right foreground, Joe Links sits between his sisters, with Frank and Betty van Zwanenberg to their left.*

(Below) *D.W., Joan, Mervyn Baron and June Head*

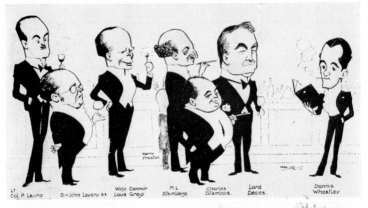

The Gourmets' and Connoisseurs' Circle dinner in South Audley Street.
Caricature by Fred May in The Graphic

Very early television at Alexandra Palace. Lord Donegall, D.W., and
Lady Eleanor Smith

I dared not answer truthfully because I did know in a general way about Gordon Eric's criminal activities in the past and feared to compromise him.

All these activities necessitated my absence from the office for such long periods that I had to give my father an explanation. He had always disapproved of my friendship with Gordon Eric and we now had a furious row. He actually threatened to turn me out into the street unless I ceased to take any part in the affair. Nancy apart, there was nothing more I could do to help in tracing Gordon Eric; so I reluctantly gave way; and I never again saw him or Dyer.

Some months later I met by chance a pretty doctor's wife with whom Gordon Eric had been having an affair on the side at the time of his disappearance, and she assured me that she had seen him in Madrid. This reinforced a theory I had formed myself: that for some reason of his own – perhaps because the police suspected him in connection with the burning of the racing stables – he had, after careful preparation, vanished overnight, for in such a case he would certainly have used one of his favourite conceptions – the succession of cul-de-sacs. But that was not so.

It was not until several years later that the truth came out. His father, an Irish Protestant clergyman, dreamed that he saw Gordon Eric's body at the bottom of a well, came to London and pressed the police to renew investigations at Kenley. They did so, and it emerged that, while walking behind him, Dyer had shot him through the back of the head, then thrown his body down a disused well at the racing stables.

I would like to have seen Dyer hanged, but Fate had already caught up with him in a curious way. He was staying at an hotel in Scarborough a year or so after Gordon Eric's death. The police came to interview him in connection with some small local fraud. Believing that they had found out about Gordon Eric and were after him for murder, he fled upstairs. Halfway up, he pulled out a pistol and shot himself.

For a while after Gordon Eric's disappearance I was greatly distressed, but fortunately I had much to distract my thoughts from him. Nancy and I were to be married in a few weeks' time; there was still a lot of shopping to be done to complete the furnishing of our flat, fittings for wedding clothes, invitations to be sent out and arrangements for our honeymoon to be made.

We intended to spend the first two nights of it at the Savoy Hotel and I booked a suite there – then £4 4s. od. per night. On the morning of the great day, 17 June, my father wanted me to come to the office and have drinks there with some of his friends, but I somewhat churlishly refused as I wanted to spend the morning alone, and I did so strolling round the beautiful old walled garden in Brockwell Park.

Soon after midday I went up to the Savoy to see that the flowers had been well set out in our suite, and to change into my wedding garments. Later, Bertie Davis, whom I had asked to be my best man, Tanko Moat and my three other sidesmen arrived to drink a glass of Champagne with me. They then escorted me to the church.

We had decided to get married at St James's, Spanish Place. It was a beautiful church and would have held many more than our 500 guests; but, as it was a mixed marriage, the Fathers meanly decreed that we should only be allowed two vases of flowers on the altar. Moreover, the service was so brief that when we left the altar rails there was consternation among our friends, as 95 per cent were Protestants and they jumped to the conclusion that some terrible hitch had occurred at the last moment and that Nancy and I had not been married but dismissed from the altar.

The reception was at the Great Central Hotel and it could not have been a more cheerful party. But a churlishness entirely contrary to my nature seemed to have got into me during the early part of the day. In the morning I had refused my kind father's request to come and have a drink with his friends; now, after the huge cake was cut and the health of the bride and bridegroom drunk, I flatly refused to reply to the toast. I cannot plead acute shyness or sheer inability to make a speech, as after I became an author I made many public speeches. But some contrary devil had got into me, and when Nancy had changed I hurried her away as quickly as I could.

Overwhelming desire to get Nancy into bed played no part at all in this. Nevertheless, as soon as we reached the Savoy we did go to bed, and remained locked in one another's arms until we had to get up to dine in our private sitting-room. After we had dined, knowing that my best man, the bridesmaids and sidesmen were having a dinner party in the restaurant, we went down and joined them, then brought them all up to our suite for more Champagne.

We spent the whole of the next day there; then on the following morning took the train for Dover. I see from my papers that the expenses had led to my being £114 overdrawn. But I could not have cared less.

5

MY FIRST MARRIAGE

NANCY and I had decided on Belgium for our honeymoon. We spent the first few nights at the Hotel Splendide at Ostend, then went on to Bruges, Antwerp and Brussels, from which, of course, we drove out to Waterloo.

We were home again just in time for me to display Nancy in all her glory at the wedding of Barbara and Cecil, which took place in mid July. Installed at 20a Trebovir Road, we led a joyous life. As a maid we had secured a girl who was the daughter of a police inspector, cheerful, willing and a good cook. In those days a young couple could live very pleasantly on about £1400 a year. We gave little dinner parties and went frequently to the theatre, but our seats were paid for more often than not by the generous Amy. She would book six or eight stalls for members of her family and friends, then take us all on afterwards to Champagne suppers at the Carlton or Ciro's.

Before I became engaged to Nancy she had half a dozen young men begging her to marry them. Two became life-long friends of mine. One was Cyril Eastaugh – always known to us as Bobby – who had won an MC as a machine-gun officer in the war. At the time we met he was secretary to Maundy Gregory, who ran the *Whitehall Gazette* and later became notorious as the middle man for Lloyd George's sale of honours. Bobby had a religious bent, and a rich, elderly lady paid for him to go up to Oxford, so that he might study there with a view to later entering the Church. He was duly ordained and became in turn a vicar in Kennington, Bishop of Kensington, then Lord Bishop of Peterborough with a seat in the House of Lords. During over half a century we have spent many a happy evening enjoying good conversation and the finest wines.

My other lasting friendship made through Nancy was with Frank van Zwanenberg. Many rich Jewesses frequented Amy's bridge parties and Frank's mother was one of them. Many years earlier two Jewish friends, van Zwanenberg and Jacob van den Berg, had come to London and made fortunes, the one out of bacon and the other out of margarine. Frank's mother had first married van Zwanenberg, but he had died comparatively young, so she then married van den Berg.

They had the only really fine house on the front in the Cliftonville part of Margate, in which they had house parties nearly every weekend and Nancy and I were asked many times down there to stay. Later Frank married his cousin, Betty, a very pretty girl from South Africa. As they were related there was great opposition by the family to the match. But I am happy to record that I was largely instrumental in securing Frank's mother's consent by the argument that the Pharaohs had always married their half-sisters yet produced perfectly normal children.

At Margate I made two other Jewish lifelong friends; Mervyn Baron, whom I later portrayed in my de Richleau books as Simon Aron, and Joseph Gluckstein Links. When I first met Joe he was only seventeen. His father had established quite a small wholesale furriers in the Barbican. Knowing himself to be dying from an incurable disease, Joe's father had taken him away from school at the age of sixteen to learn the business. Joe's mother, being a Gluckstein, was one of the family which, with the Salmons, controlled Lyons' nationwide tea-shop business. When Joe's father did die his Gluckstein relatives said, 'Joe, don't be a fool. Sell that silly little business and come into Lyons. After a few years' experience in various jobs we will make you a director, and you will be rich for life.'

But Joe doggedly maintained that, his father having taught him his business, he intended to remain in it. A few years later he moved to large new premises just off Regent Street. He had no shop but, in addition to his greatly increased wholesale trade, he supplied a limited number of private customers. Among them were Elizabeth the Queen Mother, our present Queen and other ladies of the Royal Family. He also became a Director of the Hudson's Bay Company. In the war he became a Wing Commander and an OBE. He has written several books on Venice and one which should prove the definitive work on the paintings of Canaletto. I am very proud to have had such a man as an intimate friend for over fifty years.

After eighteen months of marriage Nancy gave birth to my only child, a son. Admiring as I did the civilization of ancient Rome, I wanted him christened Anthony Marius, but Amy upset my applecart by insisting that her late husband's name, Thomas, should be included, which made the poor baby's full name sound ridiculous.

He was a healthy child except for the fact that he had exceptionally large adenoids, and within a week of his birth a specialist insisted that these must be removed, otherwise it was possible that the infant would choke. To operate on such a very young child put Nancy and me in terrible fear that we should lose him. But he survived, in due course married and gave me six grandchildren.

Anthony was duly christened in the Catholic Church of Our Lady of Victories in Kensington; and, as the only other Catholic in the family, Baba Lucas was asked and gladly agreed to act as Godmother. He was later educated at Worth and Downside and has remained a practising Catholic. My three grandsons have in turn followed their father to Downside, the well-known Catholic public school run by the Benedictine monks; and I understand that my great-grandson, Guy Hoogewerf, my grand-daughter Antonia's son, has also been put down to go there.

At about this time, Louis Newton had become Lord Mayor of London. As a great friend of my father, he transferred to us the whole of the City Corporation's wine requirements. The King of Rumania paid a state visit to King George V, and the City entertained him to lunch at the Guildhall. On the same day the Rumanian King entertained King George to dinner at his Embassy. We supplied the wines for both these parties.

The Rumanian Ambassador was then Monsieur Titulescu, a brilliant man, afterwards Prime Minister of his country. My father was away, so I took the Ambassador's order. He brought three of his staff with him to decide which wines to order. Hardly anything I suggested was good enough. He kept on exclaiming: 'Do you not understand, it is my King who entertains your King? Every wine must be superb.' I produced an 1815 Waterloo Sherry and, after several 'phone calls, dug up some Moet of a special *cuvée* that had been produced for King George's Coronation. We opened innumerable bottles of my finest Hocks and Château bottled Clarets. The tasting went on the whole morning. We finished on some superb Brandy and Original Chartreuse. On the two parties I took over £1000. Real money in those days. What a day!

Every winter now my father and mother spent a couple of months in the South of France. Although my father wrote to me every week or so giving instructions about the business, for most of the first quarter of the year I virtually ran it; as I did during their annual stay at Harrogate.

My principal assistants at the office were Percy Thurgood, our very knowledgeable Manager, who had trained as a wine merchant in a long-established East Coast firm; Cooper, an able man at figures who wrote up the ledgers, and young Tom Hayward, who did the odd jobs. We all acted as salesmen when occasion required, and had no typist secretary. When my father was there, he wrote all letters in his own hand.

We bought many old cellars from the heirs of deceased customers. One I recall particularly was that of Lord Michelham, at Strawberry Hill, the neo-Gothic mansion which had been built in the eighteenth century by Horace Walpole. The cellar left by Michelham was peculiar in that it held 385 dozen of fine Brandy and 307 dozen of Port. Apart from a small bin of Sherry there was not a bottle of anything else in it at all.

I made several trips on our lorry down to Twickenham to help collect it, and, naturally, had a look round the large library. Among the many hundreds of books there was not one that I would have particularly liked to own. Michelham had not been interested in books, but on buying Strawberry

Hill and finding the library empty he said the shelves must be filled, so he had sent his secretary to Charing Cross Road to buy second-hand books, literally by the yard. Horace Walpole must have turned in his grave.

Trying to get in long-outstanding debts was part of my work. One such debtor was Count Pocklewski-Koizel, a Polish nobleman who had taken refuge in England after the war. He was a fine-looking man of about thirty-five and received me most charmingly. When we got to the reason for my call, he spread out his hands and said: 'I am so sorry, Mr Wheatley, but since I have been in England I have found things very difficult. You see, in my own country I own great estates and was a millionaire. If I wanted anything I asked for it and it was bought for me. I knew nothing about finance. Until I took a house in London I had never signed a cheque.'

But I am happy to think that, somehow or other, this nice man survived. I saw him again some years later. We were sitting in the same row of stalls at a theatre, and his companion was Princess Margaret.

Mention of theatres reminds me that I must have been born vain, as whenever I went out for the evening I wore a white tie and tails and still sported the rimless monocle that I had used throughout the war.

In February 1924 my Uncle Dennis died. He lived in Belsize Park and was walking down to Swiss Cottage one morning when he fell dead without the slightest warning – a wonderful way to die. At the time my parents were in Florence, and as soon as I could I sent them particulars of my bachelor uncle's Will. He had a year or so earlier taken as a partner a Mr Chuter, from Jackson's; so there were no problems about his business. He had left handsome legacies to the members of his staff and the bulk of his money to his girl friend, Mrs Hoare. From Venice my father wrote to me that he thought it a very fair and sound Will; but the Wheatley aunts, cantankerous as ever, kicked up hell's delight about the money going to that '(W)hoare woman'. There was much legal correspondence, but my father, wisely, refused to be mixed up in the matter.

I continued to be perpetually hard up; so hard up that in the summer of 1924 I told my father that, now I had to pay a nurse for Anthony, I could not possibly afford a holiday. Reluctantly, having twice paid my debts since the war, he said a holiday was essential to my health. But he gave me enough only to lodge at a boarding house in Broadstairs for a fortnight.

Pushing Anthony in his pram along the promenade, while economizing on food and drink, I was bored to tears. When the fortnight was up I decided that never again would I go on that type of holiday.

The next holiday Nancy and I had was a brief stay in Paris. We were accompanied by John Troman and his wife, Alma, who were great friends of ours. As none of us had much money at the time we economized by staying at a very cheap hotel and spent such money as we had going out on the town. Johnny took us to the Bal Taberin, the Moulin Rouge, the Folies Bergères and other hectic haunts which, of course, had been outside my parents' orbit when I had stayed in Paris with them.

We lunched several times at the original Prunier's and particularly enjoyed the lobsters washed down with white Loire wine. From this I learned a lesson. On our last morning, on our way to the Gare du Nord, we picked up a couple of hen lobsters and a couple of bottles of the wine to have for our supper that evening in London.

The lobsters travelled perfectly but, to our surprise, the wine tasted thin and indifferent. There could have been no cheating. The change had taken place only when the corks were drawn and the wine exposed to the moist atmosphere of England. Light wines in their natural state simply cannot stand up to it. That is why they all have to be fortified with extra sugar before being exported to us.

In the autumn of 1925 my father did strike a winner. A short, round, soulful-eyed Polish Jew came to see us. His name was Stambois and he was trying to sell some quite exceptional old Brandies. They were so expensive that no one Stambois had tried would buy them; but my father took a gamble.

The Brandies were Louis XVIII 1820, Roi de Rome 1811, Napoleon I 1802 from the Palais de Compiégne, Reserve Royale 1825 from the Czar Alexander I's Summer Palace in the Crimea, Bignon (the famous Paris restaurateur) 1800, Grande Fine Champagne not less than 115 years old from the cellars of Marshal Ney, Napoleon, Palais des Tuileries 1818, and Marie Antoinette 1789 from the Palais de Versailles.

That Christmas my father once more paid £100 to clear my overdraft, wrote me a not very nice letter ending: 'I hope you have a happy Christmas on the money you have not got', and, shortly afterwards, went off with my mother to the South of France.

I then also took a gamble. In the twenties wine merchants' lists had many pages but were rarely more than six by four inches in size; normally the best Brandy one could buy was Hennessy, Martell or John Barnet at 35/– per bottle. I designed and had printed a catalogue with gold lettering on thick brown paper, ten by eight inches in size but having only eight pages. Each page had a brief essay of two or three hundred words describing the historic associations of one of the Brandies, illustrated with coats of arms, branded corks, and so on. The prices ranged from two and a half guineas a bottle to £100 per dozen.

That catalogue was the most costly ever produced in the wine trade. I had not written a word to my father about what I had done and was pretty scared about what his reaction might be. When he got home the catalogues had just been delivered. On my showing him one he gave me a very queer look but neither praised nor condemned me.

We sent the catalogues out. On the morning they were delivered Lord Wilton, who had never before even bought a syphon of soda from us, sent his man along with a £100 cheque for a dozen of the Marie Antoinette. Then the orders poured in. Of some of the Brandies we had only a limited stock so were soon sold out, but of others, particularly the Tuileries 1818, Stambois had a large quantity.

Most of the bottles had what were then unusual features. The Tuileries, for example, had an embossed medallion containing an 'N' with the Napoleonic crown above it. But what really mattered was that the old Fine Champagne Cognacs in them were truly superb. I have never tasted finer. But in a year or two imitations were appearing in every restaurant. The bottles had the 'N' medallion and were often covered with fake cobwebs; but the brandy in them was indifferent stuff. Whenever a waiter produced one at my table I used to say: 'Take it away. Bring me some John Barnett or Delamain.' Unintentionally, I had started the old Brandy racket.

Stambois became a frequent visitor at our office. He persuaded me to join the Ambassadors Club, which was started by a friend of his, a famous restaurateur named Rizzi. Its premises, just off Bond Street, were most attractive. Like Ciro's, round its ballroom it had a broad balcony supported by tall marble pillars on which one could dine if not wearing evening dress. Stambois took Nancy and me to the opening night. The place was packed by the most fashionable crowd in London and continued to be for several weeks. But then came the General Strike, during which it was almost empty and, soon after, it collapsed.

Another victim of the General Strike was the Splendide, in Piccadilly opposite the Green Park. That, too, was *grande luxe* while it lasted and it was there that I first made the acquaintance of Joseph Vecchi, who was the *Maître d'Hotel*.

Vecchi had already had an adventurous life. He had started as a young floor waiter at Claridges in London, then moved on for a spell at the Adlon in Berlin. From there, although still under thirty, he went to the Grand Hotel, St Petersburg, as restaurant manager. In a private basement dining-room he had on numerous occasions superintended dinners for one man and thirty or forty of the most beautiful or high-born ladies in what was then the Russian capital. The one man was Rasputin.

Some years later Vecchi moved to Kiev, where he opened his own restaurant. The Revolution came. The Bolsheviks looted his restaurant and threw him out into the gutter. For a while he fought with the Whites, then when they were defeated walked the 2000 miles to Murmansk, where he was brought off by a British Destroyer. Having arrived in England, he decided to make it his permanent home. After the collapse of the Splendide he went for a while to the Piccadilly. There he met Beneni. Together they opened the Hungaria Restaurant in Lower Regent Street and made a great success of it. I went there countless times and Joseph Vecchi became for many years one of my personal friends.

Naturally, I was anxious to take a hand in defeating the General Strike, but I did not think my strength would be up to unloading sacks of grain from ships in the docks; so I rang up my old friend Frank van Zwanenberg and asked if I could give him any help in his office. Zwanenberg's were the biggest bacon importers in Britain. He and his cousin then ran the business and he said he would be very pleased to have me.

His office was near the Port of London and I found them there in grievous trouble. They had a dozen or more shipments of bacon on the way from Holland and Denmark. The problem was where in Britain these could be unloaded. All the larger ports had been closed by the strike; but some of the smaller ones were still open, or batches of volunteers such as university students would in some cases defy the strikers and get the cargoes ashore. The job I was given was to sit at a telephone for hours on end enquiring of the local authorities in the towns along the coast whether they could receive a cargo, then diverting the ships by wireless to such ports as could take them.

Several times I went to the docks to see how the volunteers were getting on with the unloading. One such occasion nearly provoked a nasty incident. I went down sitting next to the driver in the cab of an empty lorry. On the Bermondsey side of the river our way was blocked by a mob of angry strikers who threatened to lynch us. Fortunately I had brought with me one of the automatics I had carried in the war, and it was loaded. Pulling it out, I pointed at the ringleaders, intending, of course, only to fire, if need be, over their heads. But at the sight of my pistol they panicked, turned tail and let the lorry through.

In 1926 the great event of my year was our removal from 20a Trebovir Road. My father adored Anthony and felt that the little boy should have both a night and day nursery instead of the single spare room which was all we had for him.

Two years earlier it had been declared illegal to use part of the Baker Trust to buy me a partnership in the business, but this prohibition did not apply to property with a long lease; so a pleasant little house was acquired for us in Bayswater, 12 Chepstow Place, a quiet street leading south from Bradley's corner.

Amy Robinson was that summer going to Biarritz, and she wanted Nancy and me to take our holiday there too. I told my father, but he wrote me an angry letter saying that he had no money to spare and, if I had none, I should ask Amy to pay for us. That I did not do, but we went to Biarritz for a fortnight in September all the same. Amy stayed in *grande luxe* at the Hotel Palais, Nancy and I at a small hotel up in the town. The generous Amy paid nearly all our expenses and we had a grand time.

But when I got back home again I was in serious trouble. On top of the expenses of moving, our recent holiday and a threat from the landlord to sue me for two quarters' rent of 20a Trebovir Road still outstanding, I had early that year acquired a beautiful mistress. Somehow I managed to stave off my creditors through the last months of 1926 and the spring of 1927. Then I was unexpectedly saved. On 4 May my father died.

6

THE RISE OF WHEATLEY
AND SON

My father died of cirrhosis of the liver, which is the occupational disease of wine merchants. My grandfather Wheatley died of cirrhosis, and my father suffered from it for a long time before he died. As far back as 1923 he had written to me from Harrogate that his doctor there allowed him only a lager for lunch, one glass of wine for dinner and a whisky in the evening. Yet he never appeared to be ill and came up to his office as usual until about a week before his death.

By and large he had not had a bad life. His youth – while his own father, who arrived in London penniless, had been saving money to acquire four shops – had undoubtedly been that of a drudge; but soon after he took over at No. 26 he became highly respected in the Trade and made enough money to live well in a commodious house with three servants. Then, for the last seven years of his life, my mother having inherited a small fortune, he was able to enjoy two months a year in the South of France and many shorter stays at other places.

During my childhood and teens I positively hated him; and even after the war, when we worked together in South Audley Street, I remained in constant fear of his disapproving stare and the frequent lectures he gave me about overspending. In fact it was not until about two years before his death that I realized he had any real affection for me.

Ronald Cunningham, the agent for that best of Champagnes, Louis Roederer, had called on us. I saw him to the door and just as he went out into the street I made some casual remark about my father being disappointed in me because, unlike him, I did not think only of business.

Cunningham swung round, stared at me in astonishment and exclaimed: 'But Dennis, you are entirely wrong! He is very fond and proud of you. Only a week or so ago he said to me: "How lucky I am to have a son still in his twenties who can be trusted to run the business while I go away for months at a time." '

This gave me much food for thought, and I realized how, behind his humourless stare and reproaches about my being a spendthrift, he had been most generous to me in a score of ways. I then adopted a more friendly attitude towards him, to which he responded, and I am happy to say that during the last years of his life our relationship improved enormously.

In the early months of 1927 this bore fruit. He wrote to me from Menton that our accountants had sent him figures showing that our turnover in 1924/5 had been £24,000 odd and for 1925/6 it had gone up to nearly £28,000. This was largely due to the way in which I had handled the Stambois brandies, so he intended to make me a partner.

When he got home early in April a deed was drawn up but, owing to the usual delays of lawyers, it had not actually been signed when his illness caused him to take to his bed. It was not until he was removed to a nursing home that I realized he might die. If he did so before the partnership was actually signed, as he had willed everything to my mother, the business would go to her.

I knew her well enough to foresee that I would remain no more than her Manager and that, however well the business did, I should be lucky if I could get her to increase my salary by more than a hundred or two a year. I put urgent calls through to our solicitor and my father's doctor, explaining the situation, and the three of us went to the nursing home. We found my father barely conscious, but the solicitor was an old friend and fully convinced of his intentions. My poor father was propped up in bed and succeeded in scrawling his signature on the document with the two others as witnesses. Next morning he was dead.

He was very fond of making lists, and in his desk I found one assessing the assets of his wife and himself. They totalled £124,000. By far the greater part of this was my mother's and she had paid for all their holidays. But I had succeeded in getting the business. Unfortunately, there was very little capital behind it, because my grandfather Wheatley had left most of his money to his wife, and she in turn to my two aunts. It had fallen on South Audley Street to pay out the bulk of this money; so the business had no reserve of capital.

Nevertheless, I was determined to make it one of London's leading wine merchants. Obviously the first thing to do was to make the premises suitable for that role. I did away with the beer counter, replacing it with two big glass cabinets to display exceptional wines, boarded over the staircase that led down to the cellar, substituting a circular one of iron in a hidden corner, then covered the whole floor space with a dark blue carpet. I had my own office panelled in mahogany and a smaller one that led into it in light cedar-wood as a cigar department. I scrapped the old-fashioned, high desks at which clerks used to sit on stools and bought a set of eight Chippendale-pattern chairs to distribute about the shop and office. I replaced my father's old roll-top desk with a beautiful oval piece which had drawers each side and a space for one's legs under its centre.

I have always thought it a good thing to have a nap in the afternoon whenever possible, so I had a curved panel made to fill up the front of the open space. I could then lie at full length under the desk without anyone seeing me. At times one of my staff would come in, look round and say to anyone behind him: 'That's queer! I could swear I saw the boss walk in here ten minutes ago. He must have slipped out without my noticing him.'

All these alterations and improvements cost a lot of money and we lost most of our ready-money beer trade with house-keepers and porters, but on the whole it paid magnificently and I started many new activities.

The first was the sale of cellars I created. At home my father normally kept only six or eight dozen of mixed wines and spirits. My mother kept what was there, but I sold what purported to have been his private cellar through Knight, Frank and Rutley. It had become at least a hundred dozen of the finest Vintage Ports, *Château* Clarets, Champagnes, old

Brandies and so on. Even at auction prices and after paying commission they brought me a very handsome profit.

A similar project was brought to me by Keld Fenwick, a Captain in the Life Guards who, from being a customer, became a close friend. He asked me down to his lovely home, Wickham Abbey. It was the first time I had ever been to a house party in a big country house and I enjoyed it enormously. Among the guests was Jumbo Jollif, once a Corporal-of-Horse in the Life Guards, later an officer, and after the war the head salesman for Booth's Gin. He was a huge man and could drink bumper after bumper without batting an eyelid. We all drank pretty heavily and on Sunday mornings Keld used to walk round his garden with a glass in one hand and swinging a decanter of Port in the other. He said it was the best time of the day to appreciate Port, and I am inclined to think he was right.

Keld was a raffish character and great spendthrift. There had been times when he filled the house with his brother officers and half the Gaiety chorus. One weekend he told me that he was terribly hard up and must raise money somehow. As his big cellars were nearly empty I suggested that we should fill them, sell the contents and share the profit. He jumped at the idea, so I sent down several lorry loads of wine, had it binned away, then advertised it for sale through Knight, Frank and Rutley.

A day or two after the advertisements had appeared Keld came to my office looking a little worried. Rosa Lewis, who was an old friend of his, had seen the advertisement, upbraided him for getting so badly in debt, then asked him how much he thought the cellar would fetch. He replied: 'About two thousand pounds.' She said she felt sure the auctioneers would do him down, went to her desk and wrote him a cheque for two thousand. He could hardly refuse to take it, but that put me in a fine mess, for I had to explain to the auctioneers about the sale having been called off, pay for the useless advertising and bring all the wine back from Wickham to deliver it to Rosa in London.

Rosa Lewis was a famous character. She started life in Lord Rosebery's kitchen, became for a while, so it was said, one

c

of King Edward VII's many mistresses, then started a hotel in Jermyn Street. It was like no other, as it was really a house of accommodation where men could have romps with other men's wives. They confided their secrets to her and, if any possibility of embarrassment arose, there were half a dozen ways by which customers facing discovery could be swiftly smuggled out; one was through a tailor's shop in an adjoining street.

The walls of her parlour were covered with signed photographs of young men who had since become great – Generals, Cabinet Ministers, Ambassadors and so on. It was her custom to hold a small *levée* every evening about six o'clock. She would sit in a chair having her finger- or toe-nails manicured while half a dozen young men formed a court round her, drinking Champagne. I did not go there often as it was a dicey business. Six or eight bottles of wine would be consumed, but nobody knew who was going to pay for it until Rosa suddenly said to the waiter: 'You can bring the bill to Mr So-and-so this evening.' So one might find oneself having to fork out fifteen to twenty pounds.

My installation of a cedar-panelled room and *humidor* for cigars was due to Mervyn Baron. His firm were lead-smelters but he was a great connoisseur of cigars and a close friend of Cecil Hart, of Melbourne Hart & Co., the sole importers of Punch and Hoyo de Monterey. Mervyn pointed out to me that it was absurd for a well-connected wine merchant not to sell fine cigars instead of the few odd boxes for casual customers. He offered to put up half the capital, and we formed a company called Baron Wheatley Ltd; then placed an order with Melbourne Hart, mainly for Hoyo de Montereys, which were considered the best cigars in the world.

To run such a business a man really knowledgeable about cigars was essential and Mervyn produced a very pleasant man named Monty Sternberg.

Another addition to my staff was Robin (always known as Bino) Johnstone. I met him through Myles Corry, an ex-officer of my old Brigade who, with his elder brother, owned the bulk of the shares in the Cunard Company. Myles had a house in Eaton Square where he held court every morning for a bunch of spongers whom he afterwards took out to lunch. I went to these parties but only occasionally and because Myles bought all his liquor from me.

Bino was well-born, good-looking, witty and charming. He had twice coxed the Cambridge eight to victory and had many friends among the nobility; so with my now rapidly expanding business I took him on as a means of securing still more rich customers.

It was not long after my father's death that I added a new side to the business. This was thanks to a Mr H. N. Gilbey, who had broken away from his big family concern and developed a wholesale business of his own. His main lines were Golden Guinea – a by no means first-class Champagne a French white wine, La Flora Blanche, and a White Port. For all these the retail price was high, but Gilbey induced many firms to stock them by giving to the merchant buyer one or two cases in ten free.

Considering them not good value, the leading West End wine merchants would not handle them and I, too, had refused. But one day Gilbey called with a proposition. If I would put at least a case or two of each of his brands on my list, he would secure for me the business of several night-clubs. As this would enable me to buy larger quantities of certain brands and so secure higher discounts, I agreed.

Now that we were doing a semi-wholesale business, Cooper, who for several years had written up our ledgers, came into his own. He had connections in the Quartermaster General's department who introduced him to a number of Messing Officers who were willing to buy many thousands of cigarettes from us at a small discount.

I also greatly increased our retail business. Naps Derouet, a charming friend of mine who was agent for Offley's Ports, offered me a range of quite exceptional Tawnys from the famous Quinta da Noval. The oldest was guaranteed to have been one hundred years in cask. But the trouble was the price. The best Tawny wine we sold was a Cockburn, retailed at 12/6 per bottle, and most of Derouet's would cost us more than that.

After some thought I devised a way in which we might sell them and make a handsome profit. I sent an old, square-shouldered, eighteenth century bottle with a raised crest to a glass manufacturer and asked his price for making me two gross. His quotation worked out at sixpence per bottle. I provided him with the crest of the original Wheatley family and told him to go ahead. When the job was done I issued a leaflet with a photograph of the bottle and stated frankly that I had had the bottles made because the wines were so exceptionally fine. There were six kinds including a wonderful White Cucucha, and I priced the top one at 25/– a bottle. We sold the lot and they brought us many new customers.

Another venture was in liqueurs. For years people had come to us asking for comparatively rare liqueurs which they had enjoyed while abroad, such as Izzara at Biarritz. Our reply had always been: 'We are sorry to say we don't stock it, but you might try Fortnum & Mason.' Irritated by this situation, I got in touch with every liqueur importer in London and compiled a list of two hundred. They ran from Abricotine to Zwatschgenwasser. The average price of liqueurs in those days was 17/6 per bottle, but my list included Chartreuse in *carafon*, made in the eighteenth century before Chartreuse was ever sold commercially, at £25 per bottle.

And it was no ordinary list; only five inches wide but six feet long. I sent it out round a cardboard tube, like a thin roll of lavatory paper. After its issue, if Fortnums did not stock a liqueur they sent the enquirer to Wheatley and Son.

A venture that brought us additional prestige was the purchase through Messrs Sichel of all the Imperial Tokay from the Royal Saxon cellars. In the old days Imperial Tokay left Austria only as a gift from the Emperor, either to fellow sovereigns as a birthday present or to Ambassadors who were leaving after having served for many years at the Court of Vienna.

The quantity accumulated by the Kings of Saxony was about twenty dozen and the vintages ran from 1649 to early in this century. The really great Tokays are too sweet to drink until they have been in bottle for a quarter of a century, and I found the best among those we obtained was the 1806. Years later I drank one of the dumpy bottles of 1649 ; the year King Charles I had his head cut off – with my friend Ronnie Barton, the owner of Château Langoa Barton. It was no longer a great wine and had gone almost as pale as water; but when first opened it still had a delicious perfume and was quite drinkable.

Another parcel of Imperial Tokay I acquired cost me far more than it should have done. After the death of Napoleon III his widow, the Empress Eugenie, lived at Farnborough Hill in Hampshire. When the old lady had been dead for some years her cellar was advertised to be sold by auction. I went down to view it.

It was one of the most distressing sights I have ever seen. There were hundreds of dozens of the finest clarets – Château Latours, Château Lafites of 1868, 1870 and 1874 – that for many years had been uncared for. The great majority of the corks had rotted, two-thirds of the bottles were half empty, only perhaps two in a dozen had remained unullaged and were still drinkable. But there was a bin of old Imperial Tokay and another of 1870 Château Yquem still in good condition.

I thought these two lots worth another journey so went down to the auction. It was being conducted by a local firm who had not the sense to sell the almost worthless Clarets off in six dozen lots; they were auctioned by the dozen, so the sale dragged on interminably. The buyers were obviously only small boarding-house keepers from the Aldershot district and private people. Lot after lot started at nine shillings and was knocked down for eleven or twelve.

At last the d'Yquem came up. I let it run until it reached 15/-, then chipped in. The bidding rose – 20/-, 30/-, 50/-, 80/-, 120/-, 160/-, 200/-. I let it go at 240/-. An hour or so later the Tokay came up. The same thing happened, but I was determined to have it and it was knocked down to me at 360/-.

As I was leaving the room a stalwart figure came running after me. It was an Austrian named Stulich. He owned the

White Tower Restaurant in Percy Street, which was reputed to have the finest cellar in London. 'Oh Mr Veatley, Mr Veatley!' he cried. 'Why did you not let me know that you were here? These others are ignorant people; of wine they know nothing. If you and I had got together we could haf had these splendid wines for a shilling a bottle.' Ruefully we laughed over not having noticed one another, then agreed to split our purchases. He let me have half the Yquem and I let him have half the Tokay.

I had on numerous occasions enjoyed Stulich's excellent cuisine, but I think the food was even better at a little restaurant on the south-west corner of Leicester Square. It was run by a man named Artaz, who had previously been at Ciro's. It had only about a dozen tables ranged round its walls, but his clientele was most distinguished. Several times I saw one or other of the King's sons there, dining some celebrated beauty of the moment, and the Princesses with handsome escorts.

For Artaz I produced a special wine list for wealthy connoisseurs. It had on it only thirteen items. They included Clos de Vougeot 1899, Château Lafite (in magnums) 1874, Château d'Yquem 1870, Madeira 1849, Berncasteler Doktor 1895, Sherry 1750, Imperial Tokay 1763, collected from the cellars of the Kings of Spain, Saxony and Napoleon III, the Duke of Northumberland, the Marquess of Lansdowne, and the Earl of Breadalbane.

But such lists and ones like that which I designed for my two hundred liqueurs were not the only ways of advertising with originality. I had a large gilded flagon set up above the entrance to the shop, and on our notepaper, beneath the firm's name and address, had embossed a little gold flagon with the words 'At the sign of the Flagon of Gold'. I had the firm's telephone number changed to 3355, which made it easy to remember, and changed our telegraphic address to Bacchus.

Another happy inspiration was to send diaries at Christmas to all our most important customers. But they were not ordinary diaries. They were eight by five inches in size and an inch thick, providing a whole page for each day, bound in full morocco and gilt-edged. On each in gold letters I had printed the name of the recipient – 'HRH the Duke of York, KG', 'J. B. Joel, Esq.', 'His Excellency Baron de Cartier de Marchin' (the Belgian Ambassador).

They had no advertisements in them, but every day of the year these tokens of appreciation from Wheatley & Son lay on the desks of their distinguished recipients. Secretaries started ringing us up before Christmas to ask if they might have a diary for the following year, because their masters wanted to enter engagements for the coming January.

Stambois continued to figure prominently in my business life. He made prolonged calls at least once a week and wheedled me into buying more of his old Brandies than I really wanted. Early in 1930 he started a new venture. It was called The Gourmets and Connoisseurs Circle. This was not a club and there was no subscription, simply a series of dinners. The first was at the Park Lane Hotel and a few others followed, then in May Stambois persuaded me to give one in my office.

How this fat, rather tattily dressed, little Polish Jew succeeded in getting to know the people he did I have no idea, but Lord Decies acted as Chairman, and among those who attended were Sir Louis Greig, then the Duke of York's friend and official companion, Sir John Lavery, the famous painter, Colonel Sir Percy Laurie, chief Commissioner of Police, Harry Preston and several other well-known characters.

I had the whole shop cleared on the afternoon of the party. The Mayfair Catering Company installed a long table to seat thirty of us and made arrangements for cooking the dinner down in the cellars. We were all dressed in white tie and tails. The meal opened with Plover's Eggs and the main course was roast Sucking Pig. Among the wines I gave them was Château Lafite 1889 in jeroboams. The evening was a great success and the publicity it brought me was immense.

In ten years Mayfair had changed enormously. In Park Lane the Dorchester and the Grosvenor Hotels had replaced private mansions. Big blocks of luxury flats had gone up in Grosvenor Square and the streets adjacent to it, where before there had been town houses of the nobility, most of them occupied for only a few months each year. This meant a great increase in the wealthy population, from which we benefited.

Our turnover for the year 1925/26 had been £27,800 odd. By 1929/30 I had pushed it up to over £58,000.

7

PRIVATE LIVES

FROM the summer of 1926 we continued to live at 12 Chepstow Place. It was a pleasant little house. At the rear was a small garden. In it I built a complete trench system from boxes covered with plasticine, manned with scores of khaki soldiers. With toy guns that had lead bullets we shelled it, and in the background a toy train ran between two tunnels across an open space. By hitting the rear carriage one could derail it. Anthony enjoyed the fun immensely.

Nancy and I went out a lot but not always together. Passionate as our first years of marriage had been it became gradually more obvious that we had no basic interests in common. Hers were dancing and tennis. I was quite a good dancer but did not really enjoy it. I danced only with girls who attracted me with a view to getting to know them better. And having been gassed ruled out tennis for me. I got my fun from reading books, parties and dining out with my men friends.

So, while Nancy and I continued to be the most affectionate friends, who never in all our years together had a quarrel, we drifted into a situation where I did not object to her going out dancing now and then with men I knew and liked, while she never made any fuss about my going out for an evening without her.

Although Nancy and I were no longer inseparable, we continued to take our holidays together at various seaside resorts so that we could teach Anthony to swim. I built wonderful sandcastles for him. I was anxious that he should grow up a knowledgeable man so, as soon as he was old enough to understand I read him such books as Lamb's *Tales from Shakespeare*, Kipling's Jungle Books and stories of the

Greek Gods. I also painted on one wall of his nursery a great map of the world and in suitable spots stuck postage stamps – a tiger on India, a giraffe on East Africa, a bison on North America, various types of ships on the oceans and so on.

When two passionate people have lived together for several years it seems sadly inevitable that their desire for one another should gradually wane; and, should they still be young, one or both of them is likely to seek sexual satisfaction elsewhere. This was the case with me and, some months before my father died, I acquired a permanent mistress.

Her name was Gwen and, like her predecessor, she was an artist's model; but a greatly superior one in both her career and intelligence. I met her first in August 1926.

I was walking down South Audley Street and she up it towards Grosvenor Square. At a glance I saw that she was strikingly beautiful; dark, curly hair, large eyes, magnolia skin, rich mouth, a lovely slim figure and smartly dressed. As she passed me, I turned my head to look at her again. At the same moment she turned her head to look at me. I went on for a few paces, then again looked back. She had just reached the corner of Grosvenor Square. By then we were fifty feet apart. Before crossing the road she turned her head to look at me a second time. I could hardly believe it to be an invitation. But nothing venture nothing have. Turning about I followed her and caught up with her halfway along the Square. Politely I asked her where she was going on this lovely morning. 'Nowhere particular,' she replied. 'I'm just out for a stroll.'

I took her to Selfridges, where we ate chocolate sundaes, and we were soon laughing together. I learned that her name was Gwen, she was unmarried and had no special boy friend at the moment. She happily agreed to dine with me one evening and gave me her address. By then we had been talking for well over an hour and I was bold enough to suggest that it would be more fun if we could dine somewhere alone together. She gave me a wicked little smile and only said that I must not take too much for granted.

That evening I saw a friend and arranged to borrow his

flat, as I did not want to take Gwen to a *maison de rendezvous* in Soho.

After that everything went like a bomb. I telephoned Gwen at a house in Norfolk Square where she was then living and fixed a suitable date. With me to the flat I took a sumptuous cold supper and two bottles of Champagne. Gwen arrived on time, and after we had enjoyed our regal picnic she showed no objection at all to being made love to. I learned later that this was her favourite pastime, so we both enjoyed ourselves enormously and for over a year and a half we spent many happy evenings together.

Gwen read a great deal and was highly intelligent, so made a most pleasant companion, out of bed as well as in it. She also played the piano, so when her birthday came in August I made her a present of a baby grand and had it delivered in the morning so that it should be a pleasant surprise for her when she got home that evening.

She was an exceptionally passionate young woman and, not being content with my only spending an evening with her once or twice a week, we agreed that on some days in between she should come to my office just after closing time at six o'clock; and we spent an hour or so making love there. This led to an unforeseeable disaster.

Earlier in 1927 Nancy had acquired a permanent boy friend. He took her to dine and dance at the Savoy regularly every Thursday and sometimes on other evenings when I had engagements. He was a doctor at a big hospital and was always called 'Doc' by us. By nationality he was Irish, but without any doubt descended from one of the many Spaniards who had been cast up on the beach when their galleons were wrecked by the terrible storm that drove the Armada right round the north of Scotland into the Atlantic. He had the slim, wiry figure of a *torero*; his complexion was olive; he had black hair and eyes and one of the finest beak-like Roman noses I've ever seen. He was a rather silent man, but very handsome and a beautiful dancer.

One evening in November when I was expecting Gwen at my office and was waiting at the side door to let her in, to my surprise Doc drove up with Nancy in his car. Being in the neighbourhood, they had kindly thought of giving me a lift home. With Gwen liable to appear on the scene at any minute, what the hell was I to do?

Given time to plan there are very few situations in which I can't think of a way to get out with colours flying; but taken by surprise I'm utterly hopeless. Gwen had many good qualities. She would have been perfectly justified in asking me to make her an allowance, but she preferred to keep herself and never suggested that I should buy her expensive presents. On the contrary she always wrote to thank me most gratefully for anything I sent her, even gifts of flowers, with which I kept her constantly supplied. She was tidy minded and kept her flat in perfect order. Her clothes were always in good taste; her undies spotless. She abhorred dirt and smells and the skin of her beautiful body was always as fresh as that of a nymph who had just emerged from a crystal-clear pool. She never used bad language or sulked. But there were times, when upset, that she displayed the most violent temper

At the thought of the ghastly scene which might occur if she met Nancy there on the pavement I felt there was only one thing to do. I dashed inside for my hat and coat, padlocked the door, jumped into Doc's car and let myself be driven to Chepstow Place.

But that was far from the end of the matter. Another of Gwen's virtues, and one of mine too, was punctuality. Neither of us ever forgot a meeting we had arranged or were late for it; so I knew she would create a fine fuss when next we met; but I was not prepared for what happened.

Within a few minutes of my getting home the telephone rang. I picked up the receiver and it was Gwen – Gwen almost delirious with rage at my having stood her up. She had never met Nancy but her love for me made her bitterly jealous of her. She positively screamed at me down the telephone and it was evident that she had just come round the corner as we drove off. Having seen a photograph of Nancy in my office, she had recognized her from it.

In vain I pressed the receiver hard against my ear. Nancy was sitting within a few feet of me. She would have been stone deaf if she had failed to hear a woman's voice hurling abuse at me for not having waited for her at my office.

I hung up. Nancy naturally demanded an explanation. Fortunately Doc had had a professional appointment so after dropping us had driven off. I saw no alternative to coming clean, and told Nancy frankly that for a long time past Gwen had been my mistress. She was naturally terribly upset.

Most fortunately I had arranged to dine out that night. I had never met my host, whose name was Norman Penzer. He was a writer with a special knowledge of the East and well known for his excellent translations of French versions of eastern classics into English. For Messrs Sawyer of Grafton Street he had translated a vast work of ten volumes called *The Ocean of Story*. Upon this Indian work had been based, and given an Arabic setting, *The Thousand and One Nights*. When it was published I had written to Penzer asking him to autograph my copy for me. He said he would be delighted to and, after a brief correspondence, invited me to dinner. This excused my leaving the house and thus escaping a most distressing evening with Nancy.

Norman Penzer was only a few years older than myself. He was extremely knowledgeable and had a great sense of humour. I introduced him to my men friends and he frequently joined us when dining out. His knowledge of cigars was considerable, so at Mervyn Baron's suggestion I took him on to assist Monty Sternberg in that side of my business.

Shortly before Nancy found out about Gwen the latter got herself in the family way. Fortunately we were put in touch with a very nice elderly doctor who got her out. His consulting room was in Shaftesbury Avenue, so particularly well situated for him to assist ladies of the chorus, which was his speciality. But Gwen's short stay in a pleasant nursing home was a very anxious time for me.

For a long time past I had suspected that Gwen was being unfaithful to me. Jealousy is a horrible thing, but I must confess to being very prone to it. In consequence, earlier that summer I had Gwen watched and received a considerable amount of information about both her past and present.

I had suspected that she was Sir Frederick Mills's mistress as well as mine or, perhaps, his illegitimate daughter, but neither theory proved correct. Her mother, an Irishwoman, was Sir Frederick's housekeeper and her father, an Italian, was his butler–valet. They had previously lived at Weybridge and later Reading. At the tender age of fifteen Gwen had got herself in the family way by an engineer, who then married her. But her mother-in-law, with whom they lived, had hated her so virulently that she had left her husband and his present whereabouts were unknown. She had given birth to twins, both of whom had died. There was some reason to suppose that during her teens she had lived for a while in Italy, Spain and New York. But she was extremely secretive about her past and never disclosed even a hint of any of this to me. One definite fact about the present emerged. She had a boy friend, who visited her at St George's Square on evenings when she could be certain I would not be there.

We had one hell of a row. She was an inveterate liar and denied practically everything; but she had to admit that she had been seeing him, pleading that he was a very old friend and she was sorry for him. She swore never to see him again and we made it up.

But one evening in July when I was at St George's Square the bell of Gwen's flat rang. Looking out of the window she saw a car below in the street and turning, white-faced, to me, she exclaimed in horror: 'It's my boy friend!'

'All right,' I said. 'I'll go downstairs and tell him I won't allow him to bother you.'

'No!' she cried. 'Please don't! Please don't! He knows about you, of course, and he's terribly jealous. He's come here deliberately to beat you up. He's half a foot taller than you are and up at Oxford he was a boxing Blue. He'll half-murder you. Please, please, don't go down. Let me, and I'll send him away.'

As I have a horror of being hurt, I then did what I always think of as being the bravest thing I've ever done in my life. Pushing Gwen aside I went out on to the landing, lit one of the three-and-a-half-inch Sullivans I used to smoke, and

walked slowly down the three flights of stairs; then opened
the front door. Standing on the steps I found a slender,
good-looking, chap slightly shorter than myself. Oh what a
relief!

Sternly I told him that if he bothered Gwen any more I
would put the police on to him, then slammed the door in his
face.

Shortly after, Gwen moved to another flat I took for her
at 183 Westbourne Terrace. For a time all went well, then
Gwen's boy friend turned up again. There was another row
and I slapped Gwen's face; the only time I ever hit a woman.
She had on many occasions asked me to get a divorce from
Nancy, but nothing would ever have induced me to marry a
woman like Gwen. In spite of her lies and occasional fits of
temper she was a pleasant companion and splendid to go to
bed with, but no more.

After this row, as an excuse for deceiving me with her boy
friend again, she said that although she loved me best I
would not marry her, whereas he was single and wanted to.
I declared that I would not believe it unless he told me so
himself. Upon which she gave me his address.

I wrote to him and asked him to come to see me. He proved
to be a young American who had been mainly educated over
here and had a job with a shipping line. He was a pleasant
fellow and we discussed Madame Gwen with no holds barred.
He had met her in the lounge of an hotel up at Oxford. After
a few drinks together she had said brazenly, 'Would you like
to come upstairs and see my room?'

At that he took her to be a high-class tart, but found her
so attractive that he agreed. They had a most enjoyable time
and no question of money arose; so from there on they had
met frequently and he had fallen in love with her. He apolo-
gized for having continued to pursue her after I had taken a
flat for her, but said that she had the effect of a magnet on
him and he could not keep away from her. He added that he
really did want to marry her.

After my many months with Gwen and all the trouble she
had caused me – incidentally, we had had to again resort to
our kind friend the doctor in Shaftesbury Avenue, although

as I was always extremely careful this may not have been due to me – I decided that the time had come when I would be wise to put an end to our liaison. So I told Gwen's boy friend that if he was prepared to pay the rent of her flat I would give her up to him. To this he agreed, so for the last few months of 1928 I did not see her.

8

THE DEWHURST PROPHECY

There was a girl I had known by sight for several years, and to myself I called her 'The Lovely Lady of Berkeley Square'. I often saw this goddess walking down Hill Street or Charles Street to the Square. And a goddess she was; tall, stately, with a firm step and the most beautiful woman I have ever seen in my life.

Her father was a peer and had an account with us. One day he came into the shop and complained that some Vichy water had been put on his bill. He said it had been ordered by his daughter and he was not responsible for her debts. When this was reported to me, it established her identity. Her name was Gladys, but I was no nearer to knowing her.

Shortly afterwards, the New Year of 1929 arrived. That evening I gave my mother and sister dinner at the Hungaria, with Norman Penzer to make a fourth. In Vecchi's time the Hungaria, with its gipsy band, was very fashionable. Seated with a man on the opposite side of the restaurant was the angelic Gladys. I could not keep my eyes off her.

Shortly after the New Year came in my mother and sister went home. Norman and I stayed on for another hour or so until Gladys and her escort left their table. I had already paid my bill and, with Norman, hurried out after them. The man had a car. There was only one taxi available and a couple were about to get into it. I said to them: 'Please do me a great service. Let us share your taxi. I want to follow that car. When it has set down its occupants we'll go to my office in Mayfair and knock off a magnum of Champagne.' In the gay spirit of New Year's Eve they agreed and we all scrambled into the taxi.

As I expected, the car was driven to a house not more than

two hundred yards from my office. Gladys was just going in and her friend drove off. The taxi then took us to No. 26. I hastily unlocked the side door, sent Norman in with our new friends to open up a magnum, then hurried back on foot to Gladys's house.

Only five minutes had elapsed; it was two o'clock in the morning so there were no servants up. As I expected, in answer to my ring, Gladys opened the door.

This bold procedure was not due to the fact that I had had quite a lot to drink, but was an inspiration of the moment. Terribly excited but perfectly sober I told her that I had admired her for years, was crazy with love for her and had hardly taken my eyes off her the whole evening; then begged her to come round to join a little party in my office for a glass of Champagne.

She showed no resentment at my impertinence, but was quite firm in her refusal, so I had to retire defeated. But having broken the ice it was not in my nature to let matters rest there. While at the Hungaria I had asked Vecchi what he knew about her. I learned from him that the man accompanying her was an Italian and that she spoke Italian fluently.

Next morning I went up to see my old friend, John Wilson – the *doyen* of the book trade – at Bumpus's. From him I bought the most beautifully bound volume of Italian love poems that he could produce and that afternoon sent it to Gladys with a passionate appeal that she would have pity on me and let me take her out to dinner one evening.

Two afternoons later she came to the office and asked for me. As she had seen me only for a few minutes in the half-light on her doorstep, it was quite reasonable that she should wish to know a little more of me before committing herself. She thanked me very nicely for the Italian book but was puzzled to know how I had learned that she even knew that language. I told her and we had a very pleasant half-hour's talk; then she agreed to dine with me two nights later.

I took her to the Savoy and I have never felt prouder than when I accompanied this superbly beautiful woman in full evening dress down the steps to the restaurant. We dined again a few nights later, then went back to my office for a final drink, and she told me a lot about herself.

She had a very great love of all things Italian and would rather have been Italian than British. Many of her friends in London were Italians and she was a frequent guest at their Embassy. She had refused many offers of marriage because she did not care enough for any of the men who proposed to her. She loved beautiful clothes and her allowance was by no means a large one; so she was always in debt and being worried by her creditors.

I asked her how much she owed. She said about £400. Next morning I went to my bank, drew that sum in pound notes and sent it to her. Her letter to thank me for getting her out of her troubles could not have been more grateful. A few nights later we dined together again and again went to my office. There, without any suggestion on my part, she offered to let me make love to her. Laughing happily we set about it, then to my utter horror I suddenly found that I had become impotent.

She was very sweet about it and did her utmost to console me; but I was terribly ashamed of myself and for one of the few times in my life burst into tears.

Only at one other time has this calamity befallen me, and that also happened when a woman that I had long desired offered to let me enjoy her.

For such unexpected failures there is an explanation. Among my collection of books I had a number of the most famous erotica. One is *Untrodden Fields of Anthropology* by a French army surgeon. He describes the sexual customs of natives in many countries and discourses at length on unusual sexual phenomena. In his book he states that he had heard of numerous cases in which a man who had been animated by a most passionate craving to possess a certain woman, when at last the opportunity arose for him to satisfy his desire, suddenly found himself impotent.

A week or so later I persuaded Gladys to have supper with me in one of the Yeoman House flats, where a well-furnished sitting-room and bedroom would be much more suitable to make love in than my office. Perhaps she would not face up to the possibility of letting me again arouse her passions, then disappoint her. But, whatever her reason, after we had supped she stubbornly refused to play.

Gladys had made it clear that, while she liked me, she had very little time for me. She had many friends, none of whom were known to me, and she knew none of mine; so we had not even a meeting ground in common. Sadly I realized that it was futile for me to continue my affair with this quite exceptionally lovely lady.

In May Gwen turned up again. She caught me one evening just as I was about to leave the office, and over a drink told me a terrible story of woe. Her boy friend had wanted to marry her and told his mother, with whom he lived, about her. His mother proved most averse to the idea but he had persuaded her to come round to Gwen's flat one evening, and meet her. Perhaps he had told his mother too much about Gwen. Anyhow, they met reluctantly and as enemies. The party ended in a blinding row and his mother hauled him out of the flat by the scruff of his neck, declaring that she would stop his allowance and throw him out of her house if he ever went to see Gwen again. Gwen then implored me to take her back.

For several months past I had badly missed my evenings with her and was sorely tempted to do so. I made an excuse to leave my office for a few minutes to make up my mind. When I returned, I found that she had taken Nancy's portrait off the mantelpiece, torn it up and thrown the pieces in the wastebasket.

'There!' she exclaimed. 'That's what I think of your wife. She is no earthly good to you whereas I am. Leave her and come to live with me. Then you'll know that I really shall be faithful to you.'

I was still very fond of Nancy, and Gwen's tearing up her photograph filled me with cold rage. It made up my mind as nothing else could have done. I told her that I would have nothing further to do with her and never wished to see her again.

Some months before this, on the recommendation of a friend, I had been to consult an occultist named Henry

Dewhurst. He was a Dane and lived not far from Chepstow Place. He always told his clients that, when they recommended others, they were never to give their names, only make appointments for them to see him.

When I arrived he opened the door to me himself. He was small, frail and about forty years old. Greeting me he said at once: 'Your initials are D.I.W.', which was astonishingly near the mark, as they are actually D.Y.W. He took me into a comfortable sitting-room. In it there was no crystal, cards or other fortune-telling paraphernalia. We just sat down in armchairs on either side of the fire, and he said:

'Now, my child, I am going to talk to you and probably ask you questions, but you must not reply to them. Just sit silent while I get in touch with your psyche.'

For a quarter of an hour or so he rambled on, saying such things as, 'You have recently crossed the water – no I am wrong, but you have been at the seaside.' Then he said I might put any questions I liked to him, and we talked about my business problems.

A little later I asked him how Gwen was getting on and he replied: 'My child, I am so glad you had the strength to break with that woman. She was sent to you for a purpose and that purpose has been achieved. When you met her your whole body was crying out for sexual satisfaction. Lack of it was dulling your brain and taking a terrible hold over your imagination. To have such a woman for a year was just what you needed, but it should have finished then. She could give you no sort of mental companionship and towards the end she was taking much more from you than she gave. You are not a child to stand still; you have to go on, to progress, to develop yourself, and she was holding you back. She has made an attempt to become your mistress again, because she knows that you are steady and reliable; but in no circumstances must you take pity on her. That child has great powers of attraction and she will always have men.'

I told him that at times I missed her most damnably.

'No matter,' he said. 'You don't really need her any more because your sex life is over.'

'What do you mean by that?' I asked apprehensively.

'For God's sake don't tell me that I'm going to become impotent.'

He shook his head. 'I mean only that sexual desire will never dominate you again. Your virility will continue but in future sex will be your servant, not your master.'

'Even so,' I said. 'It's a grim thought that I should drift through life with only a casual adventure now and again.'

'You will not do that. There is another woman who will come into your life permanently.'

'Do you mean that I shall leave my wife?' I asked. 'I've no desire to do so. We are very fond of one another and don't interfere with each other's affairs. For us to part would give pain to a number of people who believe us to be happily married; and we are both very attached to our little son.'

'The only reason you ever came together was for your son to be born. And there are no other factors. There is a man in her life who is very persistent and I think that in the end she will go away with him.'

'Can you tell me anything about this other woman I am going to become attached to? Have I met her yet?'

'No, I don't think so. I see her in your office; a mahogany-panelled room. You will know her socially but she comes to you first on a matter of business. She is small and fair. Her hair is parted in the middle. She has been married before and has children. She has had much sorrow in her life, but she will bring you much happiness because she will be such a wonderful companion for you. She is very slow to give her love but when she does she will give everything. She may be away from you at times for quite long periods, but you can trust her completely. She is passionate but will never think of another man in that way and neither will you think of another woman. She is a wonderful child and you do not know how fortunate you are to be.'

It was on 3 May that Joan Pelham Burn came to my office. I had never met her before, but shortly afterwards I did come to know her socially because she was Bino Johnstone's sister. He had sent her to me to order some Champagne for a ball that a friend of hers was giving.

Henry Dewhurst was the only true seer that I have ever known; and he did predict, with absolute accuracy, where and in what circumstances I should meet the wonderful woman who was to be my beloved companion for the rest of my life.

9

THE GREAT SLUMP

UNDOUBTEDLY my vanity was largely to blame. I need not have had my office panelled in mahogany and the floor of the shop covered with rich carpet or bought expensive showcases. I need not have shipped the finest cigars that could be obtained from Havana or gone on buying from Stambois much more old Brandy than I really required. I need not have surrounded myself with a little crowd of lieutenants – Sternberg, Banks, Penzer, Bino Johnstone – none of whom were real assets to the business; and, above all, I should not have allowed Bino to persuade me to form a company to handle only wholesale trade, for which I had to lease large additional cellarage in Kensington.

Yet even had I done none of these things I doubt if I could have weathered the storm, because the business had no capital behind it and I had no means of obtaining the several thousands needed.

It was the Great Slump that proved my undoing. Few people were shrewd enough to foresee its coming and so retrench in time. I certainly did not. I pressed ahead with my ambitious operations.

My ultimate objective was to draw into the Wheatley company so many large hotels and restaurants which would buy all their wines and spirits through us that we should be able to dictate to the Trade, and, if not given the rebates we requested, take their brands off all our lists. This sounds like blackmail but it would have been no more so than the general practice of wine waiters' saving the corks from all the bottles of brandy they served, then demanding that the shippers buy them. We would have been in a position to stop this racket and the special rebates given to us would have cost the shippers nothing, because they would no longer have had to pay corkage.

A further development of this plan was that we should supply the restaurants which were shareholders in our company with all their requirements in china, glass, cutlery, and furnishings.

Until the latter part of 1929 there were few signs of the coming trouble. I even added two more members to my staff to help cope with the ever-increasing business. Bino was married to Peggy Marais, a member of one of the leading families in South Africa, and I took on her young brother, Maynard. The other was Patrick Butler. He was a tall, red-headed youth with an unfortunate stutter. Although he was a member of the Butler family of Hedges and Butler, they would not take him into their business and his mother made a pathetic plea to me to give him a chance. I did and had no reason to regret it as, in spite of his disability, he was no fool and worked most conscientiously and with intense personal devotion to me.

In May, after Joan Pelham Burn had brought me the order for Champagne, we started to go out together. She was a widow and had been married twice. First in her teens, more or less under pressure from her family, to William Younger of Auchen Castle in Scotland. After the war they separated and she married Captain Hubert Pelham Burn, Gordon Highlanders, with whom she had long been in love. But tragedy had deprived her of him. One night when driving near Aldershot, a drunken tramp had staggered into the road in front of Hubert's car. Swerving up the bank to avoid him, Hubert had crashed into a tree and been killed.

Joan lived in a very pleasant maisonette; the two upper floors of No. 48, Queen's Gate. When she left her first husband – Billy the Bart, as we all came to call him after his father died – it had been agreed that of the four children of the marriage he should keep the eldest girl, Meg, and the two boys, Bill and Jack, while she retained the younger girl, Diana. She also had living with her at Queen's Gate, Colin, the one child she had had by Pelham Burn.

On neither Joan's part nor mine was there any immediate

falling in love, but we found one another delightful companions and went out more and more often together, to Quaglino's, the Savoy, Toby's Club and other places. She showed a most sympathetic interest in all my business ambitions and took on the Managing Directorship of my new venture, which was to supply restaurants with equipment. We called it The Burn Trading Company.

In September that year the aircraft race for the Schneider Trophy was held off Gosport. Some friends of Bino's who ran a travel agency hired the big steam yacht, *Prince Olav*, as a floating grandstand to watch the race from the Solent, then to make a week's cruise before landing its passengers at London. Bino was going in her and persuaded Joan and me to go too.

But I got much more deeply involved in the Schneider Trophy race because Nancy's brother-in-law, Fred Lucas, had obtained concessions from the Gosport Municipality for the use of the mile-deep stretch of grass coast below the town. One of these was the right to erect stalls for the sale of various items including drinks and tobacco, and, as it was expected that many thousand people would congregate there, I undertook this.

I had a number of stalls created, one of which had several compartments, including at its end a private lunch room for myself and my friends. Joan took charge of the catering, while Bino, Mervyn Baron and several of my office staff served customers at the stalls. One of these brought with him Noël Coward, to whom he introduced me, and I invited them both to lunch. 'The Master', as stage folk called him, was already at the height of his fame and I admired his plays enormously. The song 'I'll see you again' from *Bitter Sweet* had been adopted by Joan and me as the theme song of our love affair. He proved a charming guest and later autographed first editions of all his books for me.

In the evening Joan, Bino and I went aboard the yacht loaded with bundles of pound notes and sacks of silver; but, later, when we were able to get out the costs, I found the operation to have been one of my many follies. It had entailed a lot of work and I had lost several hundred pounds.

Nevertheless, the cruise on the *Prince Olav* proved great fun. By then I was in love with Joan. We were given adjacent cabins, but she would not let me in to hers. As a last resort I bored a hole with a corkscrew in the partition that separated us and pleaded with her through it; but to no avail.

Towards the end of 1929 all my ventures were going great guns. D.W. Ltd had obtained the sole concession to supply several restaurants with wines, spirits and cigars. We also had a number of night-clubs, golf clubs and a yachting club on our books. The Burn Trading Company undertook the re-carpeting of the whole of the Hungaria restaurant and Joan was selling quite a quantity of linen to other concerns. But all this required capital and I was becoming worried by my ever-increasing overdraft.

Yet in November I could not resist Bino's suggestion that I should go with him to Spain, where he had some business to transact with Myles Corry. At that time Miguel Primo de Rivera was the great man in Spain, but there was much discontent and, as we were about to leave, the papers reported riots in Madrid. But when we arrived there everything was perfectly peaceful. In fact one day when we drove out to Toledo we passed Primo being driven to Madrid. He was sitting in the back of a large car and had no armed escort of any kind.

Bino's Spanish friends were most hospitable. They took us to the Prado and to Boca's restaurant, where there was a huge brick oven that had not been out for over a hundred years, in which, on the end of ten-feet-long iron pushers, sucking pigs were roasted to a rich brown in a matter of minutes.

They also took us on the long drive out to the Escorial, and there displayed their Liberal sentiments. Taking us down to the Royal Vault under the Palace they showed us the octagonal room in which the coffins of the Kings of Spain were lying on rows of shelves. With glee, they pointed to the only remaining empty shelf, and said: 'Alfonso XIII; then finish.'

One evening Bino and I went to the Plaza Hotel. At some of the tables in the big, round lounge there were couples of pretty, smartly dressed girls. We had been told the drill. It was not the custom to accost them. To one's choice of un-accompanied ladies one sent a waiter with a note asking if they would honour us by allowing us to join them. They then looked at the table from which the note had been sent and, if they liked the appearance of the men there, would smile their consent. In this way Bino and I made the acquaintance of two delightful young women. After several drinks they asked us if we would like to accompany them to a house where they sometimes spent the night.

We got a taxi and they took us to the most luxurious *maison de rendezvous* that I had ever seen. The furnishings were of the finest quality, and adjacent to the bedroom I was shown to with my girl was a bathroom with a marble bath sunk in the floor into which one went by a flight of steps.

In the New Year of 1930 Joan, knowing the state my marriage had reached, declared that no good could come of my remaining with Nancy, so the sooner I left her the better. Nancy was most averse to our parting but eventually I persuaded her to agree and in February I left 12 Chepstow Place. We disposed of the house, she took a flat at No. 41 Chepstow Villas, and Joan found a flat for me over a garage, 11 Manson Mews, which was quite near her in Queen's Gate.

I was becoming more and more worried by the state of my financial affairs; then a friend of mine, Captain Ian Mac-donald, suggested a way out. He had been in the Scots Guards, but resigned his commission to marry an American girl named Helen, who was one of the heirs of the multi-million-aire President of Esso Oil. They had a flat in London, a country house in Cornwall, an apartment in New York, a house on Long Island and another in the Bahamas.

Now Ian suggested that fortunes were being made in rum-running to the 'dry' United States and that I might cash in on a special market. Ordinary spirits and wines were easy enough to get but connoisseurs were pining for the really fine products that they drank when in Europe. If I shipped over some of Stambois's old Brandies, *Château*-bottled Clarets and some of my finest Hocks, I could get any price I liked for them. The main rum-runners' route was via the Bahamas; as Ian had a house there he knew the big operators in this illicit traffic, so could introduce them to me and for a reasonable commission they would ship my stuff to the US.

Tempted by the possibility of making big money quickly, I agreed to go to Nassau taking several dozen sample bottles with me. Joan decided she would like to come too; so we booked passages on the ss *Scythia*, a one-class Cunarder, and sailed on her from Liverpool on 1 March.

She called first at Halifax, Nova Scotia. The town was a dreary sight as the explosion of an entire ammunition convoy in the harbour during the war had almost totally wrecked it. Most of the dwellings were still only wooden shacks and they were under snow.

On 11 March we entered the approach to New York. Joan and I finished the last bottle of Champagne we had with us and I threw the empty bottle out of the porthole towards the statue that was supposed to represent Liberty. An hour or two later, when we had booked in at the Savoy Plaza, Joan said: 'What about a cocktail?'

'Good idea,' I replied and walked over to press the bell for the floor waiter. She laughed then, for she had pulled my leg beautifully. I had already forgotten that America was 'dry'. Scared by the stories of the many people who were being poisoned by hooch, we stayed 'dry' during our few days in New York.

We took the Florida Special down to Miami. It had a most comfortable lounge–observation car and on our journey south we were horrified to see the poverty in which the Negro population existed. The villages consisted of rude huts made out of empty petrol tins, men and women were in rags and the children naked.

In the early thirties Miami had not been spoilt by hordes of trippers and we greatly enjoyed our short stay at the Pancoast Hotel. At Nassau we were met by Ian and Helen, who proceeded to entertain us royally. We went with them to bathe from Paradise Beach, to the best night-clubs, out in their motor-boat for big-game fishing and one day to picnic on Rose Island, which they owned.

This last expedition proved disastrous for me. The island

was about a mile long by half a mile wide and it had no buildings or trees on it, so no shade. We walked round it, then picnicked on a sandy beach. The heat was terrific and I was wearing only the lightest clothes. In consequence, I got sunburnt. That night, after dining, we all went to the Bahamian Club to play the old gambling game of Hazard. I was wearing a dinner jacket. By then, under my stiff shirt, my chest and arms were burning like a furnace. Joan carried me off back to our hotel and saturated my pajamas with witch hazel. For the next two days I was in agony, red from my neck down to my insteps and unable to lie comfortably on either my back or my tummy.

When we had first arrived in the Bahamas Ian had introduced me to several rum-runners; and to Mr Christy, a white man with entirely Negro features and a great power in the island. The bottles I had brought were stored in a barn and a tasting was arranged; but when I recovered from my burns I was told that the barn had been broken into and the whole lot stolen. So that was that.

We returned to New York by a coastal steamer of the Manson Line. The three-day voyage was the most unpleasant I have ever made. It happened to be the end of the season in the Bahamas. The hotels were closing down and practically the whole of the white staff travelled on the same ship as we did. Joan and I had booked a cabin but they took aboard at least a hundred passengers for whom there was no accommodation. They crammed the little lounge and many slept in the passageways. We had to fight to get odds and ends of cold food. All the hotel staff had brought liquor with them and were rolling drunk most of the time. Added to this the ship had a permanent ten-degree list to port. I was terrified that at any time an extra large wave would hit her and she would turn turtle; but, thank goodness, the weather remained good.

The only pleasure I derived from this appalling trip was when we docked at New York. The barman at the hotel had been very rude to me. The Customs officers found four bottles of whisky in his luggage. I laughed at him while they broke his bottles into a great bin they had there for that purpose.

I don't doubt they drained the liquor out later for themselves.

In April we sailed home in the ss *Antonia*, another one-class Cunarder. It had been a most enjoyable holiday, but I returned several hundred pounds worse off.

Meanwhile, the world slump had really set in and business was going from bad to worse. People everywhere were complaining about the alarming decrease in their trade.

I did what I could to economize. On going into the wholesale cigarette business that our salesman had established with several Army regiments, I found that the special discounts he was giving, the expenses of his travelling to visit camps and the commission he was receiving on sales, added up to the fact that we were losing, instead of making, money on it. When I told him and said it could not be continued, he left in a huff; so that was one saving. Norman Penzer's activities really boiled down to smoking a lot of our cigars and making for us at eleven o'clock every morning beautiful black coffee laced with Brandy; so Mervyn Baron and I went up to his house one Sunday morning and gave him notice.

On 30 June, Lady Newton having died a year or so earlier, my mother was married to Sir Louis at St George's, Hanover Square. It was a very suitable match. The first Lady Newton had been an old frump, whereas my mother wore smarter clothes, was more witty and vivacious and far better read than the great majority of Aldermen's wives, so Louis could be proud of her. She exchanged a rather dull existence as a widow for Mansion House society with its innumerable entertainments.

That summer my holiday was interrupted by a telegram telling me that No. 26 had been burgled. I found that the burglars had made off with nearly all our cigars. Seeing the general state of things and that cigars take several months to ship and mature, Mervyn was against placing an order for a new stock; so the Baron Wheatley Company's business decreased to a trickle.

As summer merged into autumn things got worse and worse. My business was particularly vulnerable because its backbone consisted of the rich, who did not buy from hand to mouth. In the past there had been many of our customers to whose country houses we used to send a lorry once or twice a year carrying up to fifty dozen bottles of good liquor and, perhaps, a pipe of Vintage Port or hogsheads of Claret or Burgundy that we had bottled for them, to be binned away. Then, in the Season, or on special occasions at other times of the year, there were ball suppers at the big houses in Mayfair where up to twenty dozen of Champagne were consumed in a night.

Now all this had ceased. The rich had enough wines lying in their cellars to keep them going for several years. There were no longer any big parties. People with money were using it to bolster up companies in which they had large holdings, or to buy up firms that were in difficulties.

In addition to this, bad debts began to pile up on the wholesale side of the business, and from many of the D.W. Ltd customers we could get only small payments on account. Then in the autumn there arose another matter for grave concern. The previous year the Hungaria had started a River Club at Maidenhead, which was run as a separate company, and we were their main wine suppliers. The club started off splendidly and Joan and I had been down there many times to dance and watch the excellent cabarets. But as the bad weather set in the club became half-empty and was no longer paying its way. Eventually, the Company had to go into liquidation and I sustained a loss of several hundred pounds.

10

THE FALL OF WHEATLEY
AND SON

By the end of the year things had become so bad that to reduce expenses I gave notice to both Sternberg and Banks. I also did so to Bino. He knew the mess I was in and had actually brought me very few new customers; but he simply laughed at me, then reminded me that I had made him a Director of Dennis Wheatley Limited with a three-year contract as an employee of the Company; so, as he could not get any other job, he meant to stay on and I'd have to continue to pay his salary whether I liked it or not.

Joan, on the other hand, proved a pillar of strength. We spent nearly every evening together, and when money was particularly short she used to drive me round to the office at night, so that I could open the late post and see if any big cheques had come in which would enable me to send something on account to my most pressing suppliers. From November on, Gordons would supply us with no more gin except for cash, so at times I was reduced to borrowing a few dozen from friends in the Trade in order to keep my private customers going. I had also been continuing to buy books up till the past summer and had many bills for them outstanding. Towards the end of the year I received a letter from Dulaus's, with whom I had spent hundreds, informing me that if I did not pay they would have to take proceedings.

It was at about this time that, having discussed matters with my accountant, I went to see my lawyer. He was Sir Louis's second son, Sidney, who had by then qualified. He had been a friend of mine for many years but now had no helpful suggestions. He advised me that my only course was to go bankrupt.

D

I went to see my mother who was then living in a flat that Louis had taken at 12 Hyde Park Place. She showed no inclination at all to help me and Louis, with his false Cheshire-cat smile, commiserated with me but said he feared it would only be throwing good money after bad.

It was then that my Jewish friends, Frank, Joe Links and Mervyn, showed true friendship by rallying round. All three declared that in no circumstances must I allow myself to be made a bankrupt. Frank and Joe each lent me £500 to stall my most pressing creditors, and Joe protected my library for me. On leaving Nancy, I had had all my bookcases and their contents removed to my office. Against the possibility of a notice being served on me and my being no longer free to dispose of my books, we had the lot taken to Joe's office off Cavendish Square. He could then say that I had made them over to him as security for the loan he had made me.

But it was Mervyn who saved me from complete disaster. The 200-year-old firm of Block Grey & Block occupied a single-storey building on the corner of Park Lane and Mount Street. The site had originally been the lower end of the garden of a house in Park Street. Now Blocks were just coming to the end of their ninety-nine year lease and all the gardens running down from Park Street had been bought for the erection of a block of luxury flats; so Blocks had to find new premises.

Cecil Melbourne Hart, who supplied us with our cigars, also supplied Blocks. This charming man was a great friend of Mervyn's and he agreed to open negotiations. Nicholas Block was the head of the firm. Having informed him of my precarious situation, Melbourne Hart suggested that to acquire my business, which was only a few hundred yards from their premises, would serve them much better than looking for others.

The result was that early in January Nick Block invited me to go round and discuss the matter with him in his office. He was an elderly, distinguished-looking man and during the whole of my association with him we remained the best of friends. At this first interview I learnt that his business formed only a part of a much larger one, Fearon, Block & Co., which had big premises in Holborn. The other directors were Fearon, Robinson and McIver. The two former held the bulk of the shares in the firm. McIver's business, which had offices in Liverpool and Malta, had been taken over some years previously as, I later learned, had Block's.

There followed further meetings at which Fearon and Robinson were present. The former was a pleasant man but I did not at all care for the latter (who incidentally was not related to Nancy's family). At Park Lane there was a lunch room for entertaining customers, and also one at Holborn. I lunched with the partners at both when we met to discuss balance sheets, staff and so on.

Meanwhile, my affair with Joan continued and she sustained me marvellously during these difficult weeks. I had for a long time wanted to get a divorce from Nancy and ask Joan to marry me, but in view of the appalling uncertainty about my future I did not feel that it would be right to do so. It was she, in my darkest hour, who said that she wanted to marry me and early in 1931 urged me to set about getting a divorce. So I wrote to Nancy and she reluctantly agreed.

By mid-March, to my great relief, I had come to an arrangement with Fearon, Block & Co. to liquidate Dennis Wheatley Ltd., Baron Wheatley & Co., and the Burn Trading Company, and make my lease of No. 26, stock and goodwill over to them. In return for this they would pay all my creditors a pound in the pound and give me a seat on their Board of Directors at a salary of £800 a year. On 22 April the document of amalgamation was signed.

The next step was to alter No. 26 to their requirements. Half of my big office was partitioned off to accommodate Nick Block, and the beautiful mahogany doors, twelve feet in height, that I had bought from an old house in Trafalgar Square, Chelsea, to separate the offices from the shop were sold. A lunch room was later made in a part of our cellars. Extra desks were installed for Nick's aide, a pleasant fellow named Hartman, and for Nick's manager, a Mr Dines. Bino and Sternberg lost their jobs but, to my relief, all my old staff were retained, with Dines and Thurgood as joint managers.

I did my best to settle down under the new regime but I was far from happy. Old Nick could not have been kinder, but he was only the nominal head of the firm. Fearon and Robinson were both what the Americans would have termed 'very ordinary people'. To my mind they were not even good wine merchants.

Under the new management all the original ideas I produced for increasing trade were shot down and I became just a salesman; but the thing that galled me most was a decree from head office that I must not take an order exceeding £50 from anyone without its being countersigned by another director. That was a positive insult.

At last all the formalities for my divorce were completed and I obtained a decree on 29 June, after having been married to Nancy for just over nine years, most of which had been very happy ones. The divorce cost me £88 in legal fees, which I could ill afford and I was ordered to pay alimony of £6 per week free of tax.

On 8 August Joan and I were at last able to get married. The legal tie was performed at the Registrar's Office in Buckingham Palace Road; then the following day our intimate friends assembled at St Ethelburga's Church, Bishopsgate, for the marriage to be blessed. I was now able to get rid of 11 Manson Mews, and, as Joan's husband, move into her comfortable flat at 48 Queen's Gate, where for so many months, as a constant visitor, she had comforted me during my terrible anxieties.

But I was far from free of worries. Since my father's death I had been living at the rate of from three to four thousand a year; now I was reduced to a salary of £800. Block's had taken over all my trade liabilities but I still had quite a number of private debts. Fortunately Joan had an income of over a thousand a year, so she paid the rent and with unstinted generosity virtually kept me which, while I appreciated it enormously, was a by no means happy position for any man to be in.

We put off our honeymoon until August and about that Nick Block was extremely kind. He said that as I had been through such a trying time I must take six weeks and get a real breather. When I told him we were going to the South of France he said in that case, as I had never been to Bordeaux, we must cross to the west coast and spend at least a week visiting the *châteaux*.

Six weeks sounded a wonderful break but, once again, I was up against the problem of money. However, I solved it successfully. One of Amy Robinson's friends was old Mrs Barnato. Her daughter, Leah, had married Carlyle Blackwell. He was a handsome and pleasant American who, in the old silent days, had been a top-line film star but now lived with Leah in London.

Nancy and I had seen a lot of them, for Leah was rich, hospitable and gay. She was also bawdy-minded, so it occurred to me to take some of my erotica round to her. I chose de Sade's most famous work, *Justine and Juliet*. My edition was in ten gilt leather 12vo volumes, published in the eighteenth century and copiously illustrated. The other item I took was a large copy of Pietro Aretino the Divine's book with really beautiful coloured illustrations. Leah cheerfully gave me a very handsome cheque for these rarities, and that paid for the greater part of my honeymoon expenses.

First, we spent a few nights in Paris and, on Betty Earle's recommendation, stayed at the St Regis in the Rue Jean Goujon, just off the Rond Point. It was a small hotel with no restaurant, but the most delightful I have ever stayed in. It was owned by that most famous of all Paris restaurants, the 300-year-old Tour d'Argent.

From Paris we went on to the little coastal resort of Cavalaire, about ten miles from St Tropez. The town was situated on a wide bay, one side of which rose to a steep cliff about half a mile away from any other building; on its edge stood the Hotel Surmer. We had been recommended by friends to stay there because it was cheap, but it was very far from nasty. It had only about a dozen rooms and one had one's meals on a balcony overlooking the sea. Its entire staff were the proprietor, his wife and two maids; but he had been a head chef at the Negresco in Nice. For three weeks we spent our days lazing in the sunshine, and once we committed the extravagance of going into Nice and lunching on the terrace of the Negresco.

From Cavalaire we returned to Paris and from there I sent off the letters of introduction Nick had given me to numerous Claret shippers, saying that we were coming to Bordeaux. When we arrived at our hotel there I found a handful of letters inviting us to lunch and to see famous vineyards. One was from a Monsieur Barton. He said that early next week the Vintage would be starting and that he was moving out to his *Château*. His sister would be acting as hostess for him and he would be delighted if we would come out and spend a couple of nights there.

For me this presented a poser as I have never been any good at languages and had only a few words in French. I visualized Monsieur Barton as a middle-aged Frenchman with a heavy black beard, and felt that I would prove a far from satisfactory guest. But while we were in Paris a crisis had occurred. The Navy at Scapa Flow had mutinied and refused to haul in the anchors of their ships until they received an increase in pay. That the Royal Navy had mutinied caused consternation throughout Europe. Such an almost unbelievable event made people think that a full-scale revolution was about to take place in Britain. The pound plunged to shillings and it was only with difficulty that one could persuade the French to change English money at all. It was this which caused me to accept Monsieur Barton's kind invitation. I took comfort from the fact that Joan spoke French very fluently.

During the next few days we were handsomely lunched and wined by the Calvets, Cruses, Lebegue and other shippers. We then drove the twenty or more miles out to the Château Langoa Barton. Instead of being a large, tasteless Victorian building, like most *Châteaux* in the Médoc, it proved to be a beautiful mansion of the Louis XIII period. And what a surprise when we went inside.

Ronald Barton was not French but Irish and a few years younger than myself. His sister had stayed with friends at Aldershot when Joan had been there as Hubert Pelham Burn's wife, and Ronald had been at Eton with Bino.

Ronald's firm was Barton & Guetier and the history of the partnership is interesting. The Bartons' family home was in Ireland and their property in France always the province of a younger son. When the French Revolution became the Terror, the ferocious Talien was sent to Bordeaux to exterminate all aristocrats. The Barton of that day realized that at any time he might be seized and sent to the guillotine so, leaving his head clerk Guetier in charge, he returned to Ireland. With only one short break the war with revolutionary France lasted for twenty-three years. After all that time, when peace was at last restored, Barton decided to visit his old estate in the Médoc. Knowing that the properties of all rich landowners had long since been confiscated by the State, he did so only out of curiosity. The big cellars of the firm were in Bordeaux. When he entered them he was received by Guetier, who threw open his arms and cried:

'Ah! Monsieur Barton, how happy I am to see you! War is always good for the wine trade. We have done well. In the bank I have half a million francs waiting for you.'

And in those days such a sum must have been worth over a million pounds today. So, ever since, the Guetiers have been partners in the firm.

Life at the *Château* could not have been more delightful. It combined all the best features of big English and French country houses and had a lovely garden of fruit trees. No cocktails, but Krug Champagne before every meal; with it a succession of three or four superb Clarets followed by glasses of Château d'Yquem and old Brandy. A French chef produced dishes that did justice to the wines. We had been asked for two nights but were pressed to stay on, so we remained there for a week. It was a wonderful end to a honeymoon.

When we got home I resumed my uninspiring grind. I had little to look forward to except the pleasures of my marriage to dear Joan. But a malign fate had not yet done with me. In February I was struck by a bolt from the blue.

One afternoon, shortly after lunch, Fearon and Robinson came to see me. Old Nick had gone out to avoid this unpleasant scene. The partners from Holborn told me that their accountants had raised certain questions about the previous year's take-over. The bad debts had far exceeded those I had declared. But that was not all. I had swindled them out of £4000 by including my private overdraft in the firm's liabilities. While the lawyers looked into the matter I was suspended as a Director. I was to leave the office at once, and not return without permission.

11

IN THE WILDERNESS

BEING thrown out of my office was an appalling shock. It was true enough that many of our sales which I had considered sound early in 1931 had, in that ghastly slump year, become bad debts; but I could not be blamed for that. The thing that worried me was the accusation that I had swindled Fearon, Block by including my own overdraft of some £4000 in the sum they had paid to take over my business, without disclosing to them that it was a personal liability.

Naturally, I had had to clear my overdraft, as I possessed no capital, had numerous private debts and was to receive only £800 a year salary. I was under the impression, of course, that Block's were aware that I had used my personal account to finance various business ventures and had accepted the overdraft as a part of my liabilities. But what if the accountants had made a mess of the take-over document? If they had and a case was brought, I would find myself in prison.

I went straight home to Queen's Gate. Joan was not a 'little woman' who has hysterics or faints on being given bad news. She had stood by me through two awful years and would, I knew, continue to do so. I told her what had happened straight away and she took it splendidly.

I am happy to say, too, that I did not lose my head. There were private papers in my office, love letters and so on, that, having been thrown out without a moment's notice, I had had no chance to take away; and I had no intention of leaving them there for anyone to read. Thinking the odds were they would change the locks on the doors next day to keep me out, Joan drove me round that night. I secured my private papers and any others I thought might prove useful.

The nine months that followed should have been the most miserable in my life. They were, of course, a time of ceaseless anxiety, but made tolerable by Joan's unfailing sweetness.

Our most pressing worry was shortage of money. I was reduced to living on Joan, as my mother refused to help me, and I still had a number of debts. One very nasty matter was my liability for the rent on the cellars in Kensington that Bino had persuaded me to take when we formed Dennis Wheatley Ltd, as this was an item Fearon, Block had not taken over. Other liabilities I could not escape were two quarters' rent still outstanding on 11 Manson Mews and income tax on the past year, for which I was summonsed; but luckily my accountants were able to save me by putting in certain allowances that had not been claimed. Fortunately, during my ten months with Block's, I had managed to pay off most of my debts, but I was still harassed by demands for sums I owed my tailor, haberdasher and hatter.

Joan was an excellent manager and we lived very quietly, practising every possible economy. She sacked her cook and took over the kitchen. There were no more theatres, dining out or giving cocktail parties. For drink we had to limit ourselves, except on special occasions, to a glass of Sherry each in the evenings.

But our friends stood by us nobly. From time to time Joe, Frank and Mervyn took us out to one of our old haunts for dinner. The Laurence Carrs had us several times to lunch at their lovely house just outside Richmond Park. He had been a brother officer of Hubert's and later became a Lieutenant General. Sir Lionel and Betty Earle often had us for a meal. Joan's other closest friend, Cecily Gordon Cumming, had lived with her at No. 48 until shortly before our marriage. She had then herself married Captain Christopher Vian, the brother of the famous Admiral. They bought a charming little house in Selwood Place and often asked us there.

Joan had often stayed with the Gordon Cummings at Gordonstoun before it became a famous school. Old Sir William had been at one time an equerry to King Edward VIII when he was Prince of Wales. On one occasion they had gone to Dublin, and it was decided that the time had come when the young Prince should be initiated into the pleasures of life. An attractive and suitable widow was found who agreed to receive HRH. On being informed of what had been arranged he asked Gordon Cumming two questions. 'Do I give her any money? And do I take my boots off?'

There were also weekends in the country. Joan's father. Louis Johnstone, was the fourth son of the first Lord Derwent, He had acted as agent for Major Berners, the wealthy owner of the greater part of Berners Street, who lived at Woolverstone Hall near Ipswich. It was a fine estate, occupying many acres on the south bank of the Orwell, and the Johnstones occupied Woolverstone House, a very pleasant property built by Edwin Lutyens. Joan's father had died in 1922 but her mother still lived there and for a long time past I had been down with Joan for weekends.

I recall an episode which might well have taken place in feudal times. 'Wicked Uncle Bino', as the children later referred to him, was also staying there for the weekend. He took me up to the Hall to meet old Jack Berners, who was going out to see some sheep that had just lambed. Bino and I accompanied him, together with a new shooting dog he had recently acquired. When he reached the sheep-fold the shepherd greeted his master, then stood beside him while for a few minutes we admired the young lambs. It occurred to Berners to show us how good his new dog was. Without even a glance at the shepherd he suddenly lifted his hand, snatched off the man's cap and threw it some distance while calling to his dog, 'Fetch it boy.' The dog was off like a flash and brought the cap back to his master. Again without looking at the shepherd he put the man's cap back on his head.

Mrs Johnstone was a tiny, very spry, elderly lady. She was a fine gardener, deeply religious, but not without a sense of humour, very well-informed and always most kind to me. Her one failing was habitual impatience. She was a genuine aristocrat – for she was directly descended from Richard de Talbot, who came over with William the Conqueror, and, through centuries of marriages, connected by blood with practically every Royal family in Europe – yet she would start eating before the men at her table had even been served and later sat with her fingers poised over the bell on the table, ready to press it for the next course the second the last person there had finished. Her vitality was extraordinary. She continued to prune her roses up to within two years of her death, and her sight, hearing and walking were still perfect when she did die at the age of ninety-nine.

Her family consisted of four children; Gran, a pleasant but not very brilliant Gunner officer who had won a DSO; Dorothy, a spinster whom Joan always declared to be much cleverer than herself, which was by no means the case; Joan; and the clever, witty, charming, unscrupulous Robin – known to everyone as Bino. This Benjamin was the apple of his mother's eye. Nothing was too good for him. In addition to making him a handsome allowance she paid his debts again and again; so by battening on her and his successive wives, he escaped having to do an honest day's work all his life.

We also spent several weekends with the Laurences down in Surrey. He had just retired as a Colonel from the Coldstream Guards and was a great character. When he was only twelve years old his guardian had sent him abroad accompanied only by another little boy of the same age. They were given a small allowance, told to take any odd jobs they could get and not to write home for more money except in an emergency. Wearing bowler hats they wandered round France, Germany and Italy, were several times mothered by kind-hearted tarts and acquired much unusual knowledge for their age.

Apart from these short breaks, being at Queen's Gate all day as well as in the evenings, I saw much more of the children and I did what I could to help with their education in ways that are outside the usual school curriculum.

One of my happiest ideas for them was making what we called my Historical Kite. The object of this was to demonstrate the growth of civilization. To tell a child that Rome fell in 410 and that the British Colonies in North America became Independent in 1776 cannot really convey the lapse of time between these two major events. I took a number of

strings. The longest was ten feet and its end represented the
dawn of civilization in Egypt and Chaldea. Others, propor-
tionately shorter, represented China, India and Central
America. Each string joined the longest at dates when these
separate civilizations became known to one another, the last
being Mexico–Peru. Two inches on each string represented
100 years, thus covering 6000 in all. Along the strings were
tied small labels giving outstanding happenings such as the
building of the Pyramids, Athens becoming a democracy,
Julius Caesar's conquest of Gaul, the births of Confucius,
Buddha, Jesus Christ, Muhammad and so on. For the last
2000 years the strings were pasted on a kite-shaped piece of
paper so that further information could be written against
key dates. In this way one was able to show the children such
things as that if 10 feet cover 6000 years of history the French
Revolution was only 3 inches from 1932.

A friend of Joan's who was on an Educational Committee
saw my Kite and was so impressed with it that she insisted on
its becoming more widely known. This resulted in an extraordinary experience for me. That year the annual Conference on Education was being held at Hoddesden, Hertfordshire. I was persuaded to go down there with my Kite and
lecture on it to some 200 school teachers.

Shortly after I was thrown out of South Audley Street, two
important changes took place in my affairs. My Jewish
friends said that I must change my solicitor and took me to
a cousin, Reggie Mesquita of Goulden, Mesquita & Co.,
who from then on very ably handled all the negotiations. I
had also been, of course, to see my mother and Sir Louis and
given them full particulars of my unhappy situation. Neither
of them was willing to help financially, but Louis did one
thing which later proved greatly to my advantage. He said
he had no faith in the accountants that had handled Wheatley
& Son's business for many years and sent me to his own man,
a Mr Stephens, whom I found very pleasant and most helpful.

I was still under the obligation to pay Nancy's alimony
and, although I cashed in my Life Insurance policy, I constantly fell behind. She wrote to me several times about this
as she was hard up herself. But, knowing my situation, she

was deeply sympathetic and her letters could not have been kinder.

Another obligation was Anthony's school fees; but in this I had a lucky break. I received a document from the Vintners' Company announcing that the Court had decided to allocate each year a sum for educational purposes to be distributed among Liverymen who found school fees a burden. I went down to see Commander Tuffel, the Clerk of the Company, and told him of my misfortune, upon which he kindly agreed to make me a grant from the fund.

Meanwhile, I was perpetually harassed by letters from my new solicitor and accountant, enclosing long statements from Fearon, Block & Co. giving particulars of ways in which they claimed I had defrauded them. One item was regarding book debts. Of those that I had declared good at the time of the take-over in April 1931, some £1000 was still unpaid in March 1933. I had acted in good faith, but the Slump had played the very devil with nearly everybody's finances, and it was still continuing. There was, above all, the matter of my big private overdraft. Eventually, they produced a balance sheet in which it was claimed that the final deficiency for which I was liable was six thousand, five hundred and sixty-two pounds.

My miserable position was further aggravated by the fact that I was still technically a Director of Fearon, Block & Co. and bound to them by an agreement. Therefore I was debarred from offering my personal goodwill and knowledge of the wine trade to any other company. I could only sit, brooding, day after day in the flat.

It was my wonderful Joan who saved me from this ghastly, futile existence. I had shown her some of the short stories I had written years before, just for fun. One day she said: 'Why don't you write a book? I'm sure you could.'

I had little faith in my ability to do so and even if I did, and succeeded in getting a publisher to take it, I could not hope to make out of it more than about fifty pounds. But having a shot at it would at least take my mind off my worries; so I bought some paper and sat down to write a thriller.

My feeling that it was Louis's meanness and influence over my mother which stopped her giving me at least some help led me to portray him as murdering her for her money by drowning her in a bath in a Curzon Street flat. But the book's real interest for my readers is that in it, on the night of the murder, the Duke de Richleau, Simon Aron and Rex van Ryn all met for the first time. And it was by the creation of those three characters that I made my name as a writer.

Joan typed the book for me and by mid-July it was finished. The next thing was to try to find a publisher. In this Bino repaid me to some extent for the hundreds his friendship had cost me. Incidentally, he had owed me £157 for drinks supplied by the firm before I sold it. Knowing that he could not pay and that his mother would have to do so, I did not include this among the list of creditors I produced for Nick Block. I simply removed the sheet recording Bino's account from the ledger and destroyed it.

Now, it so happened that one of Bino's friends was Gerard Fairlie, to whom Sapper was to leave, in his Will, the right to use his famous character, Bulldog Drummond. Fairlie's literary agents were A. P. Watt & Son, the most distinguished firm in the business. Joan gave a little lunch party for Bino, Fairlie and Bill Watt. Watt took my manuscript away to have it read, and, if possible, find a publisher for it.

Early in August it occurred to me to pay another visit to Henry Dewhurst and find out what he could predict about the outcome of my awful wrangle with Fearon, Block, which was still dragging on. The seer opened his front door for me, flung up both his hands in the air and, to my amazement, cried: 'You've written a book! You've written a book!'

'You certainly are a marvel,' I smiled. 'You're right, of course; but I haven't even got a publisher yet. It's only got as far as a literary agent.'

'No matter.' He took me by the arm and pulled me inside. 'You were never meant to be a businessman. You are on the right road now. Of course your book will be published. Let me see. Yes, you will receive good news about it on the 22nd of this month. And it will prove a great success. You will become famous. Your name will become known all over the world.'

The Laurences had taken a villa at Lyon-sur-Mer that summer and asked us over to stay for a fortnight in August. Naturally, I waited for the 22nd with the greatest impatience and was then bitterly disappointed. No good news about the book reached me. But it would have had I remained in London. A day was lost by forwarding a letter from Watt's to France. On the 23rd I learned that Messrs Hutchinson had accepted my book for publication.

What remained of August and the whole of September went by with no decision about the take-over and with me still under the threat that I might be brought to Court as a swindler and sent to prison. Then, early in October, I had a piece of real good fortune. When once again going through a great mass of papers concerning the business I came upon a carbon copy of the list of liabilities with which I had provided Fearon, Block. Among them was my personal overdraft.

I rushed off with it down to Mr Stephens. He was delighted and agreed that it cleared me completely on this major charge of fraud. But, alas, it was too late to use it to the greatest advantage because, behind my back, Sir Louis Newton had entered into negotiations with Robinson, the partner whom I disliked. And they had recently come to an agreement that my mother should pay the firm £5000 in settlement on my behalf.

Had I had my way I would have fought this, but the arrangement had already been made. Moreover, Sir Louis led my mother to believe that she was paying the sum from her capital right away, and for many years she held it against me that she was losing the income that this money would have brought her. It was not until years after Sir Louis's death and a year or two before her own that the matter again arose and I was able to prove to her that the transaction did not cost her a penny. Fearon told me himself that his firm was not to receive the £5000 until after my mother's death.

Nevertheless, now that it could be proved that I had not deliberately defrauded the firm, Stephens and Reggie Mesquita were able to wring considerable concessions from them. They agreed to hand over to me all my personal possessions, including some valuable furniture, that were still at No. 26; to allow me to transfer all my old customers who were willing to make a change to any other firm of wine merchants; and to issue a letter regretting my resignation from their Board of Directors.

In spite of Dewhurst's prediction about my success as an author, I felt it would be most unwise to abandon the wine trade; so early in November I went to see the partners of Justerini and Brooks. They were then still in the office that the firm had occupied for nearly 200 years. It stood on the corner of the Haymarket and Pall Mall and formed an enclave in the Carlton Hotel. But it was so small that there was room in it only for the partners: Arthur Kemp, young Eddie Tatham and dear old Stanley Brown. In consequence they could not take me in, but they willingly entered into an agreement to pay me a handsome commission on all the customers I could bring them. In this I was very successful, and although it is over forty years now since I have been active as a wine merchant, I have never ceased to enjoy most friendly relations with that splendid firm's Directors.

But now the writing bug had got into me. I wrote with tremendous enthusiasm several short stories and another thriller. This second book was *The Forbidden Territory*. Its principal characters were again the Duke de Richleau, Simon Aron, Rex van Ryn and Richard Eaton. I thought it much better than my murder story and Hutchinsons agreed, so it was decided that it should be published as my first book.

In spite of what Dewhurst had said about my not being at my best as a businessman, I was determined to do all I could in helping to market the book, and, now that I had some money from the sale of furniture and pictures that I had got back from No. 26, I invested a good part of it in salesmanship.

I had 2000 postcards printed; on one side they had the pictorial end-papers of the book, on the other, alongside the space for the address, simply the title, date of publication and a request that the recipient, if he enjoyed adventure stories, should ask for the book at his library. I sent several score of these to friends and acquaintances, asking if I might send them a dozen or more for them to send to their friends. The response was so good that Hutchinson had a further 15,000 printed for me.

Fearon agreed to send a letter to all my old customers, and to all of Fearon, Block's that I had met during the months I was one of their partners, which read:

Dear Madam or Sir,

We have to inform you that as Mr Dennis Wheatley's time is considerably occupied with literary work, he has asked us to accept his resignation from our Board of Directors, and the Board have with regret acceded to his request.

Mr Wheatley's first novel, *The Forbidden Territory*, will be published by Messrs Hutchinson in January.

J. Granville Fearon

The book was published on 3 January 1933. To celebrate the occasion I gave a lunch party in Justerini's cellars in the arches beneath Charing Cross Station. My good friend Joseph Vecchi did the lunch. The leading gossip writers from *The Times*, the *Telegraph*, the *Express*, the *Mail* and the Sunday papers were among the guests, also the Belgian Ambassador, Sir Lionel Earle, Woolf Barnato and Harry Preston, who proposed a toast to 'The two best s/cellars'.

On 5 January we had a little party of intimate friends at No. 48 for which we had thought out a series of games connected with the book, and with copies of it as prizes. Among our guests were several of Hutchinson's people. One of them was Mr Langbridge, then their publicity manager. He brought exciting news. The first printing of *The Forbidden Territory* had been 1500 copies, but only 800 had had the pictorial endpapers pasted in. The demand of the trade had been so large that the other 700 copies had had to be rushed out without endpapers; and orders to reprint the book had already been sent before it had even been published.

I had become a best-seller overnight.

12

THE ROAD TO FORTUNE

The Forbidden Territory was not my only triumph early in 1933. In the same month as the publication of the book both *Nash's Magazine* here and *Cosmopolitan* in New York published my first short story.

The editor of the former was Richard Mcland, a very friendly man who later took several more of my stories. It so happened that George Doran, the *doyen* of the American publishing world and the overlord of both magazines, was in London that January; and he sent for me to come to see him at the Savoy.

When I called he was not very well, so I found him in bed. He asked me about my work. I told him that during the past year I had written two novels, several short stories and that I was now writing a private life of King Charles II.

'Too much,' he said. 'Your work will become slipshod. You should do as my old friend, Arnold Bennett, did. Every morning he spent walking in Hyde Park thinking about the novel he was engaged on. Then he wrote for two hours in the afternoon.'

I must confess that I did not take this great man's advice. I continued to write for as long as I could keep awake.

The book went like a bomb. I made a round of the bookshops and bookstalls, modestly asking the managers if they stocked my book and had sold a copy of it. Now such visits are common practice, but in those days few booksellers and railway bookstall managers had ever before seen an author. After my visit to King's Cross Station and a friendly talk with the manager over a drink in the bar, his stall alone sold 700 copies of *The Forbidden Territory*.

I was still far from well off but I wrote to Walter Hutchinson that, as the book was doing so well, I would put all the royalties it had so far earned into further advertising. Walter was a queer fish but he believed in advertising. His reply was: 'Splendid! For every pound you put into this I will put two.' The book was reprinted seven times in seven weeks.

The royalties these big sales would bring me were a great comfort, as almost every day I was still receiving letters pressing me to pay debts that were long overdue. In the good days before the Slump I was already having my suits made by Scholte in Savile Row, my shirts by Beale & Inman in Bond Street, my shoes by Lobb, and Scotts had long supplied my hats, and some of them were tiring of giving me such long credit.

However, early in 1933 I had managed to free myself from my most serious liability, the £460 per annum rent for the cellars in Kensington I had acquired for the wholesale business of D.W. Ltd. The landlord generously agreed to relieve me of the lease for a payment of £250. I talked about it with dear old Stanley Brown, the Director of Justerini's who looked after the customers I sent them, and he very kindly offered to lend me £200 against my future commission.

But my immediate success as a thriller writer had by then fired me with literary ambitions. Having heard that Edgar Wallace had been able to write a book in a week, I decided to find out the speed of which I was capable. In order that I should remain undisturbed, Joe Links lent Joan and me a cottage on Cutmill Common, near Godalming, in Surrey. There, although I worked all out, I failed to complete a book in a week; but I did so in a fortnight.

I called it *Such Power is Dangerous*. It was a blood-and-thunder story set mainly in Hollywood.

Back in London I met with a delightful surprise, which later proved to be the only serious setback during my career as an author. Alfred Hitchcock had long been a friend of mine and I had seen him make films in the old silent days. He and his wife, Alma, then lived in Cromwell Road. We had often dined with them and they with us. Just as a friend, without any ulterior motive, I had sent him a copy of *The Forbidden Territory*. He rang up and asked us to dinner. When we arrived, he said at once:

'Dennis, your book is terrific! I'm going to make a film of it. But I'm tied up at present with Maxwell at Elstree and I don't want him to buy the rights, because I'm leaving him for Micky Balcon in the autumn. Hang on to the rights for a few months, then I'll get Balcon to buy them.'

Naturally, I was overjoyed. Hitchcock was already in the front rank of directors and I knew he would make the film of my book a world-wide winner. But, alas, things did not turn out that way. When Hitch left Maxwell in the autumn, Balcon insisted that his next film should be a musical starring Jessie Matthews. Then in the winter Hitch telephoned me again. Balcon still refused to buy the rights for him to make my book, but he had found a man who would. This was Richard Wainwright. He and his father had been Ufa Films in Germany, but now that Hitler had come to power they were transferring their company to England. They would make *The Forbidden Territory* as their first film here.

I lunched with Hitch and Wainwright at the Carlton Grill. The latter was most enthusiastic; he went straight from the Carlton to A. P. Watt's and there acquired the film rights. Gerald du Maurier was signed up to play the part of the Duke de Richleau, Gregory Ratoff that of Commissar Leshkin and Tamari Desni that of the Princess Marie-Lou.

Now comes the sad end to the story. Du Maurier died and was replaced by Ronald Squire, an excellent light-comedy actor but hopeless for the role of the Duke. Then Balcon postponed releasing Hitch to make the film for a further three months. By then Wainwright had signed up his full cast and engaged expensive studio space. The one thing we had not put in the contract was that Hitchcock was to direct the film. Wainwright could not afford to wait. As director he brought over from Hollywood a cameraman named Phil Rosen, who had never been to Europe before. Rosen's wife 'discovered' a 'real great little alley' to go shopping in. It was called Bond Street.

The film did not even get a West End opening. If only

Hitch had made it, Hollywood might have bought the rights of every book I wrote thereafter. But it was not to be.

In April, owing to the success of *The Forbidden Territory*, Hutchinson asked me if I had another completed manuscript that they could publish in the summer. Reluctantly, I submitted *Such Power is Dangerous*, but said I did not want it to be published because it had been dashed off and was a very ordinary thriller with no informative background. After having it read, they said they wanted to publish it.

In those days publishers and printers worked fast. On 8 June we threw a party to launch *Such Power is Dangerous*. The book was reprinted again and again.

I was a long way yet from having my work published in some thirty languages, but Bill Watt had secured an Italian publisher for me, and with my first foreign royalties I bought Joan a lovely coloured print of Edinburgh in early Victorian times.

In July I joined the PEN Club, and at the first of its dinners I attended H. G. Wells was Chairman; but I was much surprised to find very few other well-known authors present. I later learned the reason: anyone could join, even if they had had only a few articles or a short story published in the local paper. At the second dinner to which I went a young woman stood up and proceeded to make a public confession of what she considered to be her sins. It transpired that she was a member of 'The Oxford Group', a revivalist movement which, at that time, had achieved a certain notoriety. A feature of the PEN Club was organized tours for its members to visit other European capitals and fraternize with other organizations of authors. It seemed sad that Britain should be represented by such people. After that second dinner I resigned.

In August we took the children for a holiday to St Jacut de la Mer, a charming small seaside resort in Normandy. Some way from the shore there is an island to which one could walk dry-shod at low tide. Later, I used it in one of my books about Gregory Sallust during the Second World War.

At our hotel we met and spent a lot of time with a delightful character, Captain Magee RN Retd, and I later portrayed his cheerful personality as Captain Andy Nelson McKay in my book *They Found Atlantis*. Magee's last command had been a flotilla of destroyers and he gave me much valuable information about such craft for use in my third thriller, *Black August*, upon which I had just started. In the Second World War I met him again and gave him lunch at the Hungaria. He had returned to the Navy as a Rear Admiral in command of Atlantic convoys.

In September my *Old Rowley – A Private Life of Charles II* was published. It was a very light biography of that clever and lovable King; but the *Sunday Express* made it their 'Book of the Week', and it had many excellent reviews, which pleased me greatly, as it proved that I was capable of writing non-fiction books as well as thrillers.

The book had one unusual feature. I felt that readers must be sick to death of reproductions of portraits of Nell Gwyn and her contemporaries, so I got that most gifted artist, Frank C. Papé, to do a number of drawings for use as illustrations. Those he had done for John Lane's special editions of books by Anatole France and James Branch Cabell had delighted me, and his drawings for my *Old Rowley* added immensely to it for collectors. One depicts the famous duel in which the Duke of Buckingham killed the Earl of Shrewsbury. Buckingham was the Countess's lover and during the encounter she held his horse. As Joan is a direct descendant of the Shrewsburys, Papé drew a portrait of her in this scene as the Countess.

In October there occurred an event which brought further good luck to me. During a visit to New York, the well-known author, Bruce Graeme, had been entertained to lunch at the Dutch Treat Club, where publishers, authors and critics met once a month. With the idea of starting a similar means of contact in England, Bruce gave a lunch for some thirty people at Anderton's Hotel in Fleet Street. He was a Hutchinson author and Joe Gaute, the member of the firm who dealt with authors, had me included in the list of guests.

Bruce's proposal was received with acclaim and all those present became founder members of a Club that we named The Paternosters. George Harrap was elected Chairman, and after that we met every month at the Cheshire Cheese. When a year had passed we held an annual general meeting to elect a new Chairman. Several people were proposed, but when hands were raised there did not appear to be sufficient supporters to justify their election. Then Cadness Page, the Chief Librarian at Harrods, stood up and said: 'Let's have Dennis Wheatley.' To my surprise and delight, nearly everyone present cried: 'Yes, let's have Dennis.' So I became Chairman for the following year.

During that year it was my job to invite guest speakers to each monthly lunch and I was fortunate in being able to secure an impressive succession of well-known men. We had made it a rule that no mention of anything said at the Paternoster lunches should ever be reported in the press.

Another matter that concerned me was the fact that nearly all the members were associated with Hutchinson or Harrap, and I wished to broaden the basis of the club. I was able to bring in not only Directors of several of the leading publishers but also a number of gossip writers; among them Tom Driberg, then William Hickey of the *Daily Express*, Bunny Tattersall of the *Daily Mail* and Lord Donegall of the *Sunday Dispatch*. It will be readily understood that for every person who reads literary criticisms in their papers, ten read the gossip column; so mentions of new books in such columns are of great value to an author.

As Chairman I derived very special benefits from the Committee which met monthly in George Harrap's office and afterwards lunched together, fortified by many rounds of drinks. It consisted of George, Bruce Graeme, Joe Gaute, who looked after my interests at Hutchinson, Cecil Hunt, the literary editor of the *Daily Mail*, who bought the serial rights of several of my books, Freddy Richardson of Boots, who bought more books than anyone else in Britain, Bertram Blunt, a big public library supplier, and the author, Victor McClure, who put me up for the Savage Club.

The club occupied a fine building in Carlton House Terrace and there I met many other prominent men who earned their living by the printed word; but after a while my visits became somewhat infrequent because I found that so many rounds of drinks at the bar before lunch made me incapable of getting down to serious work for the remainder of the day; so eventually I resigned from it.

It had taken me fourteen days to write *Such Power*. On *Black August* I spent the best part of forty weeks. As a subject I chose the biggest canvas I could think of – red revolution in England in an unspecified future. Actually, I had in mind about 1960. Strangely enough, I referred to 'the mob burning all Queen Elizabeth's lovely furniture in Buckingham Palace' although as her present Majesty was then only a little girl and the daughter of King George V's second son, I could not possibly have supposed that she would become our Queen.

Gregory Sallust made his first appearance in this book as its hero. His physique and personality were based on those of my dear, unscrupulous friend of the First World War, Gordon Eric Gordon-Tombe. The heroine, Lady Veronica Wensleydale, was a portrait of Joan's closest friend, Betty Earle, later the Marquise de Chasseloup Laubat.

Black August did better than even I could have hoped. The advance copies sent to librarians and booksellers resulted in such staggering orders that the book had to be reprinted six times before it was published. There was no question about it. I had gone up to the top of the form and I was there to stay.

PART TWO

Ink

LARGELY ABOUT BLACK MAGIC

AFTER the great success of *Black August* and the tremendous pressure of work during 1933 we felt that we deserved a holiday; so when Bino, who had gone to live in South Africa, invited us to come out and stay for as long as we liked, we accepted. His wife Peggy had been a Marais and her cousin was married to Charles de Water, the South African High Commissioner in London.

With us to Cape Town we brought a number of introductions. Colin Bain Marais, who had served in the Coldstream Guards and was now a Minister, took me to a session of the House of Representatives where we heard General Smuts speak. Midge Marais, who had acted as hostess to the Prince of Wales on his visit to the Union, and her husband, Sonny, we had already known when they were in London. We were taken up Table Mountain, to bathe at Muizenberg, across to look on the Indian Ocean at False Bay and to lunch with the Bairnsfathers in their lovely old Dutch Colonial house.

In Johannesburg we stayed with Bino, whose house had previously been occupied by Gandhi when he was a practising lawyer in South Africa. We went down a gold mine and drove up to Pretoria. The Oppenheimers and the Jeppys entertained us and we were taken to visit Sarah Gertrude Millin, who had made a name for herself as a novelist. She was a pompous person and informed us that she had told John Galsworthy – who had been to see her recently – that none of the women characters in his books were true to life because he did not understand women.

Apartheid had not yet been introduced into South Africa but the Negroes were a problem. Gangs of bad ones, known as Amalati, used to roam the streets at night armed with bicycle chains. Creeping up behind a white man or woman, they threw a chain round their necks and strangled them. So, in Johannesburg, one never left the house on foot at night, even to post a letter.

Durban we found a dreary city as it was still Nonconformist English. We spent a night or two in Port Elizabeth and East London, then Bino took me up to the great game reserve in the northern Transvaal. From the Tourist Club there a friend of his was motoring down to Lourenço Marques and offered to take me with him.

At Resano Garcia we crossed the frontier into Portuguese East. It was intensely hot and we both put our coats in the boot of the car. The roads in Portuguese East were much better kept than those in the Union. At that hour there was no traffic on them so we made good going; but after darkness had fallen the car was brought to an abrupt halt by striking a big stone in the middle of the road. My companion got out and found that the near back wheel would have to be changed. Handing me a large torch, he said: 'While I'm busy keep a good look out with this. The Game Reserve is not many miles away and at night lions often leave it to prowl about.'

I had my automatic with me but did not feel that would prove much good against a hungry lion, and the jungle on both sides of the road was pitch dark. I spent a very uncomfortable twenty minutes listening to occasional faint roarings in the distance.

Lourenço Marques is the finest port in Africa, but the 'Little Englander', Gladstone, had refused to buy it off the Portuguese for the measly sum of half a million pounds. We drove straight to the Polana, a far more luxurious hotel than any other in Southern Africa. Although it was nearly midnight the manager was still up and gave us drinks in his office while a meal was prepared for us. On his desk was a photograph of Harry Preston.

Harry was one of the many friends who had not deserted me during the time I was almost penniless. From time to time telegrams would reach me: 'Will you give me the honour and pleasure of your company at lunch tomorrow at Ciro's, one thirty, do please try.'

Sometimes he gave these lunches for six or eight people at the Ritz or the Embassy. Most of his guests were well-known but there was always one who was not – a young athlete, painter or novelist – and Harry's other guests had been picked to help this young man achieve success.

A few weeks before *The Forbidden Territory* was published I chanced to meet him one afternoon in Piccadilly and told him about my book. He at once ordered half a dozen copies, then took me along to the Piccadilly Hotel to share a bottle of Champagne with him. A few weeks later he gave a lunch for me to meet half a dozen important people in the literary world. The time was to come when, as a bestseller, I should be asked to meet and help some other unknown novelists.

After supping at the Polana my companion took me to some gambling rooms. There, to my horror, I found that I had lost my pocket book. It had in it not only a considerable sum in notes but also my passport and the tickets for our voyage home. I spent a miserable night; then, on borrowed money, took the train for Johannesburg.

When I had to change trains at the frontier I went to the Passport Officer to explain why I had not got one. Miracle of miracles! The Passport Officer handed me my wallet with all my money and papers still in it. As I had taken off my coat to put it in the boot of the car, the wallet had fallen out on to the rear mudguard. It had travelled on it for over half a mile then dropped off. A Negro had found it and taken it to the Customs Office. For his honesty may that man's spirit long abide in the land of Sekhet Aru where the corn never grows less than five cubits high.

Having rejoined Joan we thanked Bino and Peggy for all their kindness to us and took ship for home. We left the ship at Gibraltar, where I was surprised but strangely delighted to see men wearing the uniforms of the English Police.

On reaching London it cheered me to learn that all my books were still selling well and that my association with Justerini's was also prospering.

The children were growing up. Colin was now at his

prep school. Diana attended Miss Spalding's famous 'academy for young ladies', where Joan had also studied as a girl. I still have one of Diana's drawings of this period, which already shows signs that she was to become a very gifted artist. It is of a huge hand, palm upwards, and seated on the edge of the palm is the very small figure of a little girl. It portrays Diana seated on the right hand of God.

Anthony had been sent to Worth, the preparatory school for Downside. From time to time Nancy and I met to talk about his welfare, and our relations continued to be most friendly.

Our family was soon to be augmented, at least from time to time. When Joan left William Younger it had been agreed that she should keep their youngest daughter, Diana, and that he should retain the other three children. They lived with their father and grandfather, who was then still alive, at Auchen Castle, Moffat, Scotland. Now that they were all well on in their teens, when they visited London they were allowed to see their mother.

Meg, the eldest of the three, then about eighteen, was the first to come and see us. She was a pretty girl and also capable and generous, but I saw less of her later than I did of the others.

Shortly afterwards Bill, then seventeen, and Jack, then fourteen, came together to see us. Bill was the smaller as at the age of twelve he had been stricken with polio. It left him with a weak right arm and retarded his growth. But what he lacked in physical attributes he more than made up for in brain power. Both of them had lively, attractive faces. I must have made a good impression on them as they took to me at once and I came to love them both dearly.

For many generations all the boys of Joan's family had been sent to Eton and she would naturally have liked Bill and Jack to go there too, but their father would not hear of it. He had a cousin who was a Housemaster at Canford and insisted on sending them there.

But the dominant factor that attracted them to me must have been the difference between my character and that of their own father. I was blessed with a happy disposition and when with me they could always be certain of a jolly time, whereas he was morose and ill-tempered.

During the First World War he became a temporary attaché in the Diplomatic Service and, taking Joan with him, was *en poste* for a while both at The Hague and in Rome. But for the rest of his life he never did another stroke of work.

Joan's father's family were the Johnstones; in the old days Scots chieftains who carried out raids across the border to drive off with English cattle. It was said that a poor woman once begged for a meal and a night's lodging in their castle. On being refused by the servitor who answered the door, she said: 'Are there any Christian folk here?' His reply was: 'Nay, woman, only Johnstones and Jardines.'

The heads of the family had long been baronets, then became Lord Derwents, their seat being Hackness Hall, near Scarborough. The holder of the title when I married Joan was Peter. I had already met him when I went to Madrid with Bino, as he had gone into the Diplomatic Service and happened then to be one of the attachés there. To me he was always very pleasant, but we saw little of him as he married Sabine, the daughter of General Iliesu, the Chief of the Rumanian General Staff, a far from pleasant woman who was extremely standoffish.

In the Second World War Peter played a most curious role. He had long since ceased to be a diplomat and did not return to that service, neither would he accept a commission. He joined the RAF as an airman but I don't think he ever paraded on an airfield. When I was in the Cabinet Offices I happened to learn that actually he was doing valuable Secret Service work in Rumania.

Shortly after the war he died in Switzerland. His younger brother, Pat, succeeded him.

As a Peer of the Realm, Pat has set a splendid example to all who enjoy that status. Unlike Peter, he attends the sittings of the House of Lords regularly and became a Minister in the Tory Government. Moreover, no head of a family could have behaved more generously to us all.

With one exception, the Johnstones were not great

E

connoisseurs of wine. The exception was one of Joan's fathers' elder brothers, Sir Alan. He was our Minister at Copenhagen and The Hague. He did not trust the Brandy at dinner parties to which he was invited while abroad. When dessert was put on the table he would say to one of the footmen: 'It's time for me to take my medicine. You will find a bottle I have brought in my overcoat pocket. Please get it for me.' The bottle, of course, contained his own superb Cognac.

There was an occasion, too, when the Lord Derwent of the day said to his butler – who had started in the house as boot boy and risen through the ranks of six footmen to a bishop-like butler – 'I think, Stone, we will send Sir Alan a dozen of that new Claret we got in the other day as a Christmas present.'

Stone raised his eyebrows and replied: 'No my Lord, Sir Alan wouldn't be poisoned with such muck.'

Stone was a great character. For years he succeeded in keeping a mistress in a neighbouring village; but no one knew it until after he was dead. At the back of Hackness Hall, looking out over the garden, there is a wide terrace on which house parties sit in fine weather gossiping while they have tea. Below the steps leading up to it is the servants' hall. One day Lady Derwent said to Stone: 'Will you tell the servants not to talk so loudly when we are having tea? We can often hear what they say.'

'Certainly, Milady,' Stone bowed. 'But it's nothing to what we can hear downstairs.'

On my return from South Africa, Gaumont British gave me a contract to write a film script. It was to be called *His Guiding Star* and that delightful couple, Jack Hulbert and Cicely Courtneidge, were to be in it. Gaumont were pleased with my script but for some reason the film was never made.

Having paid a long visit to South Africa I wrote a book called *The Fabulous Valley*. The High Commissioner, Charles de Water, gave me a subject round which to form a plot. Up in the vast wastes of South West Africa there is a small area known as 'The Place of the Great Glitter'. The sand there is sprinkled with uncut diamonds and in moonlight they give off a faint glow. Several prospectors are said to have stumbled on this field and picked up from it a fortune in an hour; but, as there is no water within many miles of it, many more have died of thirst in that arid land. Now, I believe, it is owned by the Diamond Syndicate, fenced in with electrified wire and guarded by armed sentries night and day; but then, no map showed any hint of its location. I built a story about a man who had collected a fortune there but left to his heirs only three clues that could lead to their finding it. The whole of his family went in search of this wealth and their adventures took them to all the places I had been to while in South Africa. Although the book sold well, I never thought much of it. One reviewer said rightly: 'Mr Wheatley should make up his mind whether he is going to write a thriller or a guide-book.'

After finishing *The Fabulous Valley*, I tried very hard to think of a subject for my next book that would hit another high spot. It then occurred to me that, although in Victorian times there had been a great vogue for stories of the occult, in the present century there had been very few; so I decided to use the theme of Black Magic.

Spiritualism had never interested me and to this day I have never been to a séance or participated in any magical ceremony, Black or White. I am fully convinced that no good can come of contacting spiritual entities and that in many cases it is extremely dangerous to do so.

The fact that I had read extensively about ancient religions gave me some useful background, but I required up-to-date information about occult circles in this country. My friend, Tom Driberg, who then lived in a mews flat just behind us in Queen's Gate, proved most helpful. He introduced me to Aleister Crowley, the Reverend Montague Summers and Rollo Ahmed.

We had Crowley to dinner several times. His conversation was fascinating. He gave me much useful information and several of his books, but never attempted to draw me into his occult activities. Later, when Driberg asked me what I thought of him, I replied: 'I think intellectually he is quite wonderful, but I don't believe he could harm a rabbit.'

'Ah!' said Tom. 'You are right about that now, but it has only been the case since that awful business in Paris.' He then told me about it.

For a considerable time Crowley had ruled a community at the Abbey da Thelema in Northern Sicily. There is little doubt that cats were sacrificed there to the Satanic powers. Then rumours got round that certain small children who had disappeared had been used for the same purpose. In any case Crowley was expelled from Italy and went to Paris.

There, one of his disciples owned a small hotel on the Left Bank. Crowley greatly wished to raise Pan; so the hotel proprietor got rid of his staff for the weekend and Crowley's coven of disciples assembled there. The furniture from a room under the roof was removed and it was swept clean. In the evening Crowley, in his magician's robes, went into it accompanied by MacAleister (son of Aleister), one of his disciples. He then told the other eleven members of the coven that whatever noises they might hear in no circumstances were they to enter the room before morning.

The eleven went downstairs to a cold buffet, very nervous. A little after midnight they heard an appalling racket in the upper room, but obeyed the Master's orders and did not go up. When in the morning they did go up, they knocked on the door but there was no reply, so they broke it in. Both MacAleister and Crowley had had their robes ripped from them and were naked. MacAleister was dead and Crowley a gibbering idiot crouching in a corner.

Perhaps Crowley did succeed in raising Pan and the horned god strongly objected to being taken away from whatever he was doing. Anyhow, Crowley spent four months in a loony-bin outside Paris before he was allowed about again. But it may well be that he really was able to call down power before this bizarre event. The following report certainly suggests it.

When an undergraduate at Cambridge he was brilliant and already deeply versed in the occult. He wanted the Dramatic Society to perform a play by Aristophanes which, in those days, was regarded as immoral, so the Master of John's refused to allow it. Greatly annoyed by this Crowley made a wax figure of the Master and, with a coven he had formed, took it out to a field on a night of bright moonlight. Crowley's companions formed a ring, while he stood in the centre, chanting a spell and with a large needle poised, intending to thrust it into the image in the place where its liver would have been. At the critical moment one of the undergraduates lost his nerve, broke the ring and grabbed Crowley's arm. In consequence his aim was deflected and the needle pierced the image's ankle. The following day the Master of John's fell down some steps and broke his ankle.

The Reverend Montague Summers was another interesting character. It was said that he had never been ordained, but he dressed and, with white curls hanging down the sides of his face, looked like a Restoration Bishop. He actually was a great authority on the Restoration theatre and gave me one of his books about it.

He lived at Alresford; and, after dining with Joan and me, asked us down for the weekend. The bedroom we were given had a number of big spiders on the ceiling. Feeling this to be inhospitable I had no hesitation in squashing several of them into bloody blotches. In the garden Joan came upon the largest toad she had ever seen. After dinner that evening he took me into a small room on the ground floor that had nothing in it except a great heap of books piled up higgledy-piggledy on the floor. Picking up a small volume from the pile he held it out to me and said:

'Now this is rare; very rare. And I can let you have it for fifty pounds; only fifty pounds.'

I did not recognize its title, and didn't want it; and I could not have afforded to buy it anyhow. I politely excused myself by saying that I no longer collected that type of book. Never have I seen such a complete change of expression. From having been normally benign his face suddenly became positively demoniac. Throwing down the book, he stamped furiously out of the room.

Next morning I went out early to the Post Office and sent a telegram to Nanny, asking her to send me a wire at once saying that Colin had suddenly been taken ill. Her telegram was delivered shortly after lunch. We packed hastily and departed, never to see the, perhaps not so Reverend, gentleman again.

Rollo Ahmed was one of the most unusual men I have ever met. Born in Egypt he had spent the greater part of his adult life in the Caribbean and South America. He had charming manners and laughed a lot. There was little he did not know about Voodoo and he was an expert on Raja Yoga. He practised it himself, as he demonstrated one evening when we had asked him to dinner. He lived on the far side of Clapham Common and it was a bitterly cold night, but the freezing weather had had no effect on him. Having walked all the way to Queen's Gate he arrived, without an overcoat, in a thin cotton suit, and although he had no gloves his hands were as warm as toast.

He offered to teach us Yoga and we had several lessons in breathing according to the rules; but I was hard at it writing and Joan had also started to write a book; so we could not spare the time to practise and had to give it up.

On one occasion I invited a man from the Society for Psychical Research to have a discussion with Ahmed, and it proved most interesting. When Ahmed had gone our other visitor asked me: 'Did you see the little black imp standing just beside him?' Perhaps the Research man was pulling my leg, but I certainly had not. Anyway, whether Ahmed was a follower of the Left Hand Path or not, he was a jolly fellow and I got a lot of very useful information from him.

In January 1935, to launch *The Devil Rides Out*, we gave a big party at the Prince of Wales Hotel in De Vere Gardens. As a novelty, and to give my journalist friends something to write about in their columns, I sought Harry Preston's aid. In one corner of the ballroom we had a ring erected and Harry produced two well-known pugilists to fight a three-round contest in it.

But this party was not for my book only. Joan had finished her first book, the title of which was *No Ordinary Virgin*. Hutchinson had accepted it and it was published on the same day as mine. She wrote much better English than I did, and under the pseudonym of Eve Chaucer published five more books in the years that followed. They all got good notices, but her heart was not really in the game. Within a week of the Second World War's breaking out, she joined MI5, and after the war we went to live in the country. There we had a big garden, which it was her joy to make very beautiful. So after 1939 she never wrote again.

Early in the spring we went for a holiday to Greece. In Athens we stayed at the Grande Bretagne in Constitution Square and from there could admire the Evzone sentries, in their picturesque uniforms with white kilts, on guard in front of the Royal Palace. The Acropolis, the Odeon, the Theseum Temple, the Tower of the Winds and the beautiful pieces in the Museum filled us with wonder and awe. We drove out to the great ruined temple perched on the cliff edge of Cape Sounion, to Piracus, to Eleusis, where the mysteries were performed, and to the beautiful remains of Daphni, from which area there still comes a gorgeous rich wine. Our longest trip was to Delphi. We ate the honey from Mount Hymettus and enjoyed the view of the distant sea far below.

Our guides were charming and could not do enough for us. Every morning they brought gifts of fresh flowers for Joan and often a bottle of wine or *ouzo* for me.

From Piraeus we sailed in a small steamer to Brindisi, from which we took the train to Rome. Joan knew the city well as she had lived there for some time during the First World War, when her husband had been *en poste* at the British Embassy; but it was my first visit.

To my mind, in the days of her greatness, the Roman way of life was supreme above that of all other ancient civilizations. The Romans, like the British, were practical people. They conquered the greater part of the then known world and, like us, ruled with justice and toleration. As builders of bridges, viaducts and roads the Incas of Peru alone could be compared to them. And at intervals along these roads were garrisoned post-houses which made it safe for travellers to ride unmolested from the Scottish border to the frontier of Persia. The peoples over whom they ruled were allowed to practise their own religion with the exception that human sacrifice was forbidden. Wherever they penetrated they taught the natives the best known methods of cultivating the land, and how to increase their herds of cattle and make clothes instead of continuing to wear the skins of animals. The benefits they conferred upon the people they ruled were inestimable; even today the descendants of those people display a higher degree of human decency than those of the barbarians who remained outside the Roman Empire. With the fall of Rome in AD410 the light of western civilization went out for the best part of a thousand years.

I was enthralled to walk in the Forum – a great part of which had been slums for many generations until Mussolini cleared them away – and to stroll among the ruins of the great Palaces on the Palatine Hill.

We also admired the treasures in the Vatican and the mighty castle of St Angelo. But for the greater part of our stay we were very uneasy about the state of international relations. Mussolini had sent his troops into Abyssinia. Britain had protested most strongly and it looked as if any day we might be at war with Italy. I even contemplated making arrangements for a fishing smack to run us over to the South of France in the event of a declaration of war, so that we could escape being interned.

Happily, my fears were set at rest when we dined with the British Ambassador, Sir Noel Charles. He was a charming host. At the end of dinner he produced a box of Hoyo de Monterey super coronas and offered it to me. I had given up smoking cigars when we wound up the Baron Wheatley company, so I politely declined.

'What!' he exclaimed. 'I got them specially for you because they are the same as the Duke de Richleau smokes in your stories.' At such a compliment I could no longer refuse.

We were a very jolly party of about ten and decided to go on to Rome's most fashionable night-club. Down in the hall, before getting our coats, Sir Noel and I did a little dance together, and he told me that he would not be going out to a night-club if he thought there was the least chance of Britain's going to war with Italy.

Soon after we got home, I started on another novel. This

one was inspired by Charles Balfour-Davey. He had been a brother officer of Hubert Pelham Burn's in the Gordon Highlanders and was now a Staff Colonel. He and his wife, Lexy, were great friends of ours and he showed me a short story he had written about Constantinople, where he had been stationed for a time after the Turkish surrender. Two or three magazines had turned it down, but it had the germ of an idea in it, so for a modest sum I bought the rights from him.

But I had to know much more about Istanbul, as it was coming to be called, before I could write a full-length novel with that city as the background. Another friend of mine had lived there for a long time and offered to collaborate with me.

This was George H. Hill, known as Peter, and he was one of the most interesting men I have ever met. He was an Englishman born in Estonia, his father having been a wood exporter there. As a young man he went into our Secret Service, where he was known as IK8, and, being bilingual, he was sent to Russia. When the Bolsheviks gained power first our Ambassador was recalled, and then that charming and gifted writer, Robert Bruce-Lockhart, who had been left as British representative. Peter became the only source of information that the British Government had about events in the Bolshevik-held territory. His adventures as a secret agent were fascinating. Most remarkable of all, he succeeded in smuggling the Russian Crown jewels out of Rumania.

When peace was at last restored, MI6 no longer had any use for him, so he had a very hard time. He and his wife, Dorothy, had to live in a caravan in a farmer's field in Sussex, and his only source of income was as adviser to film companies who were making films about Russia. He acted in this capacity when the film of *The Forbidden Territory* was made, which was how I came to meet him.

I am happy to relate that he turned up in the Second World War as a Brigadier with three rows of medal ribbons. After the war, he became manager of the Apollinaris Company in Germany, which he reorganized so successfully that, for the last ten years of his life, he owned a fine house and was driven about by a chauffeur in his big Mercedes.

Reverting to *The Eunuch of Stamboul*, the title I gave my new story. The late spring of that year was extremely hot. Peter used to come to No. 48 in the afternoons, lie in his shirt-sleeves full length on the sofa knocking back whiskies and sodas, while I sat at a small table taking notes of all he could tell me about Istanbul and Muhammedan customs.

Joan's lease was nearly up, and she did not wish to renew it. While I was busy absorbing material from Peter, she was equally busy with carpets, curtains and decorating. In June 1935 we left Queen's Gate and moved into a very pleasant house I had leased – No. 8 St John's Wood Park.

14

THE CRIME DOSSIERS: THE CORONATION SEASON: *RED EAGLE*

S T John's Wood Park consisted of a triangular garden. No. 8 lay on its west side. In front of it the road led north to Swiss Cottage and south towards Regent's Park. The houses had been built in the 1840s and were semi-detached. Behind stone balustrades each had a small front garden and a larger garden behind the house. Ours was big enough for a fair-sized lawn, and a broad herbaceous border and had a fifty-foot oak tree at its far end. As our garden backed on to the much larger garden of a house in the Finchley Road, which was mainly orchard, in spring the room on the first floor where I did my writing looked out on a sea of blossom and, until late autumn, the leaves of the trees formed a screen through which no other house could be seen.

It was, of course, part of the original St John's Wood; and, in the old days, became with Wimbledon Common the favourite rendezvous for fighting duels. Our landlord, a charming old gentleman, came to hand over the keys of the house to me personally. He told me that as a boy he had picked bullets from the trees with his penknife.

One evening my old friend, Joe Links, asked me: 'Dennis have you ever thought of writing an illustrated murder story?'

I laughed. 'My dear Joe, firstly I don't write murder stories, secondly it has already been done in the Sherlock Holmes books.'

'No,' he said. 'I mean illustrated with photographs of real people.'

That led me to think. If photographs of people, why not also handwritten letters, telegrams – yes, and even physical clues such as bits of hair, bloodstained material and so on?

Thus were the Crime Dossiers born. I spent the next weekend with Joe at his country home on Blackdown, and walking over the moors we hatched a plot. I wrote the story, secured suitable photographs from an agency and pasted clues on sheets of paper; then took the series of typescripts, letters, etc., in a cardboard folder, with the title *Murder off Miami*, to Hutchinson.

Walter proved far from enthusiastic as the pages giving the solution at the end were sealed; so it could not be sold to the circulating libraries. He said that, not being a cloth-bound novel, it could not be sold for more than 3/6 and he would give Joe and me a royalty of only one penny a copy on sales should they exceed 10,000.

His Sales Manager was then Maurice Diamond. Maurice and I took the MS to a few leading people in the Trade. We went first to W. H. Smith, where David Roy was then the head book buyer. After looking through it, he declared: 'This is simply marvellous! My opening order will be for 10,000 copies.' Then, after a moment, he added, 'But leave it with me. I'd like to send it round for my largest bookstall managers to see.' Two days later he rang up Maurice and said:

'I'm terribly sorry but my chaps won't look at it. They all say that, as it is a cardboard folder, it won't stand up, so they can't show it properly, and anyhow there is no market for a thing like that. They will take a few copies because they are all friends of Dennis's. But I've got to cut my opening order to 2,000.'

All the other big boys in the Trade panned it, with the sole exception of Selfridges' buyer. When I showed it to him he said, 'If you can spare a few minutes, I'd like to take you up to see our Advertising Director.'

The Director looked through it and said, 'Mr Wheatley if we set up a display of the contents of this thing, will you autograph every copy we can take an order for before publication?'

Naturally I agreed. They took orders for over 1,000 copies, and I had to spend a whole day there signing them. But better still. Publishers are always giving parties to launch new books, authors often give parties to publicize a new book of their own; but have you ever heard of a bookseller giving a party for that purpose?

Gordon Selfridge did for me. The restaurant on his top floor closes at six o'clock. From that hour up till eight o'clock on the day *Murder Off Miami* was published he gave a cocktail party for 300 people.

No other big bookseller could be persuaded that this new venture would do well. Hatchards took only six copies. Queen Mary came in the day it was published and bought the lot.

Unlike the book trade, the press seized on this novelty with enthusiasm. It was reviewed in every worthwhile paper in Great Britain, and *The Times* gave it a fourth leader. We sold 120,000 copies in six months.

That summer the film of *The Eunuch of Stamboul* was made: and Hutchinson asked me to write a serious study of the Occult. I did not then feel competent to undertake such a task, so suggested Rollo Ahmed. He produced a book entitled *The Black Art*, and it is one of the best that I have ever read on the subject. Instead, I wrote *Contraband*, a second story featuring Gregory Sallust.

Contraband concerned the smuggling of Communist agitators into England. The distance aircraft could fly in those days was still very limited so I had to select a secret landing ground in Kent and chose Quex Park, which lies between Westgate and Birchington. It is a considerable estate and the only property in that area surrounded by trees. Its owner was the famous big-game hunter, Colonel Powell Cotton. As a boy I used to go there with my grandfather, who lived nearby and in retirement ran a large market garden. The head gardener at Quex Park was a friend of his and they talked together of crops. Both of them were long since dead, but I wrote to the Colonel asking if I might call on him.

He not only gave me permission to use his estate in my

story, but took me round it to show me several old towers
which might prove useful hide-outs for illicit stores.

Joan, of course, accompanied me on this expedition and,
for some reason, Peter and Carsie Dudgeon, who were old
friends of ours. Peter had been an officer in the Royal Flying
Corps and, while we were having a picnic tea on Broadstairs
beach, the question of aircraft construction came up. I said
I could not see why monoplanes should not be introduced
into the RAF, because one set of wings would cause less
air resistance than two. Peter pooh-poohed the idea as quite
impracticable. That was in 1935.

1936 was a year of turmoil. Germany had repudiated the
Locarno Pact. The Italians occupied Addis Ababa and
Civil War was raging in Spain. There were even fears of
serious disturbances in England. So, that August, for our
holiday, I rented a house on the island of Mull. We listened
with anxiety over the radio to the news every evening, and
so threatening was it of universal catastrophe that I had
even taken with me £50 in silver coin against emergencies.
But, apart from a few minor troubles, we enjoyed our stay
in that lovely island.

By the time we returned to London the crisis had passed,
and a month or so later Joan sent Diana to live with a
family in Munich and learn German. When she returned
just before Christmas she had developed the stride of a
storm-trooper and we expected her at any moment to shout,
'*Heil Hitler!*' But we soon restored her normally civilized
behaviour.

Meanwhile, towards the end of the year, King Edward
VIII abdicated. No one had a good word for Mrs Simpson:
but I never saw why he could not have followed the prece-
dent of countless other monarchs, made her a Duchess and
kept her as his mistress. Like many other people, Winston
Churchill among them, I regarded it as a violation of the
Constitution for a Prime Minister to be allowed to kick our
King off his throne. So I became very anti-Baldwin.

My book that winter was *They Found Atlantis*, one of the
best I have ever written. Ralph Straus praised it highly in
the *Sunday Times* and 'Torquemada' gave me the title of

'Public Thriller Writer No. 1' in the *Observer*. Both of them had by then become personal friends of mine, and Ralph was so distressed by the badness of my grammar that he insisted on giving me private lessons in his bachelor chambers; but I fear I proved an unrewarding pupil.

It was about this time we met Sir Charles Birkin. He was London's most eligible bachelor, rich, good-looking, generous with a caustic wit, and he later wrote gripping short horror stories. His sight was so poor that he could have evaded conscription on those grounds, but he had contact lenses fitted, served for a time in the ranks and later became an officer in the Tank Corps.

The first party of his we went to was at a flat in Hallam Street. The place was packed with lovely, but mostly brainless, young debutantes. Their conversation was solely about clothes, dances they were going to and their boy friends; so Joan and I were fish out of water. However, there was one other guest who was in the same situation, a tall, beak-nosed man in his late thirties, whose name was Maxwell Knight. The three of us settled down in a corner to talk and it transpired that, like myself, he had been a Cadet in HMS *Worcester*, although after I had left. We liked him and asked him to drinks at No. 8. From this beginning a friendship grew which subsequently completely altered the lives of Bill, Joan, Diana and me. How strange are the decrees of Fate, that of all places, one should have met this man at a party given for debutantes.

In March Joan let Diana spend a few weeks with our friends, the Dudgeons, in Switzerland so that she could learn to ski. When motoring home through France they met with a tragic accident. Peter was a fast driver. At a cross-road he crashed into a car driven by an equally impetuous Frenchman. With Diana was another girl who had made a fourth in the party. She was killed. Diana was catapulted from her seat straight at the window of a café. Head first, she went clean through it as though fired from a gun and landed flat on top of a marble table at which four Frenchmen were drinking.

Although Peter made light of Diana's injuries in the

telegram we received, Joan went out at once to the hospital to which she had been taken. It was as well she did. Diana's skull had been cracked and she was suffering from severe concusssion, yet that imbecile Peter was giving her red wine to drink.

When poor Diana was well enough to be brought home, she was swathed in bandages from chin to crown, which was rotten luck for her as arrangements had been made for her to be presented that season. Fortunately, her lovely face had sustained no damage and, although she suffered severe head and back aches, she showed great courage. The top of her head had had to be shaved, so she was still in bandages when in April we gave a party for her to meet some of her fellow debs. Later, when the wounds in her skull had healed, she was able to wear little round Juliet caps to hide the patch of newly grown hair, and luckily they had not cut off the golden curls at the sides of her face.

As we could not afford to have a dance for her at Claridges, or somewhere of that kind, and could entertain only about a hundred people at No. 8, Joan handled the situation very cleverly. Normally, each girl was accompanied by a chaperone, but Joan evaded this by hiring several coaches which picked up the debs and took them home under the supervision of a single chaperone, Marise Derwent; so we were able to give a dance for about fifty couples.

As it was the Coronation Season it was a particularly brilliant one; but very tiring for poor Joan. Night after night, for weeks on end, she had to chaperone Diana and sit for hours on hired gilt chairs while the young people danced. We had also to give our share of dinner parties for eight or ten debs and their 'delights'. The Brazilian Ambassador's daughter was one of the debs being presented that season and we were asked to a ball for her at the Embassy. Joan and I gave a dinner party for five young couples, then took them on. The Embassy was a fine old house just round the corner from Grosvenor Square. When we arrived I found the hall crowded with people waiting to go upstairs to be received on the first floor. On the twenty-foot-high staircase, too, people were packed like sardines in a tin. And it was not

Marriage of my mother and Sir Louis Newton, St George's, Hanover Square, 1930

Amy Robinson, my first mother-in-law, with Anthony and his cousin, 1930

Joan at the time of our marriage

Joan and D.W., at Anthony's first home, about to attend the ball given by the Brigade of Guards at Hampton Court Palace for Her Majesty two nights before her coronation

Jacket, designed by Joan, for D.W.'s first novel, published in 1933

D.W. at his desk at 'Grove Place'

Bill Younger

Jack Younger as an ensign in the Coldstream Guards, 1940

one of those double-horseshoe-shaped staircases that one sees in many great houses; it was a single stairway without supports against one wall. There must have been at least sixty people on it. Under such a weight – about five tons – I felt that it might collapse at any minute. Rather than risk my party I took them off to supper at the Berkeley. Normally, even in those days, that would have cost me not less than £20. But I had told Ferrara why I had brought this little crowd. He was a great *maitre d'hôtel* and a good friend of mine. When the bill came I found that he had charged me only five shillings a head.

In addition to the unceasing succession of dances – on some nights we spent a couple of hours at two, or even three – we made up parties with other parents for events in the daytime. One was to see the Derby, for which we hired an open-topped London bus, that made an excellent grandstand. I had been many times to Ascot, as old Amy Robinson always took a box there, but never before to the Derby. It proved my lucky day. A horse named 'The Duke' was running in one race. With de Richleau in mind I backed it and it came in first.

In due course Diana was presented, but at Balmoral because she insisted on her claim to be a Scot.

Another amusing party I went to that summer had nothing to do with debutantes. It was given by Lord Donegall. He invited a number of crime writers to his house in Marsham Street and challenged them to find his safe. If I remember, Peter Cheyney was the first to do so.

Peter was an extraordinary character. He claimed to be descended from an ancient Irish family named du Cheyney. But in fact his real name was Leper. He started as an East End barrow boy, graduated to small part actor, then became a solicitor's clerk. The plots of his thrillers were very well worked out and, as a companion, he was great fun.

My summer book that year was *The Secret War*, and Joe and I had a second Crime Dossier, *Who Killed Robert Prentice?*

Our first Crime Dossier had stolen the thunder at a Foyle lunch which Christina gave for a book called *Six Against the Yard*. In it Dorothy Sayers, Margery Allingham, Freeman

Wills Croft, Russell Thorndike, Father Ronald Knox and Anthony Berkeley had all written short murder stories and these had been given to ex-Superintendent Cornish to solve.

Christina had asked me to take the chair at this lunch and as a great stack of *Murder Off Miami*, which had just been published, was there on sale, it scooped the pool at the expense of the book for which the lunch had been held.

That July Joan and I went to Central Europe for our holiday. It was our first visit to Vienna. We stayed at Sachers. The city in those days before the coming of the Nazis was wonderfully gay.

Prague, by comparison, was a dull, bourgeois city. Although Czechoslovakia was still independent, it had already fallen under Communist influence and the hotel we stayed at was named after Karl Marx's collaborator, Engels. The glory of Prague had ended some hundreds of years earlier when, after being defeated, almost the whole nobility of the country was condemned to death.

Budapest, although very different from Vienna, was equally enchanting. The whole steep hillside of Buda was covered by splendid private palaces. They were, alas, almost entirely destroyed near the end of the Second World War, when the Germans elected to make a last stand in them. In the great city of Pest hundreds of thousands of Jews still lived happily; they were very prosperous because no Hungarian 'Magnet', as the nobles were termed, would soil his hands with trade. Along the Corso were dozens of cafés and scores of good restaurants where goulash, duck and even *foie gras* were quite inexpensive. I brought home half a dozen tins each containing a whole goose's liver. Budapest had lain within the Roman Empire so for many centuries its people had inherited a civilized mentality.

Owing to the success of my *Private Life of Charles II*, my publishers had for a long time been urging me to write another biography; but I could think of no character I admired sufficiently to make a book out of his life story. Then, for what reason I have now forgotten, it occurred to me to write about a man of whom very few of the British public had ever heard. His name was Klementy Voroshilov, and I called my book *Red Eagle*.

He started as a mechanic working in a factory in the Don Basin. Like many young men of his day he became a fanatical revolutionary. When the first revolution erupted he went to St Petersburg and was among those on the station platform to welcome Lenin when the Bolshevik leader stepped out of the sealed train in which the Germans had sent him back to Russia.

Very soon Russia was in turmoil. The army was falling to pieces; there were deserters by the tens of thousands. The greater part of Asiatic Russia was still in the hands of the Whites. In the south the Cossacks were fighting for the imprisoned Czar. From the west a German Army was advancing towards the north and east. An expeditionary force of French and Italians had landed in the Crimea and a British force at Archangel.

Voroshilov had returned to the Don country. There a great undisciplined rabble of factory workers had assembled, eager to support the Red Government in Moscow but leaderless and menaced by the Germans rapidly approaching from the west. A council of Party men was called. They elected Voroshilov to tell them what they should do. He declared that their only hope was to make their way to Tzaritsyn on the Volga.

Every train available was called into service. They were packed with men, women and children and the terrible journey began. Tzaritsyn was nearly 600 miles away. The trains moved at a snail's pace and there were constant breakdowns. Day after day for weeks on end Voroshilov fought off the well-armed Germans and the Cossacks. With his rabble of workers he performed the impossible and got his scores of trains through.

But when they arrived they found Tzaritsyn already in a state of siege. Moscow was starving and surrounded on every side but that of the Volga. It could be fed only by the grain barges that came up the river from the south. If Tzaritsyn fell it would be the end.

Stalin was the political Commissar in Tzaritsyn – that is

why the city's name was afterwards changed to Stalingrad. He appointed Voroshilov Military Commander. There were not enough troops to hold the perimeter. Voroshilov at once set every factory in the city to make armoured trains. This enabled him to rush a mobile force to each threatened sector in turn. He fought the enemy to a standstill and by holding Tzaritsyn saved the Revolution.

He became a Marshal and Commissar for Defence. In the Second World War, when the Germans advanced on Leningrad, he took personal command of the city. He was cut off and besieged there for two years. The people ate horses, dogs, cats and rats, but he never surrendered. In his last years he was President of the Union of Soviet Socialist Republics.

It was not easy to get the information for my book. Sir Vernon Kell, the head of MI5, was very helpful, as was also Prince Dimitri. He put me in touch with Anatole Bakilief who lived in Barkstone Gardens. In the days before the Revolution he had been a permanent prisoner in Irkutsk on Lake Baikal, through which passed every revolutionary sent to exile in Siberia; so he had met nearly all the leading Bolsheviks. When the Revolution succeeded, Bakilief was made Commissar of Siberia but he was in fact a Liberal and, after a while, became disgusted by his colleagues' murderous excesses; so he got himself made Soviet Ambassador to Japan. Then one morning he and his family walked out of the Embassy and boarded a ship for England. When I met him his son was an officer in the British Army.

Bakilief asked me to tea, which went on to drinking Tokay. With him was another man whose name I forget, but he had been the last official representative of the Czars in England. We all became a little tight. Bakilief suddenly threw his arm round his companion's shoulders and cried:

'Mr Wheatley, you may think it strange that I, an ex-Soviet Commissar, and this last representative of the Czar should be such close friends. But, you see, we are both Cossacks.'

15

OF TRAVEL, REINCARNATION
AND PREPARATIONS FOR WAR

ON 1 January, 1938, Joan and I travelled by a one-coach special from Waterloo Station to Southampton harbour. A motor boat took us out to a Sunderland seaplane. We were about to fly to Egypt; but the days were yet to come when one could do that in a few hours. On the other hand two factors made air travel infinitely more interesting and pleasant than it has since become.

The cabin contained some ten or twelve pairs of chairs and in front of each pair was a table. The chairs were like those of a dentist with foot-rests and so much space behind them that by pressing a lever one could adjust them to any angle, even horizontal, so that one could sleep in them if one wished. The chairs and tables occupied only about two-thirds of the breadth of the aircraft; the remainder was an open space in which one could walk up and down as in the corridor of a train, and the windows all along it were sheets of glass like those in a train. As the aircraft never flew much above 2000 feet, instead of shooting up above the clouds, standing in the corridor one could see the country below as though looking down on a vast map.

Early in the afternoon we landed near Marignon on the great lake. A coach took us to a first-class hotel in Marseilles where we dined and spent the night. Next morning we flew east along the Riviera and could look down on the people enjoying the winter sunshine there, then over Corsica and down the leg of Italy to Naples, where we spent a second night. On the third evening we landed in the bay of Alexandria.

We had decided to take the train straight down to Aswân,

at the First Cataract, then make our way northward by Nile Boat. I had read a great deal about Ancient Egypt so was able to discuss places with our pleasant old guide, who used to come to us every morning and say, 'What would my Lord like to see today?' In Egypt, up till the end of the thirties, every English traveller was still given the status of a Lord.

At Luxor we explored the wonders of the ancient capital. In one courtyard of the huge temple of Karnak the whole of St Paul's Cathedral could be rebuilt and it would not touch the walls. Of the many temples there, only one small one contains a figure. It is that of the God, Set, and when looking at it I felt a definite sense of evil, although I sensed nothing of that kind in any of the Tombs of the Kings.

These lie some distance from the city on the far side of the river in a group of deep valleys. The longer the reign of a Pharaoh the deeper into a mountain goes the passage to the burial chamber, as the priests continued to excavate the tunnel until the day of his death.

In addition to the principal tombs I went down into one that is normally visited only by archaeologists. This was that of Thotmes III, the Napoleon of Egypt. Its entrance is at the bottom of a deep valley into which one has to descend by a rope ladder and the burial chamber lies 300 feet underground. It is unlit so one has to go down carrying a candle. Part of the stairway had fallen away and in places the roof is badly cracked, so it is considered dangerous; but I thought that after 3000 years the odds against it collapsing the day I went down were pretty considerable.

When walking across the area we were lucky enough to come across a French archaeologist who had just discovered and opened up the tomb of a noble's wife, and he allowed us to go down into it with him. The mummy, Ka figures and other objects were all there and, but for a light film of dust, just as they had been left when the tomb had been closed thousands of years ago.

From Luxor we continued down river until we landed at Cairo. We were fortunate in having an introduction to Russell Pasha, who looked after us most kindly. Among other people he introduced us to Count Almashey, an

Austrian airman who had been engaged by the Egyptian Government to fly to and fro across the Libyan desert, which is larger than Great Britain, in search of the lost treasure of Cambyses.

Having conquered Egypt the Persian monarch made his headquarters in Luxor, then sent a large part of his army west across the desert to conquer the rest of North Africa. As he intended to follow he sent with them the fabulous treasure that had been accumulated in Luxor. After eight days' march the Egyptian guides left the Persian army lost and stranded. Every single man died of thirst and the treasure lies with their bodies somewhere beneath the windblown sand. Almashey failed to find it, so it is still there. It was on a search for that immense wealth that I based my story *The Quest of Julian Day*.

We went on to Alexandria, where we stayed with a nephew of the famous author Captain Marriot. With him I went to an annual ball given by a Mr McPherson a millionaire cotton broker. As a young clerk on a modest salary he had lived in one of twelve flats that formed a block overlooking the beautiful bay. He suddenly had a stroke of luck and in a few years became rich. His wife said that they ought to move to a house. He refused to leave the place where his luck had changed but took the flat on the opposite side of the landing so that they would be better able to entertain. Then he took the two flats on the floor below, then the two flats on the floor above. When I went there he owned the whole block, had gutted the centre, installed a beautiful staircase brought from a Venetian palace and turned the whole of the top storey into a magnificent hundred-foot-long library.

And what a ball it was! The rich of Alexandria, British, Egyptian and Greek, all in fancy dress. Pharaohs, Cleopatras, Mamelukes, Romans, all arrayed in gorgeous garments. Enough costly foods to feed a Legion, and an inexhaustible supply of Pol Roger Champagne. I got away at six o'clock in the morning; our aircraft left for Athens at eight.

My winter book that year was *Uncharted Seas*, and in April we brought out a third Crime Dossier, *The Malinsay Massacre*.

I had written the story before leaving England but had had to leave the photographs to be taken in my absence. When I saw them I was livid with rage. The script was about mass murder in an ancient castle in Scotland. Joe had allowed the photographs of the characters and bodies to be taken in the Carlton Hotel, and the backgrounds could not have been less suitable.

At about this time there was an interesting development regarding Bill. Maxwell Knight had become a close friend of ours and fairly early in our acquaintance confided to me that he was an officer of MI5. Up at Oxford a motion had been passed by undergraduates that they 'would not fight for King and Country', and a Pacifist movement was rapidly gaining ground. MI5 were anxious to learn which out of scores of silly idealistic youngsters were really dangerous agitators, secretly paid by Moscow or the Nazis. Max Knight whom we afterwards always referred to as 'uncle', asked if we would object to Bill's being asked if he would undertake a secret investigation. Naturally we agreed and so did Bill.

J. C. Masterman was Bill's tutor and we had met him in Oxford. It was not until some years later that, when a member of the Joint Planning Staff of the War Cabinet, I met J.C. again and learned that he had long been one of the top men in MI5, and I realized what an excellent tie-up had existed between him and Bill. Masterman's book, *The Double-Cross System*, is one of the very few truthful accounts of cloak-and-dagger work carried out in the war.

That May, Christina Foyle's lunch consisted of a Spelling Bee. I took part in it and, of course, proved absolutely hopeless. I spell so badly that I even spelt my middle name as Yates for the greater part of my life. It was not until my mother died and I went to her funeral that, from the marble erected over the family grave, I saw that it was really Yeats.

In October 1937 I had met Joan Grant shortly before her first book, *Winged Pharaoh*, came out. Having always believed in reincarnation, I reviewed it enthusiastically in *Current Literature*. Still better, I sent a copy to Howard Spring who then did reviews for the *Evening Standard*. The week the book was published he devoted the whole of his space to it and ended, 'If people will accept the teachings of this book it could lead to a new age of chivalry.'

That was in the days before Howard became an author. A friend of Lord Beaverbrook said to him one night, 'I can't think why you have Spring as your reviewer on the *Evening Standard*. What can he know about books when he's never written one?'

The Beaver sent for Howard and said, 'Your capability as a critic has been questioned because you have never written a book. Go home and write one.'

Howard did. Its title was *Shabby Tiger* and it became a bestseller. A few years later his books were selling by the tens of thousands.

Reverting to Joan Grant. It was not until 1938 that Joan and I became intimate friends of hers. A year or so later she left Leslie Grant for Charles Beatty, with whom she had fallen in love.

On the death of Charles's father, his uncle, the famous Admiral, had become his guardian. When 'The Troubles' started in Ireland, the Admiral had made him go off to occupy Borodale, the family mansion in Ireland, to prevent it from being burnt down. The great house was almost bare of furniture and there were no servants. Charles lived there for many months in one room, mainly on tinned food. Apparently, he had always been interested in the Occult, so he made a study of ancient religions, particularly Buddhism, and used to sit naked cross-legged on the floor, his eyes fixed on his navel, meditating. Later he wrote a book on this subject, the title of which was *The Golden Flower*. It was this common interest in the world of the spirit that brought him and Joan together.

Joan always dictated her books while in a semi-trance. *Winged Pharaoh* was taken down by Leslie Grant, who was a barrister, and it is generally admitted to be her best. Of the others *Life as Carola* and *Return to Elysium* are very good. But Charles, who took down all her later books, although a man of the utmost integrity, was so obsessed with traditional occult symbols and ceremonies that, in my view, his influence caused a decline in her direct communication with the Powers of Light.

I think the only logical belief is that all of us have lived on Earth many times, as a man or a woman gradually acquiring knowledge, but having to pay for the evil we do in one life in a future life, or being rewarded for good deeds by promotion to higher responsibility. It is difficult to believe that after a single life we are in due course judged and either rewarded by eternal bliss among the Saints or cast down to roast in the flames of Hell for ever.

In 1938 Joan Grant, as she was then, produced a Mr Wyeth and a Mr Neal, who made their livelihood by lecturing on Reincarnation. On half a dozen evenings I had them expound their belief to twenty or thirty of our friends in the drawing-room of No. 8. What effect these talks had I cannot say.

My book that summer was *The Golden Spaniard*. The main theme was a plagiarism of Alexandre Dumas's *Twenty Years After*, in which during the war of the Fronde, the four friends take opposite sides for political reasons; d'Artagnan and Porthos siding with the Court; Athos and Aramis with the Frondeurs. In my book de Richleau and Richard Eaton sided with Franco, Simon Aron and Rex Van Ryn with the Socialist–Marxists. This enabled me to put them in many situations where duty and personal friendship clashed. The book covered all the opening phases of the Spanish Civil War and is one of the best I have ever written.

Bino and Peggy had parted. He then married Louise Chalkley, an only daughter with a very rich father, so Bino continued to 'live in clover'. That autumn Diana went out to stay with them. When she returned, her pretty young face was smothered with make-up as heavily as that of the worst type of chorus-girl at forty. We were not pleased.

In February, 1939, I had an interesting experience. Television was then in its infancy. Very few people had sets and Alexandra Palace was the only place in Britain from which TV was beamed. I was invited to take part in a programme with Tom Driberg, Lady Eleanor Smith, Lord Donegall and Patrick Balfour. What we talked about,

I forget, but the producer rashly showed a copy of the current *Who's Who* as a prize for the best performance. Lady Eleanor was voted the best and claimed the prize. The producer said, 'Oh, that was only a gambit for the show.'

But Lady Eleanor seized the book and declared; 'I've got one, but I won this and mean to sell it.' I laughed and offered her a pound for it, which she promptly accepted; with my fee in addition I had a not only very interesting but also profitable evening.

During the spring of that year Lord Donegall and I saw a lot of one another because for three months I also became a gossip writer. Reggie Simpson, the Editor of the *Sunday Graphic* asked me to do the weekly Personalities page. I was sent free tickets for every First Night, big boxing matches and the cabarets at the best hotels. I was much amused by the attitude of the *maitres d'hotels*. Previously, I had always paid in full for everything. Having learned of my new status they sidled up and suggested that I and the friends at my table should be their guests for the evening, or would I be kind enough to accept a magnum of Champagne?

On one occasion I went to a boxing championship organized by that able and charming impresario, C. B. Cochran. He had been a customer of mine in South Audley Street and was an old friend. When the boxing was over my journalistic colleagues were all going to a big dance at the Holborn given by the Dolcis Shoe Company for their employees. They expected me to go with them but I had not received an invitation. 'Never mind about that,' they said 'The Dolcis people will be delighted to see you.' So I went.

It was a grand party. Towards the end of it a few of us got together and discussed how we could return hospitality with publicity. Someone suggested that we should create a devastating beauty. So we agreed to say in our columns that at the Dolcis dance there had been a girl named Ermintrude Wraxwell, who was one of the most beautiful we had ever seen.

The result was startling. I and the others who had mentioned Ermintrude were rung up on the Monday morning by half a dozen film companies and theatrical agents who wanted to sign her up right away on a handsome contract. The Dolcis people, of course had, never heard of her, nor could enquiries among their staff trace anyone who had brought her to the dance. It shows, though, how had we named a real girl, we could have made her fortune for her.

At the time I was writing these articles the Home Secretary Sir John Anderson, was issuing his home Air Raid Shelters, so in one of my pieces I suggested another precaution that could be taken against the distresses of war. I recalled that in the First World War the only period when Britain had been in serious danger of defeat was when German submarines nearly succeeded in starving us out by cutting our Atlantic lifeline. Now, I said, Hitler has many more U-boats, so heavy sinkings of our merchant shipping are certain to create a shortage of food. Therefore, everyone ought to buy all the tinned goods they could afford for an emergency store cupboard. While we are still at peace this is not hoarding but good for trade. I then offered a prize of £5 for a list of the most sustaining items to that value.

The response was staggering. The *Sunday Graphic* received 14,000 entries. A score or so of the best were sent to me and I gave the prize to a woman at Margate who had based her list scientifically on calorie content.

In April war was very much in the air, and I invented a game called *Invasion*. It was played with small counters of three shapes, representing Naval, Army and Air Forces, on a large coloured map; the moves depending on throws of the dice by each player in turn. Geographia, a subsidiary of Hutchinson, published it and it was a great success.

In May I undertook a new activity. In preparation for war the Government had decided on a drive to secure volunteers for the Territorials, the RNVR, the RAFVR, the Air Raid Wardens and the Nursing Services. Talks were to be given in cinemas in the principal cities on Sunday afternoons. But it was realized that comparatively few people would turn out at such an hour to listen to their local MP, so Sir John Anderson formed a panel of men whose names were known throughout the country. Among them were Charles Laughton, Ralph Straus, Sir Norman Birkett and Herbert Sutcliffe, the famous Yorkshire cricketer.

I was brought into this galaxy of VIPs by Archie Mac-donell, who had written that most amusing book, *England, Their England*. The cinemas in which we spoke were crowded out. At each meeting we were supported on the platform by the local MP, his Opposition candidate, the Mayor, the Matron of the local hospital and the Colonel of a Territorial regiment.

I wrote a speech that took me three-quarters of an hour to deliver and, although I am no singer, ended up by giving the first lines of 'Land of Hope and Glory'. It was instantly taken up by the audience and I was given a standing ovation. In three months our panel secured over two million volunteers.

That summer we gave our last big party at No. 8. It was to celebrate the publication of the fourth and final Crime Dossier, *Herewith The Clues*. The cost of production prevented our publishing others after the war; but this party was, I am happy to think, a very special one. The murder took place in a night-club; so by clearing all the furniture out of our drawing-room and putting in about sixteen small tables we turned it into one.

Ruby Miller, with whom I had attended dancing classes when we were both children, came and played the piano for us. Photographs of a number of our guests were taken to represent the suspects in the story. Among them were Lord Poulett, Doris Zinkeisen, Sir Malcolm Campbell, Christabel, Lady Ampthill, Sir Charles Birkin, the Marquis of Donegall, Gilbert Frankau, Lady Stanley of Alderley, Peter Cheyney, Sir Harry Brittain and Val Gielgud of BBC fame, flat on his back in the hall, as the Body. It was a great party.

When the question of our summer holiday arose, in view of the threat of war I wanted to take the family to Ireland, to which none of us had then been, but they would not hear of it and insisted on going to the South of France.

On the way back, we did not head for Paris but drove to Amiens, as I wanted to see again the little house I had built in 1917 against a wall of the garden of a ruined *Château*. The Hôtel du Rhin at which we used to stay when on twenty-four-hour leave to Amiens seemed very small compared to how I remembered it, but the Salon Godbert provided us with an excellent lunch, although only the small room in front was open; the great reception room behind it where a hundred or more officers used to dine every night was used only for occasional local celebrations. Next day we vainly drove about what had once been a part of the Western Front, but few signs of it were left and we failed to find the village near which I had built 'Crooked Villa'.

Two days later we were home, and within a week after that we were at war.

16

THE OPENING OF THE WAR

AT 11 a.m. on Sunday 3 September, 1939, a sadly disillusioned Prime Minister told those who listened to his broadcast that we were again at war with Germany.

I was then forty-two and Joan one year older. We heard the announcement in our drawing-room at No. 8. With us were Bill Younger, who had recently come down from Oxford, Diana and Colin.

Immediately Mr Chamberlain had finished speaking we heard for the first time the banshee wailing of the sirens and went down to the basement. During the few days since our return from France I had taken reasonable precautions.

No. 8 was an old house and, lacking steel girders, would almost certainly have collapsed into a heap of rubble if hit by a bomb. But running along the back of the semi-basement there was a three-foot-wide, four-foot-deep stone trench, and the bay of the drawing-room window jutted out above it supported by two stout pillars. This, therefore, was the site I chose to make an air-raid shelter.

I had Justerini and Brooks send me a load of empty Champagne cases, and my builder a load of rubble and some sacks of cement. Having filled the cases with rubble I stacked them between the pillars and along the outer side of the stone trench, then used more rubble with the cement for concrete to reinforce them. With other cases I made three stacks to support the ceiling of the servants' sitting-room, through the window of which we could climb out into the shelter. In it there were bedding, food, wine, books and ample space for ourselves, our Scottish cook and two pretty young Irish sisters who were our maids.

Down we all went into the shelter, satisfied that, short of a direct hit on it, even if the house did collapse alongside us, we would be able to crawl out through one or other end of the stone trench. But, of course, the sirens proved only a false alarm, so up we came again. I collected a magnum of Louis Roederer 1928 – to my mind the finest *cuvée* of that magnificent vintage – then up in the drawing-room we drank to a speedy victory and the safe survival of our friends and other members of the family; Anthony, who was fifteen and at Downside; Meg, who a few years before had married Captain John Moller and lived in Scotland: Jack, who only a few days earlier, had entered Sandhurst as a Gentleman Cadet preparatory to going into the Coldstream Guards; my mother and Joan's mother.

On that Sunday afternoon my oldest friend Joe Links, looked in to see us. During the past sixteen years, he had built up the finest mink business in London. He later became a director of the Hudson's Bay Company and furrier to the Queen. To my amazement Joe was wearing the uniform of a Flying Officer.

Believing war to be inevitable, he had in 1938 joined the RAFVR and was now in charge of a Balloon Section up at Hampstead. How as the sole owner of a big business he had found time to do the drill I cannot imagine, and it was typical of his modesty that he had not told us a word about his new activities.

It was with envy that I saw him in uniform, that being the proper dress for any gentleman when Britain is at war. But he was ten years younger than I, and I had already reconciled myself to the thought that in this new war I could best serve my country in a civilian capacity. I assumed that I should be asked to continue on Sir John Anderson's panel, or alternatively, as my books were already published in eighteen languages, be immediately employed on propaganda.

As the latter activity seemed to me the best use I could make of such talents as I possessed, when I saw in Monday morning's paper that a Ministry of Information was to be formed I immediately wrote and offered my services.

As a precaution against Hitler getting the whole of my cellar with one bomb I split it up into four. One part I kept with me for immediate use wherever I moved, till the war was over; another Justerini stored for delivery any time I wanted to replenish my own stock; a third I sent down to Joe Links's country home at Blackdown and the fourth to Charles Beatty's house at Welshpool. By the grace of God I never lost a single bottle, and there were over two hundred bottles left when I collected what remained in 1945 to form the beginning of my cellar in my new home at Lymington.

For supplies of food we were very well off, as I had laid in such enormous stocks earlier in the year when I had advised readers of my articles in the *Sunday Graphic* to do so. We had also laid in a big quantity of soap, bandages, cotton wool and every sort of medicine we were likely to require.

In my storage operation I made one error. I had expected that if war did come, during the first three weeks Hitler's bombers would create hell in London by concentrating on our docks and marshalling yards, with the result that supplies would be so seriously disrupted that there would probably be food riots. To guard against having to participate in such a dangerous state of confusion, I had planned to make my household, of myself, and five women, self-supporting until the Government had got things under control. In consequence I had laid in large quantities of flour, cereals and dry biscuits. There proved to be no need for them; so I would have done better to buy more *foie gras* instead.

There was one other item that I had tinned by Fortnum and Mason, after the war had actually broken out – twelve dozen pairs of silk stockings for Joan and Diana, and to give as Christmas presents to my secretaries.

Within a few days of the opening of hostilities, Joan and Diana, as well as Bill, were, owing to 'Uncle', both in MI5. Before leaving for the South of France, I had asked 'Uncle' Max to tip me off should the situation become really threatening. It was not until a fortnight after the war had been declared that I received a letter returned to me from Cavalière, which had arrived there the day we left. It was from Max and simply said, 'If you want to see Uncle before the end I advise your immediate return to London.'

One immediate benefit of Bill's being in MI5 was that, on his account, within twenty-four hours of Mr Chamberlain's

F

broadcast, the Post Office with extraordinary efficiency, had laid on a special telephone line direct to our air-raid shelter at No. 8; a considerable comfort to me in case we had the misfortune to become entombed.

On the outbreak of war the 'Office' of MI5 had been evacuated to the recently abandoned prison out at Wormwood Scrubs. This was not a good choice, as it was very vulnerable to bombs and one direct hit might have destroyed a great part of the thousands of files recording the activities of suspected persons; and there were no duplicates. Later, the 'Office' moved to St James's Street, upon which Joan, who had a considerable knowledge of the consumption of various makes of car, was appointed 'Petrol Queen', and decreed with some austerity the exact amount that each operative should be allowed to draw for his journeys.

Diana was given a job as a filing clerk. Owing to a head injury in a motoring accident when returning from Switzerland, she was at times definitely vague, but she had an excellent intelligence, and about matters which interested her personally she was still right on the mark. Art was one of them. In addition to studying abroad she had recently been at the St John's Wood Art School, and already showed promise as a painter. She has since become a sculptress of real ability and her bronzes and wood carvings are now exhibited in the United States. Later in the war, when she had recovered her health, she did valuable work in the Secret Operations Executive, including being dropped in France by parachute.

Jack Younger, with the rest of his companions at Sandhurst, was technically reduced soon after hostilities opened from Gentleman Cadet to the ranks; but for all practical purposes his status remained the same, and he was in the war. Anthony and Colin were still too young to be accepted. I alone remained on the shelf.

On 5 September the names of the two senior Civil Servants who had been appointed to select the personnel for the Ministry of Information were announced. I wrote again to both of them, stating my qualifications and offering my services. I did not even receive a postcard in reply.

The Minister had been a High Court Judge, used to prolonged deliberation over knotty legal points, and the two Civil Servants must have been hopelessly incompetent. They staffed the Ministry of Information with nine hundred and ninety-nine men and women, *only thirty* of whom had ever been journalists or professional writers. One might as well have sent a newly-launched battleship to sea with a crew of a thousand, only thirty of whom had ever been trained as sailors; then told her Captain to seek out and destroy the enemy.

As further evidence of the Chamberlain Government's incompetence to wage a modern war, instead of keeping in being Sir John Anderson's panel of well-known public speakers to inform the public about air-raid precautions, war work, rationing schemes and so on, they disbanded it and we were informed by the Home Secretary that he had no further use for us.

I went to 'Uncle' and asked if he could not find some niche for me in MI5. As I already knew its brilliant Chief, General Sir Vernon Kell, who had started this branch of our Intelligence from scratch in 1909, and he had generously helped me two years earlier when I was writing my biography of Marshal Voroshilov, I had good hopes in that direction. But they were doomed to disappointment.

Max told me that no post suitable to my capabilities was open; and that I should thank God that I had not got myself mixed up in the incredible muddle resulting from the formation of the Ministry of Information. Moreover, I must not commit myself to any minor job of war work, as the time would surely come when I should be wanted, and perhaps quickly, for some post where my abilities could be used to the best advantage. He then urged me to remember that war and the black-out had put an end to most normal forms of entertainment, and that henceforth countless thousands of people in camps, in hospitals, in isolated stations and sitting up all night in air-raid posts would depend for their sole enjoyment on reading; so the best service I could give for the present was to continue writing my thrillers. For me, in September, 1939, that was a poor consolation.

17

OF BOOKS AND SPIES

BEFORE leaving for the South of France I had written several chapters of a new book. I had heard about a school in Devonshire which was co-educational and run on ultra-modern lines. The pupils were allowed complete licence to attend classes or not as they liked, lie in bed all day if they wished and even abuse teachers that they disliked. It was rumoured that the pupils were encouraged to attend Satanic gatherings in a ruined church near by. Sir Pellinore should send Gregory Sallust to the neighbourhood to carry out an investigation. The book was never completed. But I used the idea many years later in *The Haunting of Toby Jugg*.

I decided that now there was a war on an up-to-the-minute spy story was the thing, so on the 6th September, I sat down to write *The Scarlet Impostor*.

The previous day, after a visit to my publishers, I made my way back to a small restaurant at the bottom of St Martin's Lane where the Paternoster Club was holding one of its monthly lunches.

While we were having drinks before lunch we heard the strains of martial music and went to the window. Coming down St Martin's Lane was a small band, a man carrying a French flag and following him, a straggle of men in civilian clothes. They were French reservists who had been called up and were making their way to the station.

I recall the incident only because it brought home the extraordinary difference in the attitude of the public at the opening of the two World Wars. In 1914 there had been intense excitement, crowds in the streets eagerly awaiting the latest news bulletins about the situation in France, everyone stopping to line the pavements and cheer marching bands, thousands of Territorials in khaki going to and from their headquarters, East-Enders wrecking the German bakers' shops and coming up West to stone the windows of the German Embassy, long queues of men waiting to join up outside every recruiting office and Union Jacks flying everywhere.

Now there were no marching men, no queues of volunteers, no flags, no waiting crowds no riots, hardly a figure in khaki anywhere, and this was the first band I had seen. The majority of the public had accepted the inevitable with distressing apathy, and this spirit of gloomy resignation was, after lunch, demonstrated by our Chairman.

His name was Eric Hiscock and he was on the *Evening Standard*, where he handled all the book advertising contracts. Having opened his speech by remarking that he was not surprised to find that comparatively few members had turned up, he went on to say that, as many of us would be joining the Forces or too fully occupied to attend lunches in the coming months, he thought it would be best if the club ceased to function until the war was over.

Eric was a good friend of mine, but the moment he sat down I was on my feet. I said that, on the contrary, those of us who remained in London would more than ever wish to meet and learn how our fellow members were faring; that it was the duty of those who stayed behind to keep the club in being, so that when our younger members who joined the Forces came on leave they could attend a lunch and get news of their old friends; that in 1914 Britain's slogan had been business 'as usual', and this applied to pleasure too; that only by maintaining such a spirit could we all give of our best and be certain of achieving victory.

Old Freddie Richardson, the head of Boots' Library, had, since the Club's formation six years before, given a great deal of his leisure to its affairs. Jumping up with passionate ferocity, he seconded my contention. Poor Eric looked terribly embarrassed; for, apart from him, my motion was carried unanimously.

The war was still not a week old when Uncle Max rang me up to ask what I knew about William Joyce. I replied that I knew no one of that name. 'Oh yes, you do,' Uncle replied. 'He was at one of your parties.' I still insisted that I had never even heard of the man, but 'Uncle' said, 'It's in his files. Search your memory.' Then he gave me a description of Joyce.

That did not ring a bell either; which was not surprising as in pre-war days we gave many parties. The mentions in gossip columns and the photographs of these parties which appeared in the *Bystander* and the *Tatler* were valuable publicity. We gave young people's parties for Diana, too, and many smaller ones. No wonder I never had any money!

People often used to ask if they might bring a friend to our parties, and that, it transpired, was how Joyce had come to one of them. When I described him to Joan as a small man with a round, pale face, she recalled him and that he had got unpleasantly tight. I remembered him then as having been brought by W. H. Tayleur, who had corrected my proofs very efficiently for some years past. I remembered, too, that Joyce had talked a lot about Germany. He had lamented the fact that my books were not published there, and told me that was because in my Duke de Richleau series one of the heroes, Simon Aron, was a Jew; but that Goering was a great fan of mine and read all my books. Then he urged me to come over to Germany with him some time and meet the Nazi leaders.

I knew Tayleur to be in sympathy with the Fascists, if not one himself. But I thought no worse of him for that as I also inclined towards them. To my mind Mussolini had done a splendid job in cleaning up Italy, making his nation far more prosperous and introducing the beginnings of the first Welfare State; and that with very little persecution – no more than confining a few hundred really dangerous Communist agitators in a prison island. It was one of the greatest tragedies in history that later megalomania led him to throw in his lot with Hitler.

As for General Franco, he had my vote every time. Although violently opposed by many of my friends in Fleet Street, I had preached his cause from the outbreak of the

Spanish Civil War. To me it was inconceivable that any sane person should wish to see Spain in the hands of the Communists.

But the Nazis, with their vast concentration camps in which millions of Jews, Liberals and other opponents of the regime were systematically tortured, starved and done to death, were a very different matter. William Joyce was my guest, so I was not rude to him. And anyway, as he had already had one over the odds, I took his boasting references to being the friend of Goering and other prominent Nazis with a grain of salt. As soon as he had left the house I forgot him.

I telephoned 'Uncle' to tell him what we had remembered about this unpleasant little man; so he came round that evening to be given such details as we could supply. It transpired that the previous week Joyce had made a bolt for Germany, but had left in such a hurry that, when MI5 raided his flat, they had found that he had destroyed none of his papers.

There was a file on myself in which were copies of his reports to his Nazi masters. In one of them he said that, as I had a number of Jewish friends, I was not quite clean on that aspect of policy. But that, in all other respects, after the invasion, when able collaborators would be needed, I should make a first-class *Gauleiter* for North-West London.

This unrequested testimonial by an enemy agent might, in other circumstances, have done me no good at all, and caused me to be regarded as suspect throughout the war. But fortunately Max knew all about me; so we had a good laugh over it. Wiliam Joyce, of course, afterwards achieved a dubious fame as 'Lord Haw-Haw'. After the war he was hanged as a traitor.

'Uncle' then raised another matter with me. An Austrian girl had recently arrived in England as a refugee. She had been sent over as a Nazi agent, but actually she loathed the Nazis and was anxious to work against them. As a double agent she could therefore be of considerable value; but now that we were at war, unless some respectable citizen could vouch for having known her for several years, and she could

be guaranteed employment, the law decreed that she must
be interned. No one in MI5 could give her cover in case a
real pro-Nazi agent discovered her connection with the
'Office'; for then her 'double cross' would be 'blown' and
her future activities rendered useless. So 'Uncle' asked me
to sponsor her.

Naturally I agreed, and Fritzi, as she soon became known
to us, was asked to No. 8 for a drink. I interviewed her
privately and signed her papers. Then it was agreed that,
for a certain sum each week, she should do research for me,
and for many months afterwards she spent a good part of
her time supplying me with translations of accounts of the
Nazi leaders; their beginnings, backgrounds and rise to
power. For my Gregory Sallust spy stories this data proved
invaluable. And I got all this for nothing, since I gave
Fritzi her salary by cheque each week while 'Uncle'
reimbursed me for its value by sending me pound notes.

During the previous season Diana had met the Honourable
Brinsley le Poer Trench, son of an Irish peer who had run
through a big fortune and, some years earlier, had his
affairs placed in the hands of trustees. Brinsley was a splendidly made young man; over six feet tall with broad shoulders and slim hips. He had dark curly hair and was
extremely handsome.

He had been out with Diana a lot in May and June and
one day, after we returned from the South of France, he
threw the bombshell at me that they wanted to get married.
I knew, of course, that Diana was in love with him, because
she had had several earlier romances and always told me all
about them. This I believed to be just another; so at Brinsley's announcement I was amazed, not only because he
seemed to me unsuited as a husband for a girl like Diana,
but because his sole income consisted of four pounds a week
which he earned as a junior clerk in the Bank of South
Africa.

I rarely lose my temper but I rounded on him. Shortly
after my outburst Diana came on the scene. All the arguments of her mother and myself were of no avail. She said
she loved Brinsley and meant to marry him. So that was that.

All we could extract from her was that it should be a long engagement.

Brinsley then took a room in the house next door but one to us, where the elderly sisters of the once famous performer, Bransby Williams, let lodgings; and, for the following year, became more or less one of the family. To Diana's credit, it must be said that having gained her point she made no attempt to persuade us to let her hasten her marriage, but continued to rush blithely round the house, singing her inexhaustible repertoire of popular songs.

I had very little leisure indeed. I was concentrating on my novel, *The Scarlet Impostor*. By working most days from 10 a.m. until 2 a.m. the following morning, I got it finished on 19 October. One hundred and seventy-two thousand words in seven weeks, and one of the best books I have ever written.

Meanwhile, in a few short weeks, Hitler's *Blitzkrieg* had overwhelmed Polish resistance, and that unfortunate country had again been partitioned between Germany and Russia. No major collision had yet taken place between the opposing armies that held the Maginot and Siegfried Lines, so it began to look as though the stalemate would continue till the spring. The expected air raids on British cities had not matured and on the home front people had been lulled into a false security.

By the beginning of November they had, as far as possible, taken up again many of their old activities. Foyles started a new venture called 'The Right Book Club' and Christina Foyle asked me to become one of its Patrons. That I was delighted to do, not only because from the beginning she had been such a good friend to my books, but also because it agreed with my own principles and could be expected to counter, to some extent, the spate of subversive stuff which, for several years past, had been pouring from the Left Book Club under the aegis of Victor Gollancz.

I lunched with Joe Links at his Balloon Section Mess, which he had established most conveniently in his own very pleasant little Regency house in Pond Street, Hampstead. After lunch we all went out to a field and threw Molotov cocktails at a dummy tank. Never having been a fast, or even slow, bowler, I muffed my throw completely and the home-made bomb exploded only a dozen feet from where we were standing.

Another friend of ours, Archie Savory, had got himself a commission in an anti-aircraft battery and one night Joan and I dined in his Mess. The Colonel's name was Krohn and he had been an anti-aircraft expert in the First World War. It was typical of the idiocy of the War Office between World Wars that, although aerial warfare would so obviously prove a major factor in any future war, they decided in 1919 to scrap entirely all anti-aircraft units and, in spite of Krohn's pleading, refused to recreate them right up to the time of Munich; so that all that could be done in that crisis was to put machine guns pointing skywards on the roofs of Government buildings. It is pleasant to relate, however, that this highly intelligent officer later became a Brigadier and, during the blitz, commanded the defences of London.

Soon afterwards, I was myself given a very minor part to play in the war. At one of Charlie Birkin's cocktail parties Joan and I met a peer's wife, later known to us all as Vicki. A few days later 'Uncle', having learned by his own mysterious means that we had met her, came along and told me what MI5 believed about this very attractive little brunette.

Vicki was a Hungarian. A year or two before the war she had managed to marry the peer. By her marriage she had, of course, become a British subject and was now living in a fine flat in Mayfair. Her husband, meanwhile, had become an officer in the RAF and was stationed somewhere in the country.

'Uncle' believed that Vicki was an enemy agent and, owing to the connections she had established with many influential people, a very dangerous one. She was said to have been, before the war, the mistress of a wealthy Jewish armaments man, who now lived on a neutral ship that continued to trade between England and the Continent. Although MI5 knew enough to hang him, they had no power to have him arrested, even when the ship was in a British port; so all they could do was to keep tabs on Vicki and as far as possible prevent her passing on any information to her old boy friend. 'Uncle' wanted us to take a hand in looking after her.

Naturally we obliged and, soon afterwards, I had the interesting experience of watching a real live Mata Hari knocking back our cocktails at No. 8. To keep in touch with her without arousing her suspicions proved exceptionally easy, as it transpired that she had just written her memoirs, and I was obviously the chap to assist her in securing a publisher. Thenceforth we saw a lot of her and her bosom friend, said to have been another Nazi agent, a little black-haired Baroness. We christened her 'The Black Baroness', which phrase I afterwards used for the title of my third Gregory Sallust spy novel.

To assist us in keeping an eye of these two beauties 'Uncle' agreed that we might rope in Charlie Birkin and Captain Bunny Tattersall, DSO, as both went to many parties at which Vicki and the Baroness were likely to be present. Bunny proved particularly useful in this respect, as although he was again back in the uniform of the Inniskilling Dragoons, with a beautiful green silk-lined greatcoat, he had for many years been the 'Man about Town' of the *Daily Mail*; so he knew everyone and went everywhere.

On the last day of November the Russians invaded Finland. This was a perfectly logical sequel to their having overrun the eastern half of Poland and absorbed the three small independent Baltic States of Latvia, Lithuania and Esthonia, created in 1919/20. That should have come as no surprise to anyone who had ready my book *Red Eagle*. Marshal Voroshilov had stated very clearly, that owing to Russia's geographical situation, Germany was the only power Russia had to fear; and that in the initial stages of a war the Russian army could not hope to defeat that of Germany. Therefore Soviet strategy must be to fall back, destroying as she withdrew everything that might be of value to the enemy, even if this meant leaving many impor-tant cities in ruins. By this 'scorched earth' policy a belt of territory 300 miles deep was to be sacrificed as slowly as possible to give Russia time to mobilize her huge manpower which would later defeat Germany. In preparation for this the Russians were already removing their heavy industry and munition plants from cities in this belt and creating new and larger ones a thousand miles back behind the Urals.

Stalin's seizure of half Poland, after the Germans had defeated the Polish army, was, therefore the logical outcome of Voroshilov's policy. Why destroy your own bridges, railways and cities if instead you can devastate your neighbour's territory to form an obstacle for the enemy? So, too, was the annexation of the three Baltic States further north, whose largely Teutonic populations might well have favoured opening their ports to German forces in the event of Hitler's going to war with Russia. Voroshilov's invasion of Finland eliminated the risk of a German army's being put ashore at Helsinki.

In Britain people agitated for aid to be sent to the gallant Finns, who were fighting against great odds to maintain their independence. But for us to have done so would have been the height of madness. The 'aid for Finland' group would have shown more sense had they agitated for the internment of all British Communists, as the Party was still taking its orders from Moscow and its members were doing their utmost in our factories to cause munition workers to go slow.

As things turned out we had good reason to be thankful for Voroshilov's strategy. Had he not formed his 'Chastity Belt', so that the Germans had to fight their way over an additional 300 miles of Polish territory before they could reach Moscow and the Volga, Russia might well have been put out of the war in 1942, and Hitler still have had the forces to invade Britain before the United States could come to our aid.

In December we went to a most amusing party given by Vicki. Among the guests was the Turkish Ambassador and for the best part of an hour I sat with him, Vicki and a few other people at a small table discussing the war.

The Turk made no secret of his opinion that in the spring

Hitler would overwhelm the French, then turn on Britain, invade and conquer her. I agreed to that possibility but gave chapter and verse about what would follow if that did happen. I maintained that there was no conceivable likelihood of our accepting terms from Hitler. Although there were not the faintest grounds for my statement, I told him that plans had already been prepared. The King and his Government would retire to Canada; so would the Navy: and that from all parts of the Empire the war would continue to be carried on. Moreover, as the United States could not possibly allow Hitler to remain dominant in Europe, with all Europe's shipyards at his disposal in which to build a Fleet that would enable him to destroy the American Navy and conquer the Western Hemisphere, it could be counted as certain that the Americans would decide to fight while they were still in a good position to do so.

How, therefore, I asked, with Russia only waiting for the chance to stab Hitler in the back, could he possibly emerge victorious? As the Ambassador conceded many of my points, by the time he left I had some reason to believe that the informal talk had caused him to take a much more optimistic view of Britain's chances.

But the really great fun of Vicki's party was its composition. Among the thirty guests who were swilling her Champagne and happily devouring her *foie-gras* were Joan, Diana and me, Bill and Fritzi, Bill's colleague Grierson Dickson, Charlie Birkin, Bunny Tattersall, 'Uncle' himself and, as he told me with a finger to his big nose, several of his other aides; so cuddlesome little Vicki was more or less throwing her party for M I 5.

18

I GET AN UNPAID JOB

FOR me the year 1940 opened with a private battle. Immediately after Christmas advance copies of *The Scarlet Impostor* came to hand. As usual I supervised the advertising, scrutinized the list of review copies to be sent out and autographed another 150 copies for my friends among the gossip writers and in the book trade. Again, according to my custom, I spent the next two days in a taxi delivering personally those that were for bookshop and bookstall managers, wholesale exporters and buyers for the big libraries in the City and central London. But before I started out I knew that I was in for trouble.

In spite of my protests, Walter Hutchinson had used my autumn book, *Uncharted Seas*, as a test case in putting his fiction up from 7/6 to 8/6. If he got away with it other publishers would follow suit. That meant that the libraries would either have to accept a big cut in their profits or put their subscriptions up, which would mean the loss of a certain number of subscribers. Naturally, in an attempt to protect themselves, they greatly reduced the opening orders they would have given for my book. Fortunately, there was a big demand for it, which put them in a spot. Hutchinson then compromised by giving them a special discount on repeats; so I did not come out of it so badly in the long run.

Now, he had made a guinea pig of me again, by putting *The Scarlet Impostor* up from 8/6 to 10/6.

The booksellers accepted the two-shilling rise without protest. It was the longest book that I had so far written – 172,000 words – and highly topical, as it covered the events of the war during the autumn and even, by remarkable good fortune, a forecast of the conspiracy to assassinate Hitler. Moreover, during that first winter of the black-out people were reading as never before; so even at 10/6 it was a potential bestseller.

But in those days the four great subscription libraries bought more books than all the booksellers put together and accounted for two-thirds of most authors' sales. They were, in order of buying power, Boots, W. H. Smith, Harrods and the Times.

At Boots old Freddy Richardson sadly shook his head, and declared that he had no option but to fight. He maintained that there was no justification for the rise in price; that Hutchinson was attempting to hold a pistol to the book trade on account of the greatly increased demand for books; that he had done a mean thing in choosing me as his stalking horse because of my popularity as an author; that he had done so knowing how many good friends in the trade I had and was counting on that to help him put his racket over.

Freddy then told me that it was more than his job was worth not to cut his opening order severely if Hutchinson insisted on 10/6 as the price, and urged me to persuade Walter to change his mind, promising a bigger order than I had ever had if he would do so. But I knew that was no good because I had already done my damnedest, and once Walter had taken a decision no one could shift him from it.

Baker, the Chief Librarian at W. H. Smith, and Shirley of the Times Library took the same attitude. So did Thomas Joy at Harrods, a stranger to me who had recently taken over from his chief, my good friend Cadness Page, who had gone into the Army.

For some days I carried on this hopeless battle, but the four of them got together, with the result that they cut their opening orders for the book by no less than 66 per cent against those they had given for my last book, while the smaller libraries and wholesalers cut theirs on average $33\frac{1}{3}$ per cent. On learning this I was in despair. I thought *The Scarlet Impostor* the best book I had ever written, and that with a free circulation it could double my sales; yet all hope of this now seemed ruined.

In mid-January the book was published. It had a magnificent press. The critics acclaimed it as 'The first great spy story of the war'. Naturally this heartened me, and on the demand created by those splendid reviews Hutchinson went to war. He informed the libraries that unless they antied up their orders to at least 50 per cent of those given for my last book, they would have to pay 7/11 per copy on all repeat orders instead of the regulation trade percentage of 6/4.

Still the libraries refused to play. Yet although we did not receive a single repeat order from the Big Four, a fortnight after publication sales were down only 28 per cent on those of my last book for the same period. *The Scarlet Impostor* was standing No. 2 in the bestseller lists and I knew the demand for the book must be immense. Walter, whatever his faults, was a born fighter and spent a great sum in advertising to force the hands of the libraries. I too went into action.

I wrote direct to Sir Richard Burbidge, Chairman of Harrods, outlining the situation and declaring that if Joy continued his policy of refusing to buy an adequate number of bestselling books, subscribers would become so discontented that it would prove the ruin of Harrods library. Backed by Walter's advertising campaign I also wrote to Freddy paraphrasing the old slogan:

We don't want to fight, but by Jingo if we do,
We've got the book, we've got the quotes, we've got the money
   too.

In the end the demand created by the advertising beat them. Walter conceded that they should have their repeats at 6/4, then the orders rolled in. Once agreement was reached they let the book have its head and none of them bore me, personally, any ill-will; even Thomas Joy, who afterwards became a good friend of mine.

As yet the war had not seriously interfered with many peacetime activities and Billy Butlin approached me to write a Crime Dossier with one of his Holiday Camps as its background; but, from the beginning, I had always believed that the vast majority of my readers wanted to read about people of wealth or beauty, such as they never met in their own lives; and I did not see such characters as Sir Pellinore Gwaine-Cust or the Princess Marie Lou disporting themselves in a Butlin Holiday Camp. So, although the fee offered was high, I turned it down.

Mention of my Crime Dossiers reminds me of an amusing incident that occurred shortly after the war broke out. A security officer attached to the tented camp in Hyde Park found among the papers of a sergeant a slip with a list of names on it; among them were: Carlotta Casado, Heinrich Hauser, Pauline Vidor, Ninon de Lys, Serge Orloff and those of several Irishmen. Some names had ticks against them, others crosses and others again question marks.

These names led the security officer to jump to the conclusion that he had stumbled on the key to a spy ring; so he promptly turned the list in to MI5. It was shown to several people there but did not ring a bell with any of them. Then it was shown to 'Uncle'. He roared with laughter; for he recognized it at once as the list of suspects in my last Crime Dossier, *Herewith the Clues*; the innocent sergeant had only been checking off those he decided had not committed the murder.

Some years earlier repairs to Westminster Abbey had been undertaken which necessitated the opening of the Poet Spenser's tomb. This excited considerable interest because, in Elizabethan times, when a poet was buried it was customary for his fellow poets to cast eulogies they had written about him into his grave. It was therefore possible that an original Shakespeare manuscript might thus be brought to light.

On a Friday morning the *Sunday Despatch* rang me up and asked if I would do an article for them on the Bacon–Shakespeare controversy. I replied that I knew nothing whatever about it. 'No matter,' the editor said. 'I have a chap who does. All we want is your name. I'll send him along to you.'

That afternoon a young man arrived staggering under a

dozen weighty volumes. It transpired that he knew no more about the controversy than I did, and thrusting the volumes upon me, he said, 'Please can we have your article by ten o'clock tomorrow morning, because it's Saturday and we go to press.'

I got down to the job and my opening paragraph ran:

There have been many mysteries in history on the lines of, 'Who was the real father of the Heir Apparent, the King or the Court Musician, and who poisoned who?' But none are more intriguing than. . . .

My article passed muster and duly appeared. On the Tuesday morning, I received a postcard. It read:

Whom, Mr Wheatley. Who wrote the plays and *whom* was guilty of such appalling grammar? Bacon, Shakespeare or Wheatley?

Unfortunately the postcard was anonymous, otherwise I would have been delighted to stand its sender a good lunch.

While burning the midnight oil on this subject I felt that all the cypher interpretations upon which the Baconians built their case were the most utter nonsense, but I did come upon a very interesting fact. In one of the historical plays Shakespeare had a scene depicting a secret midnight meeting between the French and English Army Commanders. This had been thought pure invention. But as late as 1860 certain memoirs from the library of the Duc d'Orleans had been published in France showing the meeting to have been an historic fact. That Shakespeare could have had access to these archives seemed out of the question, but Bacon had. He had spent two months as the guest of the Duc d'Orleans of his day, browsing in his host's magnificent library.

In fairness to the Baconians I inserted this point in my article. That resulted in Joan's and my being asked to be guests of honour at the Baconian Society's annual lunch in January 1940.

It proved to be one of the queerest gatherings that I have

ever attended. Nearly all the members were very old and, obviously, charming cranks. But the luncheon was held in the upper room of the ancient Canonbury Tower in north-east London, and I could not help being impressed by the fact that Bacon, after his disgrace, had spent two whole years there, during which we know nothing whatever of that remarkable man's activities. Such a fertile brain, one of the greatest in all England's history, could not possibly have remained inactive for all that time. Did he, while living as a hermit in Canonbury Tower, write Shakespeare's plays?

In February that extraordinarily able assessor of what was likely to appeal to her public, Christina Foyle, devoted her monthly Literary Lunch at the Dorchester to 'Spies'. Captain von Rintelen was the principal speaker. He had been Germany's Chief of Secret Intelligence during the Kaiser's War, but having quarrelled with Hitler was now a refugee. That, alas, was the last 'gentleman's' war, in which it was still customary to treat one's enemies with courtesy.

As one of the guests of honour at the lunch, afterwards I had a talk with von Rintelen, but I did not find him a very pleasant man, or a very clever one. With Sir Paul Dukes, who was also there, I had a much more interesting chat. He had been our top secret agent in Russia in 1914 and up to the Bolshevik Revolution; and we found that we had many acquaintances in common.

One of my excursions in March was down to the big store of Arding and Hobbs in Clapham Junction. For what reason God alone knows, but I had been asked to be one of the patrons of the 'National Knitting Campaign for the Troops', and an exhibition was being held there to popularize it. Among the other more distinguished patrons were Rebecca West, Steve Donoghue, Lady Kemsley, Jessie Matthews, Sonnie Hale, Lady Chamberlain, Bobby Howes and that remarkable woman, Lady Oxford and Asquith; and I was given the pleasant task of looking after the famous 'Margot' for the afternoon.

It was she who, some years earlier, had started the vogue

for very frank political memoirs. As she had been born into political circles and was for many years the wife of a Prime Minister she had much of interest to recount. Even so, the publishers who brought out her book did not think sufficiently highly of it to give her in her contract more than a very modest royalty. Yet it sold so well that a year later they made her an *ex gratia* payment of £10,000.

Bitten by this bug, for years afterwards Walter Hutchinson paid absurd sums for any political memoirs that he could lay his hands on, in the hope of repeating this remarkable success; but he never pulled it off.

I record the meeting with the caustically witty Lady Oxford only because it reminds me of a delightful story about her. A few years before the war she had visited Hollywood. There she was introduced to Jean Harlow. That was long before the days when it became more or less common practice for people who had only just met to call one another by their Christian names. But Jean at once addressed Lady Oxford as 'Margot'.

At this the hook-nosed Countess promptly replied, 'My dear, it is pronounced "Margo". The T is soft as it is in Harlot'.

Early in March the Russo–Finnish war came to an end. The thaw, on which the Finns had counted to prolong their resistance, came six weeks late and a great Soviet offensive had opened on 1 February. After forty-two days of hellish bombardment and mass attacks, the Mannerheim Line was breached and the gallant Finns were compelled to accept terms. On 12 March they surrendered.

The Russian victory had proved immensely costly, but by it Voroshilov had completed the making of his 'Chastity Belt'. When, fifteen months later, his fears of Germany proved only too well founded, it was seen that his long-term strategy had saved Russia.

On 5 April Neville Chamberlain made the idiotic speech which revealed that he had not the faintest conception of what Britain and France were really up against. Having reviewed the whole war situation, he stated his belief that, during the eight months we had been at war, the Allies had become immensely stronger whereas the power of Germany had decreased. One thing is certain, he said, by not attacking in the previous autumn, Hitler 'has missed the bus'. Four days afterwards the Germans went into Norway.

On 10 May, Hitler at last launched his blitzkrieg against France, Belgium and Holland. Anticipating that if things went badly for the Allies on the Continent Hitler would next turn his attention to Britain, I took new precautions. Among my friends was Harold Armstrong, the author of *Grey Wolf, Grey Steel* and *Lord of Arabia*, three excellent biographies of Mustapha Kemal, General Smuts and King Ibn Saud respectively. Harold was a close friend of Lady Carnarvon and she had leased to him at a very modest rent a large cottage named 'Pen's Porch' on her estate at Highclere Castle in Hampshire.

Harold wanted to let it, so I had taken it from him for three months with an option to continue my tenancy, which I took up. We then began the dismantling of No. 8, retaining only just sufficient furniture so that we could continue to occupy it in reasonable comfort. We sent all our best pieces, ornaments of value, clothes and supplies of food and wine down to Highclere.

Actually the blitz on London did not begin until four months later, but it was comforting to know that our most valued possessions were safe. Meanwhile, 'Pen's Porch' provided a pleasant change of scene for weekends and to send Colin and Diana for a summer holiday.

With growing apprehension we listened to every news bulletin. The Germans went through the 'impregnable' Maginot Line as though it were made of butter. Rotterdam was savagely bombed, Dutch resistance collapsed and in Belgium the situation was tragic.

The Belgians were good fighters. Had King Leopold heeded the warnings of the British Government and agreed to its pleas that our Expeditionary Force should be allowed to enter Belgium earlier, there might have been a fair chance of holding the Belgo–German frontier; but Leopold would not hear of it. In consequence the Belgians had to face the

German onslaught on their own and were soon overwhelmed.

Our Expeditionary Force was sacrificed in a crazy attempt to save 'poor little Belgium' when it was already too late. The French, with a short-sightedness almost impossible to credit, had built their Maginot Line only along France's frontier with Germany, leaving that with Belgium unprotected. This was the sector of front allotted to our Expeditionary Force. They had been given eight whole months to dig themselves in, and had created a strong system of defences. Had they stood to fight there, they might have held the Germans and still been in a position to attack the flank of the German thrust that had pierced the Maginot Line. Instead they were ordered to leave their defences and advance into Belgium. With little armour and few motorized troops they were called on to fight in open country and with exposed flanks vastly superior numbers of the best-equipped and led army in the world. Who was responsible for this suicidal strategy? Daladier, Chamberlain, Gamelin and Gort must all have approved it. That the greater part of our Expeditionary Force was saved was not due only to the 'miracle' of Dunkirk, but to the miracle that any considerable number of our troops ever succeeded in getting back there.

Our only consolation throughout these anxious days was that Churchill had taken over the helm. All my life I had been a whole-hearted believer in Churchill. Now I rejoiced to think that we at last had a leader of great imagination and vigour, one who I felt sure would not waste British lives but would succeed both in conserving them and in bringing us victory.

While the great battle was raging on the Continent my book, *Faked Passports*, and Joan's last, *Silk Sheets and Breadcrumbs*, were both published.

Faked Passports was a continuation of Gregory Sallust's adventures in Germany and during the Russo–Finnish war. It was the first time that I had ever published consecutively two books about the same character and, having from the beginning seen the folly of becoming associated with only one hero – as had Sapper with Bulldog Drummond and

Leslie Charteris with The Saint – I was in somewhat of a quandary about the theme for my next book, tempting as it was to continue with Gregory, owing to the great popularity he had achieved.

In consequence I decided to let my readers choose, and inserted a note at the end of *Faked Passports* asking them to send me postcards saying whether they would prefer me to continue Gregory's adventures or give them either a story of strange happenings in the West Indies during the war or an historical romance. Several hundred replies came in, of which an overwhelming majority was in favour of 'more Gregory'. So, soon afterwards, I sat down to *The Black Baroness*.

As a matter of interest, the respective sales of *Faked Passports* (a bestseller) and *Silk Sheets* (a light novel that did reasonably) were 7926 and 1426 copies.

Towards the end of May the public knew only that in Belgium our army was making 'a strategic withdrawal'. It was not even rumoured that it might become necessary to try to bring our men home. Joan was still driving her car for MI5, and one day she was allotted as her passenger Captain Herbert Stringer. He did not say that frantic preparations were already under way to bring the Army off – or, if he did, as she was always exceptionally security-minded, she refrained from telling me. But he did tell her that our Expeditionary Force was in an extremely bad way, and it was now feared that Hitler's next move would be an invasion of Britain.

He went on to say that he had been given the job of thinking up measures for countering such an eventuality; but that his was normally police work and, apart from the routine stuff that had already been laid on, he didn't seem to be able to think of much that we could do.

Joan replied, 'Why don't you ask my husband? He has been fretting for months over not having the chance to use his imagination on some job connected with the war. He might be able to produce some ideas.'

Stringer agreed. That evening she told me of this conversation. I sat down right away and, while the little ships were bringing our men off from Dunkirk, worked with furious intensity all through the night. In fourteen hours I had written, re-written and corrected my first War Paper. It ran to nearly 7000 words. I headed it: *Resistance to Invasion*.

19

THE INVASION PAPERS

I SET out all the measures I could think of which might help
to thwart an enemy landing or, if the landing was made,
delay the advance of the enemy inland. I concentrated on
measures which could be put in hand immediately – such
as calling up every engineer in the country to supervise the
construction of beach defences, commandeering every yard
of barbed wire for that purpose, having a series of 'Invasion
Weekends' during which every man, woman and child would
help in transporting materials to vulnerable stretches of
coast, digging trenches and so on.

My excellent secretary, Dorothy Logan, typed the paper
the next day, and the following morning Joan took it to
Captain Stringer. Two evenings later he came back with
her to have a drink with us.

Hubert Stringer was a delicate, charming man and a
real patriot. Later he wrote a book called *England Expects . . .*,
urging the public to make a greater war effort. He was
enthusiastic about my paper and said that many measures
suggested in it ought to be put in hand right away, but the
trouble was that, although he had sent the paper on, it
might be weeks before it reached anyone high enough up to
give orders for such a mobilization of effort.

Encouraged by Stringer's praise of my ideas, I told him
that I had a few fairly highly placed friends and asked if
he had any objection to my sending copies of my paper to
them.

'Good gracious, no!' he exclaimed. 'Go to it and good
luck to you.'

I posted three copies; one to Admiral Sir Edward Evans –

Evans of the *Broke* – who, like myself, was an old Worcester boy, although before my time, but with whom I had a slight acquaintance; one to Colonel Charles Balfour-Davey, at that time in the Operations Section of the War Office; and one to Wing Commander Sir Louis Greig – whom I knew fairly well, and who was then Personal Assistant to the Secretary of State for Air.

Admiral Evans replied with a cordial letter. Charles Balfour-Davey rang me up and said, 'Dennis, I'm on duty tonight at the War House. Come along any time after eleven o'clock and we'll talk about your paper.'

How great a thrill it was for me to make that midnight journey through the blackout to the War Office can well be imagined, and even more to hear Balfour-Davey's final verdict, 'I cannot express any opinion on the naval and air matters, but on the military side you have certainly produced a number of ideas that have never occurred to us. And one thing I can promise you. Your paper shall reach VCIGS, [the Vice-Chief of the Imperial General Staff].

The following week I had to put work aside for a big occasion. At long last Joan and I had seen no alternative but to consent to Diana's marrying Brinsley. She had been in love with him for eighteen months and engaged to him for the best part of a year; so she had been very patient. Moreover, he was shortly due to be called up; so we could not possibly deny her a honeymoon and a few weeks of happiness before what might prove a long separation.

The wedding was at our local church, my old friend 'Bobby' Eastaugh performed the ceremony and I gave Diana away. She was just twenty, and I don't think I've ever seen a girl look more ravishing than Diana that morning in her bridal dress.

We had a reception at No. 8 for about sixty people and the Champagne flowed, but it was with difficulty that I concealed the foreboding I felt about this marriage. Neither of them had a penny; so they had to make do with going to 'Pen's Porch' for a honeymoon, then returning to live with us.

It was about this time that Jack was ordered overseas.

Joan and I went down at six o'clock one morning to say good-bye to him at Chelsea Barracks. As he was an exceptionally bad sailor he was dreading the long voyage out to Egypt, but I had seen to it that he had a couple of magnums in his luggage to tide him over the first spell of bad weather. Otherwise he was cheerful and looked immaculate in his Ensign's uniform, but very young; and as we watched him march away it was with the heart-rending thought that we might never see him again.

Then, on 28 June, my anxieties about Diana and Jack were temporarily expunged from my mind by another repercussion of my first War Paper. Sir Louis Greig rang me up and asked me to lunch with him that day at the Dorchester.

There he introduced me to Wing Commander (later Air Marshal Sir Lawrence) Darvall and Mr J. S. L. Renny, a Czech armaments manufacturer operating in this country, to whom we owe clover-leaf barbed wire and many other valuable war devices.

To know Louis Greig was to love him. His rich deep voice, ready laugh, forthright opinions and kindness of heart at once brought out the best in every sort of person; within a few minutes we were all talking like old friends.

Naturally it was of the war we talked, and of the desperate plight in which Britain stood at that moment. The greater part of the BEF had mercifully been saved, but it had had to abandon all its tanks, guns, transport and even most of its rifles. Ten days before, Italy had entered the war against us, thus jeopardizing our whole position in the Mediterranean and it was only three days since the French surrender. Winston Churchill had been Prime Minister little more than five weeks. The country was only just waking up from the phoney war, and armaments were still coming from our factories only in a trickle. It seemed obvious that Hitler's next move would be invasion, and we had not the weapons to put up a prolonged resistance.

Inspired by the Prime Minister, the best men in thecountry were now prepared to cut red tape and adopt every idea that offered any prospect of helping us meet what we felt would be the greatest crisis in our country's history since the Spanish Armada.

This was illustrated by the attitude of such officers as Lawrence Darvall. At the outbreak of war we had not a single sub-machine gun in the country. We even had to buy half a dozen from the Italians to find out how they were made. By May 1940 they were in the process of manufacture, but few, if any, had been issued to the Forces. Over lunch Renny mentioned that he had an associate in Chicago who, on receipt of a cable, would at once despatch 5000 to us, but he could get no satisfaction from the War Office, who were still arguing whether or not to buy them. Darvall, although then only a Wing Commander, told him to cable for them right away, and he would be responsible for the quarter of a million pound order.

It was in this spirit that they discussed my paper on Resistance, which both of them had read. Parts of it, of course, for reasons that I could not know, were quite impractical; but the thing about it which appealed to them was my urging that we should use resources that were readily available and gear the nation for Total War.

At the end of lunch I said, 'I feel extraordinarily flattered that you should think some of my ideas worth following up. But as far as I am concerned the war is ten months old and I am still unemployed in it. Can you suggest any way in which I could make myself useful?'

Darvall immediately replied, 'Yes. Show us the other side of the picture. Go straight home. Consider yourself as the German High Command and produce a plan for the invasion of England.'

I went first to Geographia in Fleet Street and bought two maps; one a physical map of the British Isles and the other showing density of population. These I hung up in my library and with them a map of Western Europe. I then worked at dynamo speed, with only two comparatively short breaks, for forty-eight hours. To keep going I used up over two hundred cigarettes and three magnums of Champagne.

The result of this effort was a paper of 15,000 words, *The Invasion and Conquest of Britain*. As soon as it had been typed

I sent it, as Darvall had told me to do, to him at Mr Rance's room in the Office of Works. That seemed a strange address to which to send such a document; it was not until later that I was let into the secret that it was the 'cover' name for the Joint Planning Staff's quarters in the Ministry of Defence.

I envisaged the Plan as a five-day operation. Readers who are interested will find particulars of it, and of my other War Papers, in my book, *Stranger than Fiction*, which I was persuaded to publish several years after the war.

It was my contention that if Hitler could conquer Britain, with every shipyard in Europe at his disposal his naval building programme could far exceed anything that the United States might attempt. In consequence, regardless of losses he should, logically, throw everything in; the whole of the combined German and Italian Navies and Air Forces, and as many German troops as he could find liners, cargo ships, sea-going barges and motor boats to send over; and, using the shortest route from France, the great majority of these should be landed on the coasts of Kent and Sussex.

Many months later I learned that the War Office appreation had been entirely different from my own. They had not envisaged the possibility of airborne landings designed to cut England into three sections and had placed the main landings on the coast of Suffolk. Mr Churchill had then set up a special Committee under General Denning and Air Marshal Slessor to re-examine the probabilities. My paper was studied by the Committee and afterwards Slessor told me that large parts of it had been adopted in their new and final appreciation.

After the war, when the documents of the German General Staff were seized and examined, it emerged that in Operation 'Sea Lion' – their plan for the invasion of Britain – they had intended to do exactly as I had forecast.

Having thoroughly frightened myself, I at once sat down to write a third paper of 12,000 words, *Further Measures for Resistance to Invasion*. By 28 June I sent copies of it to Darvall and to all the others who had received my first two papers.

A week later Darvall asked me to lunch at the RAF

Club in Piccadilly. When we had settled down, he said: 'Since we last met you have acquired a new, small but very exclusive public. All three of the Chiefs-of-Staff have read your papers on Invasion.'

He went on to explain that my value lay in viewing the war from a completely different angle from that of the advisers of the War Cabinet. Whether Navy, Army or Air Force, they had all been taught at their Staff Colleges to regard war as having definite rules like cricket.

But in Poland Hitler was at that very time having hundreds of people shot every day, in order to eliminate politicians, senior officers, magistrates, prelates, heads of industry, the nobility, editors, authors and, in fact, everyone who might later lead a revolt against Nazi domination. Apparently the Service Chiefs had never seriously contemplated the possibility that, if Hitler invaded Britain, he would use the same methods to subdue us here.

Darvall then disclosed to me that he was a member of the Joint Planning Staff with access to every form of Intelligence; and that, while my invasion plan for cutting Britain in three followed the pattern which the Germans had actually used in Norway, he did not think they had sufficient airborne forces to carry out such a plan here. In that he was proved right, as Operation 'Sea Lion' revealed that they had intended to land all their airborne forces in Kent and Sussex. But he went on to say that my papers had raised so many urgent questions that they had been roneoed off and circulated to all the Operational and Intelligence Departments of the Service Ministries for comment and action; and that already many of my suggested measures had been taken; such as orders for the removal of all signposts and the names from railway stations, so that German parachutists should not at once be able to tell where they had landed; and that the BBC was working out a special code so that responsible authorities in the provincial cities could be informed of the real situation, as distinct from false broadcasts put out in English by the Germans, and be able to maintain morale in their localities by announcing the truth.

All this was more than enough to make me swollen-headed,

and towards the end of lunch I eagerly asked Darvall if he could find any further use for me.

'Yes,' he replied. 'For some time past we have been recruiting men who are too old to serve in the Regular Forces as Local Defence Volunteers. Their job is to guard vital points, such as bridges, and to tackle with shotguns and pikes any enemy parachutists who may land in their area. We now propose greatly to increase their numbers and weld them into a better-organized force to be known as the Home Guard. I would like you to write me a paper on the utilization of this force for village defence.'

A few days later I sent in a first draft of *Village Defence*, and at the end of the week a lengthier and much improved version on the same subject.

From then on I had each paper typed three times with three carbons and sent copies also to: the Viscount Mansell (First Lord of the Admiralty), Sir Walter Monckton (then Chief Censor), Sir Walter Womersley (Minister of Pensions), Major General Sir Percy Laurie (Provost Marshal London District) and, as Admiral Evans had left the Admiralty, to Captain (now Admiral Sir Peveril) Williams-Powlett.

The much wider circulation of my papers in this way, and the roneoed copies sent out by Darvall from the Ministry of Defence, produced two results.

One afternoon Mr J. A. Frost, the Director of Overseas Intelligence at the BBC, arrived at No. 8. His problem was that his monitoring service was picking up broadcasts from an illegal station in this country. In tone the broadcasts were vaguely Left-Wing, but it was suspected that their text concealed a code which was being used by enemy agents to pass instructions to Fifth Columnists. Frost handed me copies of the text and asked me if I could break the code.

This, of course, was right outside my field, and I told him so at once. All the same I looked through the papers overnight, but had to return them the following day and confess myself completely defeated.

Two other visitors who arrived unannounced were officers from the Air Ministry Operations Department. They wanted to know what targets in Germany I thought it would pay us best to bomb. To this I was at least able to give an original answer. It was, in effect, the precision raids which the RAF later perfected to such a degree that ace pilots could blow down the wall of a Gestapo prison, and enable the prisoners to escape. But in 1940 the Luftwaffe was still extremely strong, so the bombing of military zones and munition factories was liable to cause us heavy losses of aircraft. I therefore proposed that we should send over single aircraft, flying very high, to swoop down and bomb specially selected, undefended targets, the destruction of which would lower the morale of the German people. Among those I suggested were: the Brown House in Munich, the Brandenburg Gate in Berlin, the Fuehrer Schools, the Denkmal victory statue on the Rhine, the Tannenberg Memorial and Schloss Johannisberg.

As far as I know my idea was not adopted at that time, but years later there occurred a sequel to it that was surprising and regrettable.

From the end of 1941, I adopted the custom of giving a small luncheon party once every ten days or so at the Hungaria Restaurant for officers with whom I was associated in my work. To these lunches I always brought wine from my own cellar, and at one of them in 1943 I gave my friends Schloss Johannisberger 1921.

One of my guests on this occasion was the then Vice-Chief of the Air Staff, Air Chief Marshal Sir Charles Medhurst. The Vice-Chief was a great connoisseur and, noticing the label on the bottles, he remarked: 'What a treat you are giving us, Dennis; but what a tragedy it is that, when the little that is in this country has been drunk, we'll never see this wonderful Hock again.'

'Oh come, Sir,' I protested. 'We ought to be able to put an end to the Nazis in another couple of years, and soon after the fighting stops we should be able to ship over new supplies.'

Medhurst shook his head. 'No; the vines have been destroyed. A little time ago we wanted to try out a powerful new bomb. In order that the pilot might have ample opportunity to register its effect it was decided to drop it on an undefended target, and some idiot ordered him to put it down on Schloss Johannisberg. He dumped it on the slope of the hill and blew the whole vineyard to blazes.'

As by that date we were sending 1000-bomber raids against the German cities, such an act could no longer have the least effect on German morale – the whole point of my original suggestion. It was instead a shocking piece of vandalism. No one could have been more distressed than I; for there can be little doubt that, when an undefended target had to be selected, someone in the Air Ministry had turned up an old list compiled from my suggestions.

However, the end of this story might be worse. In 1955 I went again for a holiday up the Rhine. The pilot had not destroyed any part of the vineyard. He had dropped his egg right in the centre of the castle.

20

GREAT STRATEGY AND
THE BLITZ

FROM July onwards 'Johnny' (as he was known to his friends) Darvall and I lunched together every ten days or so. He was a tall, well-made, handsome man with prematurely white hair and bushy eyebrows. Of all the Air Marshals that I came to know he had one of the finest and most interesting brains. There was not a subject upon which he could not produce an original opinion. Nearly always they were contrary to Government or Air Ministry policy. Some were, perhaps, too revolutionary for practical application, but most of them were entirely sound and had they been carried out we might have both won the war more speedily and placed Britain in a stronger position *vis-à-vis* the United States and Russia after it.

At lunch on 14 July he gave me a new problem. During that summer Britain's fortunes were at their lowest ebb. To maintain morale, everything possible was being done to keep the public from realizing the desperate state we were in; but a price had to be paid for that. Believing us to be far stronger than we were, and smarting under the humiliation of Dunkirk, they were clamouring for us to strike back at the enemy. Even the Prime Minister, although no one knew better than he the true state of affairs, was almost begging his Chiefs-of-Staff to propose some blow against the 'Narzies' which would show that we had a kick left in us, because he feared that if we remained entirely inactive, the Americans would believe their Ambassador Kennedy, that we were really down, and in another few months would be out; so it would be throwing assets down the drain to send us any kind of aid. In consequence Churchill ordered his JPS to produce a plan for some form of spectacular offensive.

I was not aware until long afterwards that the Prime Minister's order was resposible for my next paper. Johnny never gave me any secret information. He told me the bare facts of our need to strike a blow against the enemy, and that the JPS had examined every possibility but, with our hopeless lack of resources, could suggest no major operation which would not prove suicidal for those taking part in it. He asked me to have a crack at this apparently insoluble problem.

I went home, pinned up a map of Europe against my library shelves and sat staring at it for four hours without a glimmer of an idea. Then, late in the evening, quite suddenly, what I believed, and still believe, to be inspiration came to me.

The answer was to seize Sardinia.

That it would have been perfectly possible I am still convinced. Although Italy had entered the war against us, our Fleet still made us paramount in the Mediterranean. No tanks, heavy guns, Bren carriers or mechanized transport were required; they would only have been a hindrance in that island, four-fifths of which is rugged mountain. I envisaged a force of four Brigades, made up mainly of such troops as Highlanders and Gurkhas, with mountain batteries and mule transport. Given surprise and the support of our immensely superior Navy and Air Force, this single Division Plus, could easily have landed and would be sufficient to secure the key points of the island. Our Navy would then have made it impossible for the Italians to reinforce their garrison, whereas we could have put in reinforcements and supplies as required.

I attached to my plan a contour map of the island and detailed particulars of its terrain. Sardinia was rich in corn, oil and wine, so once our troops had seized the island they could have been practically self-supporting. Had the garrison of the island proved larger, then our troops could have retired to mountainous country in which they could have been supplied by air, and it would have proved next to impossible to dislodge them.

At the end of this paper I pointed out that, although Gibraltar was still useful, it had lost a great part of its value in modern war owing to its having only a small, very vulnerable airfield. Whereas the great island of Sardinia could provide us with many airfields and later be made a splendid base for the mustering of an army for the conquest of Italy.

It was not until twenty years later that Admiral Sir Brear Robertson, in 1940 a Commander RN on the JPS, told me that a précis of my paper had been shown to Mr Churchill who had said, 'This is a magnificent conception. You must bring Wheatley in as a planner, so that he can work for us with full knowledge of our situation.' But, alas, in the urgency of those days no action was taken.

However, this paper resulted in my learning that a most extraordinary honour had been done me. A few days after I had sent it in, Sir Louis Greig telephoned and asked me to come to see him at the Air Ministry.

For many years he had been Equerry to King George VI while Duke of York; and, although he had retired from that post before the war, he continued to be a frequent visitor at the Palace. Knowing that I was one of the King's favourite authors, Louis Greig had shown him a copy of *Resistance to Invasion*. The Monarch was, apparently, so interested that he asked to be furnished with copies of all future papers which I might write upon similar subjects.

Louis Greig went on to say that on the previous night a meeting of the Directors of Plans had been called to discuss my paper on Sardinia, and that as the JPS had only Darvall's copy on which to brief them, he had asked Louis Greig to borrow His Majesty's copy. Sir Louis had telephoned the Palace and the King had promptly sent his copy along.

His Majesty was so conscious of security that he addressed the envelope containing the paper in his own hand marking it 'Personal and Urgent'. It was typical of Louis Greig's kind thoughtfulness that he should have kept the envelope and given it to me. I now have it framed as my most precious souvenir of the war.

Towards the end of August Johnny Darvall asked me to

write another paper. The first stage of the Battle of Britain
was already under way. The Germans were bombarding
Dover, Goering's Luftwaffe was making mass attacks upon
our shipping; and although it now looked less likely that
Hitler would invade Britain in the immediate future, it was
thought that he would do so in the spring. The JPS were,
therefore, much concerned to keep up morale in the Forces,
and make the best use of the respite from invasion that it
looked as though we were to be given. Johnny wanted my
views on these problems; so I wrote a paper which I called
This Winter.

Under enemy attack from the air, civilians were now
performing feats of valour which equalled the most courageous exploits of our soldiers, sailors and airmen; so one of
my suggestions in this paper was that the King might be
pleased to consider the creation of a new decoration for civilian
gallantry which would rank with the V C.

His Majesty was regularly reading my papers and, from
time to time, most graciously sent me through Sir Louis
Greig, messages expressing his interest in them, and it was
shortly afterwards that he created the George Cross and
George Medal for civilian bravery.

At the end of the first week in September the blitz on
London opened with a very heavy attack on the docks. No
bombs fell within miles of St John's Wood Park, and from
the upper windows of No. 8 we watched the lurid glare in the
sky over the dock area. But after a few nights the bombing
became general so, from then on, when dusk fell we retired
to the basement.

When the blitz had been on for about a fortnight I became
absolutely furious at the way the Government was handling
the situation. If a single enemy aircraft came over outer
London the sirens went, everyone stopped whatever he was
doing, including the workers in the munition factories, even
the civilian personnel in the Service Ministries, and went down
to sit idle, sometimes for an hour or more, in the nearest
shelter. Household shopping for women was a long and
tiring business anyway in those days, and it was rendered
far worse when the shop assistants knocked off every time

there was an alert. Post Offices and all other Government premises shut up like clams and, greatest absurdity of all, the Tube Stations, which might have given shelter to thousands, also closed their gates immediately the sirens went.

In consequence I sat down to another paper: *Aerial Warfare*. As I was not paid for such work or under any authority, I was free to abuse the bone-headed Home Secretary, Sir John Anderson, to my heart's content and I did not pull my punches.

By the time my 11,000-word screed reached the Planners many of my most vitriolic criticisms of the Government's handling of the situation had been rendered obsolete by vigorous orders from the Prime Minister. But I was told that my paper had helped further to make certain authorities use common sense.

When October came in London had settled down to 'take it', but things were getting pretty grim. Gas became a flicker upon which it took an hour to boil a kettle, and many telephone wires were cut, and unexploded bombs blocked many streets. But people carried on, and everyone did his utmost to help and cheer others during those desperately anxious days.

Towards the end of the month *The Black Baroness* was published. It told of Gregory's adventures during the invasion of Norway, then in France to the collapse, and was, I think, the best story I had done about him so far. In spite of the blitz it sold well.

In October I wrote another paper for Darvall, which I called *By Devious Paths to Victory*. It dealt with future strategy, reviewing all foreseeable developments including the possibility that, by the rigorous application of our blockade, Hitler might be rendered so short of supplies that he would take the suicidal step of invading Russia.

We continued to make merry as far as we could and one night we dined with Joe Links at Hatchett's in Piccadilly. Hatchett's had been very popular in the First World War and, as the restaurant was down in a basement, it acquired a new popularity during the blitz. About halfway through dinner the bombs began to fall and it chanced to be the night

of the great raid on the West End of London. At the Café de
Paris, also a basement restaurant, many people were killed
when the whole building collapsed on them. We all went
up into the street to see the fireworks. Piccadilly was as
bright as day owing to Burton's the tailors, being ablaze
like a huge bonfire.

About this time Brinsley was called up and joined the
Gunners near Amesbury. To be near him Diana took a
minute ground-floor furnished flat in the town. We sadly
missed our beautiful and ever-gay Diana.

Towards the end of the month things became far from
pleasant at No. 8. The gas pressure had become so low that
it took hours to cook a hot meal, our telephone had been put
out of action, for three weeks we had no water so had every
few days to visit friends in order to have a bath, and nearly
every night we lay awake listening to the drone of enemy
aircraft overhead, wondering if the next bomb would fall
on us.

But at least we were luckier than most Londoners. We
had as much good wine as we cared to drink and a fine
supply of tinned food; so we kept pretty cheerful.

I was by then well into a new book, *Strange Conflict*. Successful
as my Gregory Sallust stories had proved, I felt that after
three in succession I must give him a rest; so this tale
featured the Duke de Richleau and his friends. As the
German U-boats had begun to inflict serious losses on our
shipping I took for a theme that the Germans were receiving
information on the astral plane about our convoys from a
powerful witch doctor in Haiti. Then I sent the Duke and
his friends out to the West Indies to deal with the situation.

I don't suppose that I should ever have left London had
it not been more or less forced upon me. So many thousands
of people had swarmed out into the country that it was
becoming more and more difficult to find accommodation
in the Home Counties for genuine refugees who had been
bombed out. In consequence the Newbury Borough Council
wrote to me that, as 'Pen's Porch' was not permanently
occupied, they intended to commandeer it.

As we had sent down there most of our best furniture and

valuable stores of all kinds, we were naturally much averse to allowing the cottage to be occupied by refugees, and the only way to prevent that was to go to live there. Joan's job with MI5 made it impossible for her to do so, but I was still officially unemployed; so it was decided that Bill should move into No. 8 to keep Joan company, while I went down to the country. On 28 October my secretary and I left London.

21

'PEN'S PORCH' AND TOTAL WAR

DURING the ten weeks I spent at 'Pen's Porch' it was not destined that I should be lonely. For most of the time I had guests. A few days before I left London the redoubtable Peter Cheyney came to see me and he was in a lamentable state of jitters. He had been caught in an air-raid one night in Fleet Street and, being tight, had missed his footing in the blackout and fallen down into an area.

He was the greatest liar unhung but a magnificent story-teller. It was enormous fun to watch this great, big, bald tough, whisky glass in hand, striding up and down our drawing-room telling the most extraordinary tales about his exploits. The top half of one of his ears was missing and that alone formed the basis of a dozen different desperate en-counters from which he had emerged with flying colours. Sometimes he would continue these monologues for over an hour, time after time diverging from his original theme to tell of other exciting situations in which he had played a part; but however tight he got he would always return in the end to conclude the story with which he had started. It was an intriguing and masterly performance.

As it was clear that they needed a break I suggested that he and his wife, Roanne, should come down to 'Pen's Porch' with me.

Before I left No. 8 I gave a bachelor dinner party for five friends representing the three services and MI5; all of whom were concerned with the High Direction of the War. This ensured fascinating conversation and, relaxed by just the right amount of my finest wine, it proved a most happy evening. It was the last dinner party I was ever to give at

No. 8; yet, had I known that, I could not have chosen more delightful guests to make it a memorable occasion.

As a contribution to our cellar at 'Pen's Porch', Peter, whom no one could ever accuse of meanness, brought with him a case of whisky and a case of Kümmel. I had already laid in there supplies of all kinds, Roanne took over the housekeeping and we had local women to cook and clean; so we did ourselves very well there.

But I had no intention of remaining out of things, so once or twice a week I went up to London to lunch with my Service friends and to see Joan; sometimes spending the night at No. 8. She too came down to 'Pen's Porch' every weekend and, in a trailer she had bought, systematically transferred more of our stores and belongings to our country refuge.

I was at this time working on another War Paper. It is a testimony to the Prime Minister's absolute confidence in victory, and his determination to secure Britain's future, that in September 1940, when our fortunes were at their lowest ebb, he ordered his Joint Planning Staff to produce for him a paper on the following problem, 'When we have won the war, what steps ought we to take to prevent Germany launching a Third World War against us in twenty years' time?'

The Joint Planners were always up to their eyes drafting recommendations on immediate problems, and often worked until two o'clock in the morning; so when this instruction from Mr Churchill reached them they were anything but pleased. Such a task entailed analysing the future potentialities of every country in Europe, and they just could not face it. But they could not say so to the old man, or altogether ignore it; so, having consulted with his colleagues, Darvall's suggestion was accepted that 'it should be given to Wheatley'.

However, as we had yet to win the war, there was no urgency about the matter and, realizing the immense amount of thought needed to produce such a paper, Darvall told me to take my time over it. It was the last paper that he asked me to write, for in October he was promoted to Group Captain and, after a short period commanding a Bomber

Station, he was sent out as Senior Air Staff Officer to Air Chief Marshal Sir Robert Brooke-Popham, who had just been appointed Commander-in-Chief Far East. But before Darvall left he introduced me to his successor, Wing Commander (later Air Commodore) Roland Vintras.

Vintras was a very pleasant little dark-haired man, who always appeared to be half-asleep, but was, in fact, a remarkably shrewd fellow. He was rather shy and retiring, not the type ever to reach High Command, but an extremely efficient Staff Officer. He entirely lacked Darvall's brilliant imagination and grasp of out-of-the-rut possibilities; but he proved an excellent friend and we had many a good laugh and meal together during the four years of our war-time association.

Vintras felt that morale could be much improved if the public were told more about why some things were being done and why others were not being done: so in November he asked me to write a paper on these lines.

It was really Ministry of Information stuff. Among other matters I raised the question of 'Books for the Forces'. This was inspired by my ex-enemy Thomas Joy of Harrods. At that time the Forces were receiving only old, unwanted books that people were persuaded to discard from their libraries. Joy had worked out a scheme by which he said that he could furnish every Mess and canteen in Britain with up-to-date fiction and non-fiction which could be borrowed for a halfpenny per volume per week. It was a splendid idea. I took it up with enthusiasm, and Vintras arranged for me to see an officer in the Army Catering Service. The old bunhead I saw there was pleasant enough but turned the scheme down flat on the grounds that he did not think it right that the troops should be asked to pay for the books they read. As though any man who liked reading would have cavilled at paying a halfpenny a volume for a good thriller or biography.

In December an opportunity to do another paper of real importance came my way. As I was at no time given any secret information I was free to show my papers to anyone I wished. In the autumn I had started to send them to another friend of mine, a diplomat who was then working in the Foreign Office, Henry Hopkinson (later Lord Colyton). The Hopkinsons asked us to dinner in Chesham Place. About ten people were present, among them Brigadier (later His Excellency General Sir Dallas) Brooks of the Royal Marines. When the port went round it transpired that Henry had passed on to him several of my papers. He expressed his interest in them, and, when the dinner party broke up, he invited Joan and myself to accompany him back to his flat for a talk.

Noël Coward was then in the United States lecturing to arouse pro-British sympathies and he had lent his delightful home off Sloane Square to the Brigadier. There we talked with him about the war till dawn.

It later emerged that he was the military Head of the Political Intelligence Department of the Foreign Office and responsible for all propaganda to the enemy and peoples of the occupied countries. His main theme was that we were not waging Total War, because the people in authority did not understand what Total War meant; and that if we were to emerge victorious we must do so. Before we parted he asked me to write a paper on that subject; adding that if I could really get to the root of the matter, he would submit it to Mr Churchill and thought he could persuade the great man to act upon it.

The Brigadier's ideas entirely coincided with my own. As soon as I got back to 'Pen's Porch' I made a start on *Total War*.

This was another immense task. Total War, I explained, would mean the complete mobilization of the nation. All property rights would have been abolished, contracts nullified, trade union agreements cancelled and no vestige of freedom left to any individual. In fact the whole population would have become slaves of the State, as in Russia.

Naturally, I was not advocating the bringing about of such an appalling situation; I was simply carrying out the job I had been given by stating the logical outcome of applying the doctrine in full and, to the best of my ability,

I outlined the innumerable measures which would have to be taken to bring it into effect.

Johnny Darvall had told me that the Prime Minister had given an instruction that every question presented to him must be so reduced to essentials that, when typed, it would not occupy more than one sheet of foolscap. In view of the scores of decisions that he had to take every day that was a very sensible order; but it was obviously impossible to compress the requirements for waging Total War into 300 words, or even 3000; so I made no attempt to do so. Instead I took the opposite line of dealing with every aspect of the matter that I could think of. This entailed many weeks' work and resulted in a paper longer than the average novel – over 100,000 words.

Many of the measures that I stated to be necessary would have aroused a storm of protest, but there were others that were compatible with the public spirit, and could be carried out without repressive legislation by the good will of the people themselves. Although this vast document naturally did not go to Mr Churchill, Dallas Brooks told me afterwards that various pieces of it had, upon which action was taken; so my time and labour were by no means wasted.

It was towards the end of the year that I paid my first visit to the underground fortress known as 'Mr Rance's Room', in which the Joint Planning Staff worked. Mr Rance was actually the elderly custodian of the War Cabinet Offices responsible for their furniture and equipment through the Office of Works. He was a charming old gentleman who had served for most of his life as a warrant officer in the Indian Army Security Service.

Although I am sure Johnny Darvall trusted me completely, he had never asked me to bring one of my papers there; but Rolly Vintras did, and I was greatly intrigued actually to see this hive of brain cells from which Britain was waging the war.

One result of this visit was that Vintras introduced me to his chief, the Deputy Director of Plans (Air), then Group Captain W. F. Dickson, in due course to become a Marshal of the Royal Air Force and Chief of the Chiefs-of-Staff

Committee. He was a short, thick-set man with very bright eyes, who talked volubly and had a very ready smile. He had read all my papers and we became great friends.

A few days before Christmas Joan rang me up to tell me that No. 8 had been bombed. The bomb fell at about six o'clock in the evening so, mercifully, neither she nor Bill was there. The bomb came down on the house opposite; but the blast made a pretty nasty mess of No. 8. All the windows were broken, the doors stove in, and soot and fallen plaster lay all over the carpets.

As the house had been rendered unfit for occupation Joan went to live with a friend of hers, Eve Cairns, who, her husband Nugent being on active service, was living with a Swedish cousin and his wife in a large flat in Oakwood Court, West Kensington; while I at once made arrangements to have all the furniture remaining at No. 8 brought down to Newbury and stored with Camp Hobson's. We had had some very happy years at No. 8, so it was sad to think it unlikely that we should ever occupy it again; but with London being blitzed we might have sustained a far more tragic loss.

For Christmas Joan and Bill came down to 'Pen's Porch' and Diana and Brinsley came over from Amesbury; so we had a very jolly party. With the new year of 1941 the blitz eased, so Peter decided to return to London. A few months later Brinsley received his commission and was posted overseas.

For some time I had been anxious to get back to London. Through the friends with whom Joan was staying at 139 Oakwood Court it was arranged that I should have the use of part of a ground-floor flat, No. 151, in the next block. So in January, I gave up 'Pen's Porch' for the use of refugees and returned to London.

22

A YEAR OF INTENSIVE WORK

OAKWOOD Court was one of the oldest blocks of flats in Kensington. It dated from late Victorian times and was a gloomy structure; but it had the sort of lovely big rooms upon which people insisted in those days.

The Swede in whose flat Joan was staying as a paying guest was called Eric and he was a member of the Society of Vikings. No one could have been less like those ferocious Norsemen with their horned helmets and yellow hair, but, of course, he became known between Joan and me as 'Eric the Viking'.

Joan and Eve Cairns were out at their offices all day, so it was arranged that Eric's wife should cook my lunch and I should eat it in her kitchen.

In 151, I had a vast front room that I had sparsely furnished and in which I daily laboured with Dorothy Logan on *Total War after the Battle*, or the book I was writing to keep the wolf from the door. As my part of the flat had no bedrooms I slept in the kitchen.

Soon after my arrival at Oakwood Court I was called on to become an ARP Warden. Early in the war 'Uncle' Max had advised me not to become involved in anything of that kind, as I might at any time be wanted for something more important. He had proved right in a way, but only in a way. Darvall, Vintras, Dickson and several of their naval and military colleagues had all said they would like to have me in a cubby-hole in their basements, so that they could throw me non-technical problems with which they had little time to deal. But the trouble was that all these chaps were regulars who had passed high out of their Staff Colleges and were the pick of the brains in their Services. No ordinary

run-of-the-road officer would ever have been considered
for an appointment to the JPS, let alone a civilian. Bureau-
cratic 'Establishment' made it out of the question for me to
be taken in; so it now looked as if I would never achieve any
official status. Moreover, although I was working half the
night as well as all day and was most reluctant to give time
to standing about watching for incendiary bombs, I did not
wish to appear a shirker, so I agreed.

Perhaps because I had been an officer in the First World
War, I was at once elected by the tenants at Oakwood
Court as a Group-Captain of Fire Fighters. I conscientiously
attended a demonstration at the Kensington Borough
Council Air Raid HQ and promptly decided that fire-
fighting was not really one of my 'things', and that I should
be scared stiff if called upon to tackle anything larger than
an ordinary incendiary bomb. But, naturally, I did not
convey this to my team; and, at least, I had the ability
to drill them efficiently and make it absolutely clear what
each of them was to do in an emergency.

By far the most co-operative members of my team were
two pretty girls who lived in a basement flat and, although
I did not explore the possibility, I had a shrewd suspicion
were tarts. Another member was a small, fat Jewish doctor
who was a refugee from Holland, and this acquaintanceship
led to my writing yet another paper.

He invited Joan and me to tea in his flat and generously
produced a whole stack of rolls lavishly spread with genuine
pâté de foie gras. My mouth watered but, alas, I was debarred
from participating in this feast because he had first spread
on the rolls an equally thick layer of butter, and cold butter
has always made me sick.

At this little party I remarked that, in view of the Jews
having been singled out for special ill-treatment by the
Nazis, it was surprising that we had not raised Jewish
battalions, as happened in the First World War, and that
there did not seem to be any concerted effort on the part of
the Jewish people to buy aeroplanes or assist in other ways
to bring about the defeat of the Axis powers.

Much to my surprise the doctor informed me that the

D.W. giving Diana away at her wedding, 1940

Anthony as an officer in 'The Micks', 1945

'*Grove Place*', *1866*

'*Grove Place*', *at the time we were living there*

Colin and Pam Pelham Burn

Anthony and Annette – their engagement photograph, 1949

'Grove Place'

(Left) *D.W. building his serpentine wall, 1948*
(Right) *On the terrace with his first grandchild, 1951*

*Exchanging memories with Harold Macmillan at
an Authors of the Year party*

New Zionist Organization had, on the outbreak of war, offered to raise an army of at least 100,000 men to fight under the Allied High Command against Hitler.

The following day the doctor put into my hands roneoed memoranda issued by the NZO, outlining its proposals for a Jewish army and negotiations with the British Government concerning this project. From these it emerged that Mr Duff Cooper, Sir Hugh Seely and Lord Lothian had all expressed themselves as in favour of the scheme, and that the Canadian Government had declared its willingness for Canada to be used as a transit training centre for the proposed Jewish Force and for the organization of recruiting propaganda in the Americas; but, in spite of this, the proposal had been definitely turned down by the British Government on 14 July, 1940.

I took the view that here was a most valuable asset going to waste, for reasons unknown to me but which now, ten months after the rejection of the project, might be overcome.

On going further into the matter, I formed the opinion that the world Jewish population, outside Nazi-controlled Europe and Russia, might well provide an army of 250,000 men, that the Jews had the money to maintain it and, apart from this military contribution, if organized and instructed, could do great service to the Allied cause by putting over anti-Axis propaganda in almost every country and language.

It was, however, clear that, in order to get their people whole-heartedly behind a world-wide campaign of this kind, the Jews required certain inducements. These were: the promise of a land of their own after the war; that forthwith the Jews should be regarded as a nation; and that they should be allowed to form their own Government in Exile, to be treated on the same terms as those of the Poles and the Czechs.

Having regard to the arbitrarily limited, but considerable, numbers of Jews who, under the Balfour Declaration, had already been allowed to establish themselves in a small part of Palestine, the Arab–Jewish question could not be ignored and the whole problem bristled with controversies. But I thought it worth grasping the nettle.

Any serious attempt to clarify the problem necessitated going to its very roots; so I went fully into the origin, history and present dispersal of the Jews, together with their characteristics and political leanings. In consequence my paper, *The Sword of Gideon*, ran to 18,000 words.

My final conclusion was that to establish an independent Jewish State in Palestine could only lead to endless trouble and probably future local wars in the Middle East owing to the hereditary hatred of the Arabs for the Jews; that the Arabs had always been our good friends and, in the middle of a war, we could not possibly afford to offend them mortally by announcing that after the war we intended to deprive them of part of their territory to create a Jewish State. I further contended that the Jewish claim to Palestine was based upon false premises, because their race had originated on the eastern coast of the Red Sea, in the Yemen. They had migrated to Palestine and colonized it only after the Babylonian captivity. The Arabs had been there long before they had.

However, to acquire this great asset of organized World Jewry for the Allied cause it was obviously essential to promise the Jews a country of their own after the war and the NZO documents had stated that, provided the country was habitable, it need not necessarily be Palestine. As the French had not only ratted on us, but their troops in Syria were actually at war with ours, I thought it perfectly just that they should be made to pay for the trouble they were causing. I therefore suggested that, after the war, the great island of Madagascar should be taken from France and given to the Jews. It was many times the size of Palestine and had far greater natural resources; so had my suggestion been adopted the Jews would be much better off than they are now and much of the trouble that has since bedevilled the Middle East would have been avoided. In February I duly sent my paper to Rolly Vintras but, of course, nothing came of it.

While we were grateful for the hospitality of Eve Cairns and her cousins, Joan and I found the position of paying guests a little irksome; so she gave some of her time to flat-hunting. The blitz was still going strong. In January, during the great raid on the city, Hutchinson's offices in Paternoster Row had been destroyed, so the staff had moved into Walter's private house, and so many people had moved out of London that the choice of flats was almost unlimited. For example, at Chatsworth Court, Earl's Court, only fifty of two hundred flats were still occupied.

Joan took me to see one on the ground floor there. Having been accustomed to big rooms, I declared in protest, 'Damn it all, one couldn't swing a cat here.'

But Joan persuaded me to take it and her choice was extremely sound. The accommodation was really quite adequate. The sitting-room was large enough for six people to sit comfortably in, and at a small round table in the window we could seat four for a meal. Having our own kitchen we could knock up breakfast and dinner if we were on our own, but there was also, for war-time, an excellent restaurant in the basement, in which we could give dinner parties. As it was on the ground floor of a modern steel and concrete block, we never had to leave our beds to go to a shelter during air raids. Later, Bill moved into a flat in the same block, and, when Brinsley was sent overseas, Diana moved into another; so we had with us the only members of our family still in London.

In February we moved into 10 Chatsworth Court, and remained there, snug as bugs in a rug, until the end of the war. For my work I retained my rooms at 151 and went there every day, as Oakwood Court was only ten minutes' walk away on the other side of Kensington High Street.

Now that we had a home of our own again we began to give little dinner parties about once a week and many an interesting evening we spent there, discussing the progress of the war with our friends who had a behind-the-scenes knowledge of what was taking place. Among our first guests were 'Uncle' Max, Louis Greig, Rolly Vintras, Dickie Dickson, Dallas Brooks, Henry Hopkinson, Charles Balfour-Davey, Peveril Williams-Powlett, Hubert Stringer and another of Joan's friends in MI5, Colonel Gilbert Lennox, with whom I was later to be associated.

In March two events that distressed me occurred. Freddy Richardson was retired from Boots. Although he had reached the age of retirement he had expected to be asked to stay on till the end of the war; but he was barely thanked for his services and given a scandalously small pension. As Chief Librarian at Boots for many years, this able and jovial little man had built up for his firm the greatest book-lending organization in Britain and he deserved better treatment; but Boots had always regarded their library service simply as a means of getting customers to visit their shops regularly.

The other blow was that Dorothy Logan gave me her notice on the grounds that she wanted to do a job that would be really useful in the war. I was decidedly taken aback and tried to persuade her that typing out my ideas, which went to the people responsible for every conceivable war activity, and were frequently accepted by them, was quite as useful as any other job she could do; but she would not alter her decision. I gave her as good a reference as any girl could wish for and she got a job with the BBC.

Finding another secretary at this time, when practically every woman who could even type, let alone take shorthand, was employed in the hugely swollen Ministries or offices of firms engaged in producing essential goods was no small problem. But in that I was very fortunate.

Joan Grant's secretary, a Miss Sutherland, was the eldest of four sisters. The youngest, Iris, was then eighteen, and having had an excellent secretarial training, was just ready to take a job. She proved to be a very pleasant, able and well-educated little girl with a fine head of red hair.

In March I wrote another paper, *The Key to Victory*. During the past nine months Britain's situation had enormously improved. The RAF had defeated the Luftwaffe in the Battle of Britain, but for us to launch an invasion across the Channel was still right out of the question. The time was now foreseeable, however, when we should be able to go over to the offensive. Great offensives take many months of preparation; so the JPS was already considering where it would pay us best to strike when the time came – a return to Norway, a landing in the neighbourhood of Bordeaux, a bid to establish ourselves in North Africa and win over the French forces there, or an attack on what Mr Churchill termed ,'the schoft underbelly of the Axis'.

To my mind the last offered by far the greatest reward. So, having discussed all the other projects and displayed their weaknesses, I developed the theme of two of my earlier papers; namely that, Italy being the weaker partner, we should endeavour to knock her out first, and that as a stepping stone to so doing we should seize the island of Sardinia. Eight months had elapsed since I had put my finger on Sardinia as the most vulnerable Axis-held territory in Europe, and now we were in far better shape to carry out its conquest. Then, of course, it would simply have been a prestige operation, but now it would be the opening move to far greater prospects. Once Sardinia was safely in our hands, protected by the Navy and the RAF, it would prove the perfect base for the invasion of Italy. By landing there we could cut off all central and southern Italy, then advance into the valley of the Po. Later, as the size of our army in Italy increased, we could take Napoleon's road, force the Ljubljana gap through the Carnic Alps to the north-east and strike with equal ease at either Munich or Vienna.

Several members of the JPS agreed that it was our best bet, and my paper was duly sent up to the Directors of Plans for consideration. In due course it was decided by the Planners that Sardinia should be our first objective when we carried the war into Italian territory.

I had taken my paper down to 'Mr Rance's Room' personally and, as Vintras was out, saw Group Captain Dickson. With 'Dickie', as the forceful and very forthcoming little man was known to his friends, I had a long talk about the contents of my paper, making it clear that, although it appeared possible for us to go into Sardinia at any time, we would obviously have to delay launching an attack against the Italian mainland until we were very much stronger. For the present we must be content to hold Hitler in his cage, and meet his land forces only if they attempted to cross water into Africa or Asia.

Dickie then paid me the compliment of letting me into

my first major war secret. He told me that although the operation was still only in preparation, the die had already been cast. It had been decided to send the greater part of our Army of the Nile into Greece. This was to do the exact opposite of my own first strategic principle. Still worse, it meant throwing away our greatest military achievement in the war up to that date. By his brilliant offensive, General Wavell had already reached Benghazi, so Tunisia lay open to him, with the possibility of inducing the big French Army in Algeria to come in on our side. To rob him of the fruits of his victory seemed madness. Moreover, as it later transpired, the C-in-C Med., Admiral Cunningham, had pointed out that to keep an army in Greece supplied would mean a great loss in ships and aircraft, as indeed proved the case. The few Divisions we could send to support the Greeks could not conceivably hope to stand up against the Germans. It could lead only to another and probably more disastrous Dunkirk. I was absolutely horrified.

Dickie sadly agreed with me, and said, that the whole of the JPS had been against it; but that calamitous man, Anthony Eden, had persuaded Mr Churchill that this gallant gesture would be worthwhile because it would impress the Americans that we really were waging the war to preserve the freedom of small nations.

Later the Prime Minister privately acknowledged that in this case he had made a sad blunder. His PA, Sir Desmond Morton, told me of an occasion when the PM had tapped Greece with his finger on a map in the War Room, shaken his head and said, 'How wrong I was to allow Anthony to persuade me into agreeing to such a disastrous operation.'

In April *Strange Conflict* was published. How, during that winter, with *Total War, After the Battle* and all these other activities on my hands, I had ever managed to write it I cannot now imagine; but, of course, for many months I had been working fourteen hours a day, Sundays included. I was also now writing *The Sword of Fate*, when I could get a few hours from my War Papers.

For this I used Julian Day, a character who had already appeared in a pre-war book of mine with Egypt as a background. In it, Julian, who had a flair for languages, became an officer of the Interpreter Corps in Cairo, participated in General Wavell's victorious campaign in Libya, and later was involved in our disasters in Greece.

Michael Arlen, long a friend of mine, about this time turned up in London. He was an Armenian by birth and, after his great success with *The Green Hat* and other novels, had spent only a few months each year in England. But, to his honour be it recorded, unlike numerous other authors who elected to save their skins by becoming refugees in the United States, Michael returned from there to help in any way he could. The Ministry of Information, of course, turned him down; so he became an Air Raid Warden and went through the hellish blitz on Coventry.

We lunched together, and when I told him that I still had no American publisher, he very kindly sent some of my recent books to Doubleday Doran, with a strong recommendation; but they replied that the American public was reading so much about the war in the papers that war novels were not proving popular and turned me down.

In May I wrote a paper on an idea of my own, which I called *Atlantic Lifeline*. The U-boat campaign had developed to a point where our shipping losses were becoming really serious, and it looked as though, should they continue at that rate for another year, Britain might be starved out. The remedy I suggested was the creation of Raft Convoys. Each convoy would have consisted of one hundred 100-foot square rafts – carrying bulk cargoes of grain and raw materials in iron containers – in ten rows linked by steel cables with another cable connecting the ten rows in front, and two sea-going tugs armed with ack-ack guns at the front corners of the square to adjust the convoy's direction.

Each raft was to have a sail four feet high from corner to corner, and there were to be two motor boats in attendance on each convoy to service the rafts.

The whole would have occupied a square two-and-a-quarter miles in extent, so the rafts would have presented a poor target for bombs, and, being made of thick layers of logs, they would have been virtually unsinkable. My idea was that we should take advantage of the Gulf Stream and the prevailing wind, which, in some six weeks would bring the rafts over from the United States to our Western Approaches, where they could have been met and towed into our ports. By this means, I contended, many thousands of tons of cargo could be brought over without loss.

My paper went to the Admiralty but the experts there pronounced it to be impracticable. Why, I have never understood, for even if certain details of the project were not feasible, surely on broad lines, the idea of making use of the Gulf Stream was sound?

On 13 June Joan's leave came round, so we went up to Wales to spend a fortnight with Charles and Joan Beatty, who were living with his mother at Trelyden Hall near Welshpool. It was a pleasant, rambling old mansion and its stables and coach-house had been well converted into a home for Joan and Charles. Up there I had one of my cellars, so a good time was had by all.

I have often said that I have never participated in any magical ceremony; but that is not strictly true, as on this occasion I witnessed the 'Ceremony of the Roses'. Charles believed himself to be an expert on White Magic rituals and, in my view, it was his influence on Joan, although exerted with the highest motives, that ruined the natural psychic link that she undoubtedly had with the Powers of Good.

She stripped herself naked, then there was a lot of palaver with a sword and roses with abjurations by Charles to the Powers of Light. Afterwards Joan lay on a sofa and, apparently, went into a trance. She then began to talk as though she were in an incarnation which she had lived through in ancient Egypt, and Charles took her words down.

The interesting thing was that when she roused from her trance, she had no idea at all what she had been saying, and I do not belive for one moment that she was lying.

At 4 a.m. on 22 June, Germany declared war on Russia. Charles had heard this in the six o'clock BBC broadcast, and woke me to tell me the splendid news. For a year and a week Britain, with her Army weaker through lack of weapons than it had ever been before and her only support the distant peoples of her Empire, had defied Hitler. Now she was no longer alone. Hitler had treacherously attacked his passive ally and roused against himself a nation of courageous fighters which could create an army larger than his own.

From the beginning of the war many of us had always had faith in ultimate victory but, generally speaking – and this includes Mr Churchill and the officers of the Joint Planning Staff – we had greatly underestimated Germany's powers of resistance. In the dark days of 1940 the JPS believed that Hitler was in such a bad way for food and raw materials that, if we escaped being invaded, Germany might collapse in 1941. It was undoubtedly these shortages that had driven him to invade Russia. Even if he succeeded in securing large quantities of grain and oil from her, it could only be at a terrible price in German manpower. Meanwhile, with a hundred Divisions of Germany's best troops occupied on a 2000-mile front, the chance was at last offered us to strike at Hitler's Europe in the West on much more even terms. Immediately I returned to London, I sat down to a new paper which I called *While the Cat's Away*.

In it I re-examined the possibilities of a landing in France, Holland and Norway and again shot them all down as too dangerous a gamble for our present strength. I also envisaged sending a British Army round the North Cape to Archangel, as had been done in 1918, and shot that idea down too, on account of our shipping losses already having been so severe that it would prove too great a strain on our Merchant Navy.

In what way then could we best help Russia? Again my thoughts reverted to Sardinia. It offered the best base in all Europe for an air offensive against German-held territories. This I proved by sending in with my paper a map, with circles showing an 800-mile range from (1) Syria, (2) England and (3) Sardinia. The circle from Syria had within it only Bucharest, Odessa and a third of Greece. That from England had within it all France and Germany but only the north of Italy as far south as Leghorn and a small part of Czechoslovakia. That from Sardinia had within it all France,

Germany as far north as Berlin, two-thirds of Greece and the whole of Czechoslovakia, Austria, Hungary and Rumania.

The most important requirement in the war was oil. Germany was drawing the bulk of her supplies from the Rumanian wells and we could not bomb them from England. Moreover, one of her major objectives in her new campaign must be the Russian oil wells situated north of the Black Sea. Owing to the barrier of the Carpathians she could send, and keep supplied, a large army to secure them only by the Orient Express route and by barges along the Danube, both of which ran south of the great mountain chain. From Sardinia both the railway and the river could be bombed by us for nearly their entire length. Therefore, I argued, the best help we could give Russia was by invading Sardinia and mounting a great air offensive from it against these targets.

My paper was entirely endorsed by my friends in the JPS, and it is now agreed by many of them who have since become Admirals, Generals and Air Marshals that, had it been adopted and followed by a landing in northern Italy, the war might have been won much sooner; but, alas, it was turned down.

In August I had great news from my agent in America, Jane Hardy. My good friend, James Hilton, who had achieved fame with *Lost Horizon* and *Goodbye, Mr Chips*, had interested her in my books. She wrote to tell me that the Macmillan Company had taken *The Scarlet Impostor*.

When the book was published in the autumn it had an excellent press and, in due course, they followed it with my other Gregory Sallust stories, *Faked Passports*, *The Black Baroness* and *V for Vengeance*.

Russia being now so much in the news I asked Hutchinson to bring out a new edition of *Red Eagle*. But, alas, I was told that the type both of *Red Eagle* and of *Old Rowley*, my only other non-fiction book, had been destroyed in the blitz on Plymouth, where they had been printed.

However, in September, Voroshilov paid me a small dividend. By then a German army advancing from Finland had encircled and was besieging Leningrad. Voroshilov was commanding there, and this happened to crop up in a conversation I had with 'Uncle' Max. This shrewd operator saw in my knowledge of Voroshilov a chance, perhaps, to get a little low-down on Russian views through the Press Attaché of the Soviet Embassy. He said that if I would write an article on the siege of Leningrad he felt sure that the *Daily Mail* would take it; but first I should write to the Soviet Press Attaché, tell him my intention, then ask him to dine with me and give me his guidance.

I acted accordingly and a most amusing evening resulted. The Press Attaché met me at the Hungaria Restaurant and proved to be the most nervous little man I had ever met. He arrived clutching a brief-case and refused to leave it in the cloakroom; instead he sat on it all through dinner. Dear Vecchi of the Hungaria had been *maître d'hôtel* at the Grand Hotel, Petrograd, and with him I had planned a real Russian dinner – Blinis, Bortsch, Saumon Koulibiac and Boeuf Stroganoff. Before the meal I gave my guest vodka and drank it with him, in spite of my personal dislike of the stuff.

To my surprise he opened his eyes wide and exclaimed, 'Vodka! How do you do this? We never get it at the Embassy. It is reserved for the Ambassador and his friends.'

He had a couple, but nothing would persuade him to drink anything further, as the poor little man obviously feared that I might make him tight; so I had to drink a whole bottle of Champagne myself. But as the rich courses succeeded one another his eyes opened wider and wider at such magnificence when Britain was supposed to be starving. Quite early he hurried away clutching his brief-case like a frightened rabbit.

I did not think that I had got much out of the Russian, but when 'Uncle' Max read my report he said I had done very well, and as he had asked me to send him my bill, I enjoyed an excellent dinner at the expense of MI5.

When I'd written the article I took it to the Press Attaché at his office off Trafalgar Square. In it I had declared that as long as Voroshilov commanded in Leningrad the city would not fall – as proved the case although it was one of the longest and most terrible sieges in history. But I also recounted that when Trotsky had sent a GPU man to spy on Voroshilov and the Marshal had found out, he had knocked the man down a flight of stairs. Further, that one night when a victory had been gained at Stalingrad (Tzaritzen) in the Civil War following the Russian Revolution, Voroshilov had driven up with some friends in a *troika* to his favourite restaurant, got drunk, thrown the waiters out into the street and danced the Trapka on a table.

I put these things in to show that Voroshilov was a real he-man. But the poor little Press Attaché was horrified and exclaimed, 'Oh, Mr Wheatley, Marshal Voroshilov is a most respectable man! He would never do things like that!' All the same I sent my article into the *Daily Mail* as it stood and it was duly published.

In September Joan and I went up to Trelyden again for a very pleasant fortnight; then in October *The Sword of Fate* was published and did all I had hoped for it. That month Christina Foyle also took my *Strange Conflict* for her Book Club.

By then I had decided that it was time to give Gregory Sallust another turn so I made a start on *V for Vengeance*. In it I sent Gregory and his friend the ex-Bolshevik General, Stefan Kuprovitch, to Paris. The book was not so good as its predecessors, although it sold very well.

My voluminous papers, *After the Battle* and *Total War*, had both gone in in the spring, but now the latter came into prominence again. The JPS felt that a pruned version given to the public, might boost morale and help increase the war effort. So I got to work on cutting it ruthlessly, then submitted my draft to Laurence Burgess, a charming Pickwickian little man who was Deputy Secretary to the War Cabinet.

A great part of the paper had consisted of stringent criticisms of certain Government Departments that I felt were not pulling their weight, and all that had to be deleted. Eventually Laurence and I reduced the original paper of over 100,000 words to 30,000; and in this form Hutchinson's published 100,000 copies of it as a shilling pamphlet.

By this time I had become quite an accepted visitor to the famous fortress-basement as well as lunching and dining

fairly frequently with several of its inmates. The usual tour
of duty for officers there was two years, but the overall
knowledge of every aspect of the war required to make
plans – which it took two or three months to acquire –
sometimes led to officers' being promoted and retained
instead of being allowed, as they all desired, to be given an
active command.

This proved the case with my friend Dickie Dickson; he
was promoted to Air Commodore, made Director of Plans
(Air) and went up to an office in the Air Ministry. His
place as senior Air Planner in the STRATS was taken by
Wing Commander (later Air Chief Marshal Sir Walter)
Dawson, known to his friends as 'Tubby' – though why I
had no idea, as he was a very short man with a good slim
figure. It was Tubby who first invited me into the JPS for
a drink; another landmark in my association with 'Mr
Rance's Room'.

But during the autumn Rolly Vintras had made little use
of me and I was getting pretty despondent, so I was delighted
when a new prospect opened for me. I had a letter from
Air Commodore Vatchell, our pre-war Air Attaché in
Berlin. In it he said that, having read my Gregory Sallust
books, he had formed the opinion that I could get into the
mind of the enemy, and if I liked the idea of a job that
entailed doing so, would I lunch with him?

I at once replied accepting and sent him copies of some
of my papers. When we met he said that reading them had
shown how right he was to approach me and that, in view
of my association with the JPS, he felt free to tell me what
was proposed. The Chiefs-of-Staff had decided to form a new
Section of the JPS, whose job it would be to assess Germany's
future intentions, and he was to be the head of it with
permission to select his own staff. Would I go into uniform
and join it?

Naturally, I jumped for joy at such a prospect. But my
elation was premature. A fortnight later we met again. In
the meantime he had put up to the Chiefs a first paper on
'enemy intentions' that he had written himself. It credited
the Germans with such strength and ruthlessness and was

so utterly different from anything the Chiefs had expected
that they decided his views could not be reconciled with
theirs; so they returned him to the Air Ministry and to my
deep disappointment the whole scheme was abandoned.

There remains one War Paper about the contents of
which I have so far made no mention. This is *After the Battle*.
It was the last I wrote at the request of Johnny Darvall.
It was also my longest – 120,000 words – and he considered
it my most important.

The question was, 'How could we prevent the Germans
from launching a Third World War against us in twenty
years' time?' My answer was that a means must be found
by which the population of the German State could be
reduced to numbers insufficient to go to war with any first-
class Power.

I pointed out that only seventy years ago Germany as
we now know it had consisted of Prussia, Bavaria, Saxony,
Wurtemburg, Baden and a large number of smaller independent States, which throughout the thousand years
preceding 1870 had never all taken the same side in any
war; so it would prove no insufferable hardship on the
German people if these clans were again separated.

There was, of course, much more to it, for I dealt with
each race in detail and anyone who is interested can read a
full account of this – and my other War Papers – in my book,
Stranger Than Fiction. But the net result was that Germany
would have been reduced from a nation of 80,000,000 to
40,000,000 and deprived of her great industrial zone in
the Ruhr, so in no state ever again to launch a major
war.

By the autumn of 1941 I had written over half a million
words for the Joint Planning Staff – the equivalent of some
six full-length novels. By then they seemed to have little
further use for me, but there I was wrong. Rolly Vintras
was, I know, largely responsible, but it was Dickie Dickson
who rang me up one day in mid-November and asked me to
lunch with him at the R A C.

His other guest was Oliver Stanley. In the Chamberlain
Government Stanley had been Secretary of State for War;

but he was now wearing the uniform of a full Colonel. The reason for this I was to learn later. During 1940/41 Mr Churchill had been considerably thwarted by the Chiefs-of-Staffs in his burning desire to hit back at the enemy. The Chiefs were, of course, advised by the Directors of Plans and the three teams that made up the Joint Planning Staff. In the hope of getting behind the Chiefs with a series of plans more to his own liking, the Prime Minister created two more teams and placed Oliver Stanley in charge of them as a sort of extra Director of Plans. Henceforth the original JPS was known as the STRATS (Strategic Planning Section) and Stanley's teams as the FOPS (Future Operations Planning Section).

But, for the object the Prime Minister had had in mind, he had chosen the wrong man. He was an able politician, had a brilliant mind and, having been trained as a barrister, could argue a case with great ability. But he was a destructive critic, and I never knew him to put up an original idea. Moreover, having served in the First World War, he had an ingrained respect for the opinions of senior professional soldiers; so, instead of contesting the Chiefs-of-Staff's view that we were still too weak to undertake even a minor offensive, he backed them up.

He was, however, a charming person; tall, slim, white-haired, with a most kindly disposition and a ready wit; so the lunch proved a very pleasant one, although I had no idea that I had been asked to meet him so that he could 'vet' me as a person. However, after lunch, evidently satisfied, he told me that a new Section of the Chiefs-of-Staff Organization was being formed to work under him and that a place might be found in it for me. If so, the question would arise as to whether it would be better to bring me in as an officer or as a civil servant. Which would I prefer? I replied that I would prefer to become an officer.

Dickie then said that if I did, owing to regulations, they could give me no higher rank to start with than Pilot Officer; whereas if I came in as a civil servant I could be given at once a more adequate remuneration.

With a laugh I told them that I would come in a chef's

hat or anything else they thought most desirable; but, if I was to work with officers, I would rather be one.

As Stanley had not read any of my papers I sent him some, and on 21 November I had a letter from him saying that he had found them most interesting and would like to see me in his office when he returned from a week's leave that he was just starting.

Towards the end of the month I received the summons and went once again to 'Mr Rance's Room' but found that only the STRATS worked down in the fortress-basement. Stanley and his FOPS had been accommodated on the third floor of the great building; so up I went.

I was first received by Commander (later Admiral Sir Ballin) Robertshaw. Smiling at me he said, 'Why, you must be the chap who wrote that splendid paper about Sardinia,' which, as I was feeling desperately nervous, put me at my ease.

Stanley then saw me, but gave me only a vague idea of what I should be expected to do. So vague in fact that when he pointed at his telephone and said, 'If that suddenly rang and I found I had the German DMI on the other end of the line, believing that he had made contact with his best agent, I simply would not know what to tell him.' I really did not know what he was talking about, but, before I left, I did gather that I was to be employed in thinking up ways to deceive the enemy; and what Stanley had meant was that, as the Chiefs-of-Staff had not yet decided where, when the time came, we should launch our offensive, he could not have given German Intelligence any misleading information.

I went home in a daze. In spite of the obvious inference made at my lunch with Stanley and Dickie, that I was to be given a definite job, I had never imagined for one moment that I was actually to be made a member of the Joint Planning Staff of the War Cabinet. Yet Oliver Stanley had just told me that I must get a uniform made at once because he wished to have me on his Staff as soon as possible.

The Prime Minister dominated the War Cabinet and his decisions were final. General Sir Hastings Ismay was

Churchill's Chief-of-Staff, Brigadier Leslie Hollis was Is-may's Deputy and Major Sir Desmond Morton the PM's PA. There were the Chiefs-of-Staff of the three Services and Lord Louis Mountbatten as C-in-C Combined Operations. Under them were the three Directors of Plans and Oliver Stanley. The STRATS consisted of nine officers and the FOPS of six, all picked men from the three services with the rank of Captain or Commander RN – or its equivalent in the Army or Royal Air Force.

I was therefore to be the only man ever commissioned direct from civilian life to serve in this strategic stratosphere. It consisted of less than thirty men, who all contributed to the High Direction of the war and so controlled the movements of 9,600,000 men and women throughout the Empire who were then wearing His Majesty's uniform.

H

INTERMEZZO

DURING the next four years I was fully occupied by my fascinating job as a Deception Planner – but those experiences I will leave for a separate volume, which I am entitling *Secrets of the War Cabinet.* The mental strain imposed made it out of the question to switch my tired mind to writing a book in the evenings, so I had become dependent on my officer's pay and such sums as the half-yearly royalties on my cheap editions might bring in. Given normal circumstances, as I already had twenty-two books behind me and now neither holidays abroad nor servants to pay for, the sales of my 'cheaps' would have kept me well provided. But there was a shortage of paper. Most of my cheap editions had already sold out, the stocks of the others were rapidly declining and Hutchinson's could make much more money by using such paper as they were allowed to publish new books than reprint old ones. So this source of income must obviously soon dry up completely.

Hutchinson constantly urged me to write a new novel somehow, declaring that, even if it was a bad one, it would at least keep my name before the public. I, too, realized that, should I fail to publish anything for several years, I should be in danger of losing my name as a bestseller. But I have always been most strongly opposed to giving anything but the best I could; and it is certain that, in the long run, pot-boilers damage an author's reputation.

In this dilemma, it occurred to me that I might put out a book of short stories. On going through my manuscripts, I found that if I padded out the dozen or two really good short stories which I had had published, with other early ones that had been rejected, extracts from *Old Rowley* and

Red Eagle, several articles, two film scripts and a one-act play, I had enough material for two books.

Accordingly, I set to work on this hotch-potch and, to gild the pill, I wrote a short introduction to each item, relating the circumstances in which it had come to be written, which were more or less autobiographical snippets. The first, *Mediterranean Nights*, was published in 1943 and the second, *Gunmen, Gallants and Ghosts*, in 1944.

In pre-war days it was accepted by publishers that a book of short stories by a well-known novelist earned only one-sixth of the sum earned by one of his novels. My surprise and delight can be imagined, therefore, when *Mediterranean Nights* brought me over £2000 in its first six months – more than any of my novels had earned in the same period up till that time; and *Gunmen, Gallants and Ghosts* did equally well. This, of course, was due to the exceptional conditions of war-time, when people's pleasures were so limited and the blackout created a tremendous demand for books. Even so, it is pleasing to relate that these 'scrapings of my bottom drawer' were reprinted again and again, are still, after half a century, in print and during the years have earned me many thousands of pounds.

Apart from these gleanings, all my writing and most of my reading were devoted to the business of our office; an endless succession of minutes and papers of all kinds, of long hours spent at the conference table and occasional crises. Personal and professional life were subordinated, as they were for so many millions of other people, to the single aim of helping to win the war. But that, as I said, is another story, which I will tell separately.

PART THREE

Autumn

1944–1977

FOR me the war ended on 22 December, 1944. During the past three years I had worked as a member of the Joint Planning Staff of the War Cabinet, in the famous fortress-basement. Colonel J. H. Bevan MC, who became Chief of the European Deception Section, came in five months after me. He and I alone thought out the successful cover plan for Operation Torch, the invasion of French North Africa. Later, others had to be brought in to assist and implement our cover plans for the invasion of Europe and for other operations; but our permanent staff was never more than seven.

Once General Eisenhower was securely established in France, he was sent a Section of British and American officers to fulfil what had been our role against the Germans, and it was decided that the staff of the London section should be reduced.

Paper still being in very short supply reprints were issued in only limited numbers. In consequence, my royalties had dwindled to next to nothing and I had become practically dependent on my Air Force pay as a Wing Commander. I therefore applied at once to be released in order to write another book.

After my three years in the Cabinet Offices I knew so many secrets that I positively dared not write another spy story from fear of infringing the Official Secrets Act; so I wrote a story, based on my Raft Convoy Plan, about a man and girl who got swept down to the Antarctic on a raft, and called it *The Man Who Missed the War*. It cost me my American publishers, Macmillan, as they had done very well with my Gregory Sallust books and refused to take any book that did not continue his adventures. But that could not be helped. When the new book did come out here I was welcomed back by the Trade, and it did very well.

Meanwhile, negotiations had gone forward for the purchase of a house in the country – 'Grove Place', Lymington. With the aid of a £5000 loan from Hutchinson I bought the freehold of this charming Georgian mansion and some four acres of garden. During the spring of 1945 we were very fully occupied arranging for the removal of our furniture from store, my wines from several cellars and arranging about curtains and carpets for our new home.

Finally, on the last day in June, we sent down everything from Chatsworth Court and, that evening, gave a cocktail party on the bare boards.

I was then forty-eight and about to settle down to a new life in the country; so it seemed to me that, apart from writing, my active life was as good as over. But more than thirty years have elapsed since then. They have been good years, full of interest for me, but perhaps of less interest to other people; so I thought that, instead of describing them in a continuous narrative, I would end with a pot-pourri of subjects.

Lymington

It was to this small, ancient town, about halfway between Southampton and Bournemouth, that Joan and I moved in June 1945. As a borough it is one of the oldest in England. After the Norman conquest it became a fief of the Earls of Devon, which placed upon them the feudal obligation of defending it from attack. Redvers, the second Earl, evidently decided that it would be a sound economy to leave the inhabitants to defend themselves so, in 1150, he gave them their freedom.

It is situated at the mouth of the Lym river, and in early times scores of small ships from the Continent sailed up the river to unload their cargoes in Winchester; but the coming of larger ships made this impracticable so, under the

Plantagenet Kings, Lymington itself became a port of considerable importance, even rivalling Southampton.

The town's principal source of wealth lay in the salt-pans to seaward of it and a great part of England relied on this source until, in 1845, the salterns had become worked out. A little over a hundred years ago Lymington sent two MPs to Parliament, among them Edward Gibbon, the famous author of *The Decline and Fall*.

It consisted of little more than a long High Street, running down a steep hill to the river, with a few short residential streets turning off it. The northern side of the High Street was once the property of Nell Gwyn, given to her by Charles II. Until the last quarter of a century it had altered very little, and is still one of the most picturesque towns in Britain.

'Grove Place'

Our new home was a square, two-storeyed Georgian mansion of modest size built about 1770. Attached to its back stood a building a century older, once a Jacobean farmhouse. This made a perfect self-contained home for our living-in couple. The main house had a spacious hall, four reception rooms and six bedrooms plus ample kitchen quarters and three bathrooms. All the main rooms were large and lofty with tall windows. The staircase led up from an inner hall in a graceful curve; period mantelpieces and fanlights added to the charm of the house.

The principal rooms faced south-east and a previous owner had covenanted with three others who owned land to the south that none of them should allow any building to be erected on their property without the consent of the other three. In consequence we had an uninterrupted view over fields and woodland to the Solent four miles away and, beyond it, the western end of the Isle of Wight. To the north our ground sloped upward to the backs of the houses in the High Street, only a quarter of a mile away; and from our stable-yard a footpath ran up to it.

A great deal had to be done to the house, and fortunately

the local builder, Mr Bower, had apparently not heard of the war-time regulation that not more than £50 might be spent on repairs or redecoration. He cheerfully put in work that cost me £1100 odd.

This very nearly landed us in serious trouble. When the work had been completed, a local dealer, who had been using 'Grove Place' as a store house came to see me one morning and threatened to inform the police that I had illegally spent a far greater sum on redecorating the house than was allowed by the regulation, unless I made it worth his while to keep his mouth shut. I said I would think the matter over and let him know of my decision if he would come and see me again at the same time the following morning. When he had gone I hurried off to see Bower and told him about the danger we were in. We then made a plan. When the dealer came the following day Bower was in the next room with the door just ajar. Having led the dealer to repeat his demand I called Bower in and said to the old crook, 'You are attempting to blackmail me and I can call Mr Bower as a witness. One word about the decorations and I'll have you in jug.' So that was the end of that.

Joan was a great gardener and had sadly missed having one during her years in London; so that being at 'Grove' was a great delight to her. By the time we had finished with it the whole area was lawn, shrubbery or flower-beds. But what a job it was to make it even presentable.

The previous owner had been a Mrs Hall, the wife of a Colonel Hall whose brother was the famous Admiral 'Blinker' Hall, the one-time head of our Secret Service. Unhappily for Mrs Hall, her husband died shortly after they had moved in to 'Grove', and the poor lady was left so badly off that she feared she could not afford to remain on in a house of that size. However, she tried it for a year, and finding that she could just make ends meet, stayed on for another ten. But she had not a spare shilling to spend on flowers so, even in 1940 when she left it, there were no more than a few beds of very old rose bushes.

Everything had run wild. The lawn was a hayfield, the terrace a sea of weeds, branches of fruit trees met across the paths, and brambles had smothered the wistarias on the walls of the house right up to the level of the first-floor windows. On the far side of the lawn to the south of the house rose several splendid trees. Behind them curved a dense shrubbery. It was not until we had been there for six months we discovered that a path had once led through it leading to a summer house in ruins. In the walled kitchen garden behind the house the fruit cage had collapsed and we had to cut our way between the once-espaliered fruit trees.

But a year or so of strenuous effort put things to rights and by the fifties we had achieved a transformation. A returfed close-shaven lawn was laid out for croquet. The 200-foot terrace overlooking it had been gravel with a low brick edge. I had it paved, replacing the brick with stone balusters with Georgian urns. To the east of the house we had another terrace and made a sunken rose garden below it.

Beyond that, against the stable-yard wall, we had a long, deep herbaceous border. To the north, to screen off the kitchen garden, Joan had a big rockery planted with scores of intriguing little cacti and flowers. Behind it I made a maze and, still further north, a glade of young forest trees. But my greatest joy was the only piece of garden that I designed and planted myself. It lay to the west of the house, opposite the front door, and was a sextant-shaped area of grass. In it I planted some hundred trees and bushes, all of which blossomed in the spring: lilacs of several shades, laburnums, peaches, forsythias, cherries and magnolias. Then between them I put in clumps of crocus, specially selected daffodils, tulips and hyacinths. From the end of February till the beginning of May it was a glory of colours such as is seen in Italian Renaissance paintings, and we called it the Botticelli garden.

Diana

During the last stages of the war, my beautiful step-daughter had fallen in love with Professor Wentworth Eldredge of Dartmouth College, New Hampshire; and had succeeded in securing a divorce from Brinsley. She came down to 'Grove' with us and lived there for some months before she married 'Went', as we all call him.

He is some ten years older than Diana and, during the war, served on General Omar Bradley's staff as a Deception expert, having been initiated in that type of work by my Section.

Later, there were several periods when he was a member of the President's 'Think Tank' at Washington. He is a brilliant lecturer and in addition is an excellent skier, a very cheerful companion and most generous to Diana.

Fortunately, he had private means in addition to – by American standards meagre – Professor's pay. This enabled them to build a large, comfortable home on the far side of the Connecticut River, in Vermont.

In her teens, Diana had shown good promise as a painter; but after going to America she took up sculpture instead. Her success in this medium proved quite remarkable and high prices are paid for her pieces.

How she finds the time for it is remarkable for, in addition to running her home very efficiently, she has two sons, both of whom are now in their twenties and the elder, Jamie, already doing her great credit as an officer in the Coast Guard.

Colin

Joan's sons, Jack Younger and Colin Pelham Burn, joined the Coldstream Guards. When I married Joan, Colin was only about eight years old and our home was his until he married; so I saw much more of him than I did of Jack, who lived in Scotland with Joan's first husband, Sir William Younger.

Colin, who always wore a kilt, was a truly cherubic little boy. He was a cheerful youngster always willing to do any chore, particularly answering the telephone; so we nick-named him the 'Second Footman'.

He was educated at Wellington, then became an Ensign in the Coldstream Guards. With them he saw active service during the troubles in Palestine and successfully passed the

tests for a Parachute officer. When back in England he
married Pam, the only daughter of Colonel Carrington
Sykes, a retired Siege Gunner who had done most of his
service in the Far East. In due course they had a daughter,
Fiona, and a son, Andrew; both of whom have grown up
to become charming young people.

Colin's career in the army was not very distinguished, but
his seniors always spoke of him as an excellent regimental
officer and very popular with his men. He had the good fortune to be sent as a Major to the Staff of the British Military
Mission in Washington. After twenty-five years' service he
reached the rank of acting Lt. Colonel, then retired to go
into insurance. As his firm did not carry out their promise
to make him a Director he left it and was fortunate enough
to be appointed Public Relations Officer and made responsible for Ceremonial Parades at the Royal Military Academy
at Sandhurst. Owing to his background and cordial disposition no job could have suited him better.

Anthony

My only child was born eighteen months after I married my
first wife Nancy, *née* Robinson. He grew up to be much taller
than myself and was not the least like me to look at. Our
personalities, too, had little resemblance except that he had
a good sense of humour and enjoyed fine wine.

His mother was, as I have recorded, a Roman Catholic, so
I had agreed to his being brought up in that faith and he has
remained a practising Catholic.

He was educated at Downside and during the war held
commissions, firstly in the Royal Marines, and later in the
Irish Guards. Unfortunately, while with the Army of
Occupation in Germany, he went down with tuberculosis
and was invalided out of the army.

In 1949, he married Annette Webb, the daughter of an
inventor and one of the most vital young women I have
ever known. She was a pretty brunette and her energy was
inexhaustible. Not only did she give Anthony three daughters, Antonia, Patricia and Nicola; but followed that with

three sons, Dominic, Gregory and Justin. She brought them all up to be a credit to her, is an excellent cook and keeps a large house in perfect order. She also helped Anthony to start a small chain of automatic laundries which she managed herself while Anthony was still in full-time employment.

She was not a Catholic but became one eight years after her marriage. On the twenty-fifth anniversary of their marriage, they had a Silver Wedding Mass offered by the same Downside monk, Dom Wulstan Phillipson, who had married them. He was assisted by the priest who had received Annette into the Church; and their three sons served on the altar as acolytes. The Mass was followed by a reception at the Vintners' Hall which I had arranged for them.

When his military career was cut short, Anthony became a trainee executive at Chiswick Products Ltd, which later became a part of Reckitt & Colman. He gained a good commercial training from this firm; but after eight years it seemed that there was no opening for him so he left and founded Luncheon Vouchers Ltd with a friend whom he had met in the Army. This wonderful idea went like a bomb; but unhappily the larger catering firms took fright at the potential power which the firm might eventually have enjoyed, and insisted on buying them out.

He then joined Burroughs Machines Ltd, where he spent ten years progressing to Area Sales Manager in their Accounting Machines Division.

Meanwhile, a desire for independence had caused him to start up a small chain of automatic laundries with the help of his wife, and after leaving Burroughs he took over the running of this small business.

He lives at Wimbledon in a Victorian house that has ample accommodation for his large family. They entertain generously and often have friends to stay. Antonia married an art dealer and already has a son and daughter. Patricia married a solicitor and has two daughters; so this makes me four times a great-grandfather.

I am often asked out to Wimbledon and always enjoy my visits; although I do not accept as often as I would like because I have so many other commitments. I often feel guilty about not having given as much time to my only son as I should have; but my life has been an extraordinarily full one, and Joan's descendants – including their husbands and wives – coupled with my own now number forty.

Anthony has proved a good husband and father, and an affectionate son.

Jack

When Joan parted from William Younger, feelings on neither side were friendly, so Joan was not allowed even to see Meg and the two boys until they were well into their teens. From then onward they came to see us when they were in London and I am happy to think they developed a deep and lasting affection for me as their stepfather.

Bill was a near-genius and I will write of him later. Jack went from his Public School to Sandhurst. He passed out in the summer of 1940 and was gazetted an Ensign in the Coldstream Guards. A year or so later Joan and I watched him march out from Chelsea Barracks with a detachment on its way to Egypt. At Mersa Matruh he was badly wounded in the thigh and spent several weeks in hospital in Cairo. They wanted to send him home but he refused, so they gave him command of the Battalion Transport, where he should have been safe from further action. But it proved most unfortunate. At Tobruk most of the Battalion fought its way out; but the Transport and Jack were captured.

There is one happening in the surrender of Tobruk by the South African General Klopper, that deserves the same immortality as Nelson's signal to the Fleet at Trafalgar. A Company of Coldstreamers was commanded by Major Sainthill. When he received the signal to surrender, he sent a signal back: 'Surrender is an exercise never practised by the Guards in peacetime so they would not understand how to execute it in time of war.' Then, with his men and some two hundred stout-hearted South Africans, he fought his way out through Rommel's encircling forces.

Jack was taken to Italy and confined for a long time in a prisoner-of-war camp. During the confusion that followed

Mussolini's fall, he escaped and got through the German lines to the neighbourhood of Parma. There he was hidden by a gallant pro-Allies farmer for many months and became the secret Commandant of the Parma partisans. When he gathered from the news that the war was nearing its end, he decided to come home. Again he made his way by night through the German lines and, to our enormous joy, arrived back in London in the winter of 1944.

After the war he served with his Regiment for some while on garrison duty in Berlin. There he fell in love with Jane Dodd, the wife of a Captain in the Irish Guards. She obtained a divorce from her husband; and in due course she and Jack were married and had two children, Julian and Joanna.

But the marriage proved far from happy; and when Jack was posted to Rome as Assistant Military Attaché, he fell in love with Marcella, the Princess Granito di Belmonte. He eventually obtained a divorce from Jane and married Marcella in the autumn of 1953.

Marcella is a remarkable product of Roman society. Her intelligence and wit make her the centre of attraction wherever she goes.

While Jack commanded a battalion of the Coldstream at Windsor he received permission to give a cocktail party on the polo ground for Her Majesty and Prince Philip. Joan and I were invited and he presented us to the Queen. It is well known that Her Majesty does not photograph well, but seen face to face she is most attractive on account of her perfect skin and lovely colouring.

Jack became a professional soldier of the first grade. After attending the Imperial College of Defence he served for a year or so in India. From then on he has been transferred from one post to another in the Ministry of Defence.

In 1941 I dedicated one of my books to Jack with the hope that in his chosen career he might one day wear the crossed swords of a General on his shoulders. It makes me very happy to be able to record that in 1974 I was able to dedicate another of my books to him as Major-General Sir John Younger, Bt, CBE.

Meg

I saw much less of Meg than of Joan's other children as she spent her early years in Scotland; and when she married John Moller, she continued to live there.

John had been a regular officer in the Cameron Highlanders but had retired as a Captain. He was both a fine shot and an outstandingly good fisherman.

He rejoined his Regiment for the war; but soon after it was over they came south and bought Hammer Court, near Liphook, where they have lived ever since.

Meg and John have three children: Caroline, Maxine and Christopher. In the late sixties John had the misfortune to suffer a severe stroke, but has since recovered sufficiently to enjoy the fishing that means so much to him. His son, Christopher, lives nearby in Hammer Vale where he has developed a trout farm. He is married to a lovely girl and they now have a daughter.

Bricklaying

In an earlier volume I have recorded how, while on the Western Front during the First World War, I built against a walled garden of a ruined *Château* a two-roomed snuggery that my friends christened 'Crooked Villa'.

It was not until thirty years later, when my wife and I went to live in Hampshire, that another opportunity occurred for me to lay some bricks.

In the Isle of Wight and South Hampshire many wavy walls are still to be seen. These were mostly built by French prisoners-of-war, at first confined on the Isle of Wight. The wars against the French Revolutionaries, and later Napoleon, went on for twenty-one years, with only one brief interval. A humane British statesman took the view that it would be cruelty to keep confined for year after year many prisoners who were still youngish men. The result was a decree that they should be allowed out as ticket-of-leave men to be employed as gardners.

It was they who built the attractive serpentine walls, said to have originated in Brittany. Such walls have practical advantages. In the first place no single depth brick wall of more than fifty feet in length can stand up against a really strong gale. Such walls must be buttressed by pillars every twenty feet or so. On the other hand a mile-long serpentine wall only one brick thick, without a single pillar, will stand up against any gale; the reason being that it has the strength of corrugated iron or paper. Wavy walls being only one brick thick, sunshine will warm them sufficiently to penetrate and ripen fruit on their north side. Espaliered gooseberries on the north of my serpentine walls used to ripen before those on the bushes in the fruit cage. A yet further factor in favour of them is that, should they face either south-west or south-east, instead of planting one's fruit trees in the centre of each bay one can plant them a little to one side so that they face south.

The bays of serpentine walls should not be too deep. I found the best measure to be about 20 feet per bay but only 18 inches deep in the centre.

Laying bricks is very suitable exercise for a middle-aged man. Any fool can lay bricks, providing he has patience. The amateur should never rush the job or attempt to lay along a line of stretched string. Every brick needs to be checked with a spirit level, otherwise the wall will become out of true. There is then no alternative other than pulling it down and starting again. A professional can lay a hundred bricks an hour. I reckoned I had done well if I averaged thirty; but once up my walls never fell down. And one of the rewards of bricklaying if done properly is that, unlike mowing the lawn or weeding, it never has to be done again.

Joan's mother

Joan's mother had spent her girlhood within a few miles of the Solent, as her father had been the Chief Verderer of the New Forest. Soon after we moved to 'Grove' she left Suffolk where she had spent most of her life, and bought a house in Lymington. She was a remarkable old lady, still with perfect sight and hearing, and pruning her roses well into her nineties. Through constantly watching TV, she could discuss all modern problems and she had a caustic wit. For Christmas dinner I always brought out my huge crystal goblets, which each held a half bottle of Champagne. On one occasion I remarked to her: 'These are suitable only for wine merchants and for kings.' Ignoring the fact that I had been a wine merchant, she promptly replied: 'They have come down in the world, haven't they?'

She died one morning of a heart attack while having breakfast in bed, only a few months after her ninety-ninth birthday.

A new friend

Soon after settling into 'Grove', we were introduced to a great personality who became for many years one of our real friends. This was Constance (always known to her intimates as Sheila), Duchess of Westminster.

She and her sister, afterwards Princess Pless, were Cornwallis-Wests, who lived when young at Newlands not far from Christchurch. Both were great beauties and, as the first wife of Bendor, Sheila had few rivals in London society.

The Duke – nicknamed Bendor from his racing colours – was to my mind the 'last of the Barons' and, as his wine merchant in the twenties, I learned quite a lot about him. He did as he wished and went wherever he wanted to go as the mood took him and without consulting anyone. He had complete outfits, from tennis flannels to tails, stored in trunks in over twenty hotels in different parts of Europe. He would drive to Victoria without a penny in his pocket, the top-hatted Station Master of those days would come scuttling out to greet him and show him into a reserved compartment on the Dover train. He would be received with equal deference on the cross-Channel boat and then in Paris. He never left word when he intended to return to London. At times when he had arranged to give a dinner party and nothing had been heard of him, this caused his staff acute anxiety, but he always turned up just in time for a bath and to put on the clothes that had been laid out for him.

Sheila loved Spain, went there many times and was a great friend of King Alfonso. Her albums of photographs taken in those days were fascinating, and when I wrote my book *Vendetta in Spain* (period 1908) she gave me invaluable help with local colour.

She was arrogant and treated her second husband, gentle old ex-Wing Commander 'Fitz', like a footman. But when she talked of the great houses in King Edward VII's and King George V's days she was spell-binding.

She was, too, a woman of great courage. On one occasion she was without the Duke on their big yacht, *Cutty Sark*, in Istanbul. It was Ramadan and she heard that a great ceremony was to be held in the St Sophia Mosque. She said she would like to go to it. The Captain replied: 'I am sorry, your Grace, but that is quite impossible. No women are ever allowed inside the Mosque at such a time.'

Sheila turned to the nearest *matelot* and said: 'Boy! Go down to my cabin and take off your clothes, then give them to my maid.' And dressed as a sailor she went to that ceremony unaccompanied, having been warned that if discovered she would be torn to pieces.

Dear Sheila died shortly before we left 'Grove'. She sent for us to come and sit with her for a while as she lay in bed slowly dying. She was a great lady and a real friend. Sadly, for the last time, we kissed her good-bye.

My mother's death

Since the death of her second husband, Sir Louis Newton, my mother had lived in a very comfortable flat at Wildcroft Manor on Wimbledon Common with my sister Muriel.

Up until about a year before her death my mother, who was then well on in her seventies, had been very fit for her age. But early in 1954 she had begun to suffer pains which were diagnosed as cancer of the breast. During the summer she spent several weeks in a nursing home having radium treatment. This appeared to be more or less successful, so when she returned to her flat, although she had to spend much of her time in bed, her doctor told me that she might hope to live for at least another year. So I went on holiday with no misgivings, and the cable informing me of her death came as a great surprise.

Since my mother's marriage to Sir Louis Newton – due I think to his influence upon her, although he showed no open dislike for me – she and I had not been on truly affectionate terms, so I thought it quite possible that she would leave everything to Muriel. On the other hand Muriel had been far from happy living with her mother and feared that if she did go to live in a flat on her own, our mother might leave the lot to me. So, a few years earlier, on one of Muriel's rare visits to 'Grove', we made a solemn pact that however mother left her money we would split it fifty-fifty.

In the event my mother left two-thirds to Muriel and one-third to me. As I was by then making a good income as an author I did not ask Muriel to keep to our secret pact; so, what with double death duties and other expenses, out of the quarter of a million that my grandfather left I came into only about £12,000.

Travels

During these years Joan and I travelled all over the world. Those fascinating journeys genuinely combined business with pleasure, since, while we very much enjoyed ourselves, I also derived a great deal of background information from them which I was able to use in my books. Just to give an example, here are two unforgettable incidents, both of which I subsequently introduced into the last Gregory Sallust novel, *The White Witch of the South Seas*.

I have often said when giving interviews that I have never been present at a Magical Ceremony of any kind, or even a séance, and this is the truth. But I came very near to doing so on my first night in Brazil. Knowing of my interest in the Occult, our friend Tony Wellington had very kindly arranged for us to attend a *Macumba* gathering. *Macumba* means communicating with the Loa (Voodoo gods) and calling them down to take possession of initiates. Crooked *Macumba* priests arrange fake parties of this kind to make money out of gullible tourists. But this was to be the real thing.

As a member of the British Embassy staff Tony had a pull with the police and he had arranged a police escort for us in case it was discovered that we were not members of the cult, and so be set upon by the crowd. Being white, of course, means nothing, as many thousands of rich, white people in Brazil are nominally Roman Catholics but, in fact, worship the *Macumba* gods.

After drinks with the Chief of Police, Joan and I, Tony and Pussy Wellington set off with him, accompanied by two detectives and two policewomen, all in plain clothes, in two cars and drove several miles out of the city through the dark forest. We pulled up at a place where there was already a long line of cars at the roadside, then walked up through the trees by a narrow stairway, made only of short boards kept in place by pegs of wood on which there were several chickens whose necks had been wrung, to the meeting-place. It was a little larger than a tennis court with tiers of benches on two sides; a third was occupied by a Voodoo altar with the usual offerings – fruit, flowers, Coca-Cola, rum and crude pictures of Christian saints.

Here the women were separated from the men. None too happily I watched the two policewomen lead Joan and Pussy to the benches at one side of the court while the policemen took Tony and me to seats on the other. We sat there for a time while the place filled up and several hundred people were jammed side by side on the benches. The ceremony then began.

An old, white-haired Negro smoking a pipe, in which we were told was marijuana, wearing dirty white clothes and a battered straw hat, walked out into the centre of the court, supporting himself with a stick. He was followed by a string of girls, mostly coloured. They were all wearing white frocks of the same pattern, with high collars, tight waists, then long skirts right down to their ankles. The old priest started a slow, shuffling dance; the girls formed a line with linked arms and in time to the beating of drums swayed backwards and forwards.

Then it began to rain. The night was very hot and there was not a breath of wind. Big drops of warm water splashed straight down upon us all. In a few minutes their intensity increased to a tropical downpour. Through the curtain of rain one could only just make out the figures on the court. Soaked to the skin they abandoned their slow, rhythmic movements and ran for cover. The spectators, too, left their benches and crowded towards the entrance of the enclosure. It was only with difficulty that we found Joan, Pussy and the two policewomen. The narrow staircase leading to the road had become a waterfall. Somehow we managed to get down it and find our cars. So I never witnessed any occult manifestations after all.

The cloudburst did not last long, but the following night the British Ambassador, Sir Leslie (Bunny) Fry, gave a dinner party for us, and on our way to the Embassy it began to rain heavily again. It emerged that the Ambassador had served in India under my wartime colleague, Colonel Sir Ronald Wingate. He was also a great fan of mine and wanted to talk to me about my books. This led to a rather curious arrangement at the dinner table, to which about twenty of us sat down. Instead of Joan being put next to the Ambassador, and myself at the other end of the table next to his wife, I was put at his end, with only a Brazilian lady between us; so that after a few polite words with her, he could talk across her all the time to me.

The Embassy was a fine Regency mansion, as diplomats had not yet been forced to go up and live at Brasilia, the grandiose new capital in the interior. No sooner had we joined the ladies for coffee in the *salon*, and Bunny made pleasant remarks to a few of them, than he drew me into a corner and continued, over a succession of brandies and sodas, to talk to me for over two hours. He had been our Ambassador in Budapest at the time of the uprising against the Russians and was most interesting about it. We had a number of friends in common, and I was pretty well up on the international problems of the day; so I had a very pleasant evening; but poor Joan had nothing in common with Bunny's wife and among the other people had met only Pussy, so she had a pretty dreary time.

When at last, well after midnight, I did get her away, we found that it had been pouring in torrents ever since we arrived. The drains were now choked and the street awash with water. Tony's car was in dock, so he had ordered a hired one, but it had not turned up and a very pleasant Brazilian couple offered to run us home.

The Wellingtons had an apartment high up in a big new block immediately behind which was the sheer cliff of a mountain. In front, below it, lay a small park, on one side of which was the President's Palace. It was a delightful situation, but to get there from the Embassy we had to go down to the waterfront before turning inland again. The road along the coast was axle-deep in water and in quite a number of cases it had swamped the engines of cars so that they stood there abandoned. To avoid a similar fate our driver had to go on to the hidden pavement, which gave him a few extra inches of height above the water. We then had to cross a large open space where monuments rose among flower-beds. It now appeared to be a bay, for one could not tell where the sea normally ended and the land began. Here were more abandoned cars, but beyond it the land rose slightly, so the water became shallower until we reached the limit of the flood, and our Brazilian friend got us safely home.

Yet this was only the beginning of the terrible calamity suffered by Rio that winter. For four days and nights the rain never ceased. Bridges were swept away by the torrents streaming down from the mountains. The city was cut off from all communication with the interior except by air. Every cellar, except for those of buildings high on the slopes, was flooded. Hundreds of cars in underground garages were ruined. Millions of pounds-worth of stores, edibles, clothes, books and other property in basements and ground-floor rooms were rendered useless. On the slopes fringing the city that ran down from the mountains were thousands of shacks made of dismembered packing cases and empty petrol tins. They were called *favelas* and in them lived the very poor. The rushing waters swept away these flimsy dwellings and their occupants with them. Hundreds were drowned and many thousands rendered homeless.

High up in the Wellingtons' apartment we were safe but besieged, as all the streets below had become rivers. Fortunately Pussy had a good stock of tinned things and Tony of drinks. There we waited and watched the unceasing rain streak down, until at last the weather cleared and we were able to resume our travels.

On another occasion when we toured the South Seas, we visited Suva, the capital of the Fiji Islands. Some twenty-five miles south east of Suva lies Beque Island famous for its fire-walkers. But the ceremony takes place, only a few times every year. A party of rich Americans had hired a steam yacht to take them over to see it, and we managed to get ourselves included in the party. The ship had to anchor some distance from the land and we transferred to motor-boats for the last two miles. Even then it was so shallow that we had to be carried several hundred yards to the beach by natives who waded out to meet us.

There the Chief was waiting to receive the party. Although there was apparently nothing to distinguish us from the rest of the rough line facing him, the old man walked straight up to Joan, bowed to her, gently took her arm and with me on his other side led us along a path up the hill.

We walked inland for a mile or so to a bowl in the hills where the natives danced and sang for us. On the bowl's far side there was a miniature grandstand – just two rows of about a dozen seats each. Fifty feet below us was a circular pit, roughly forty feet in circumference, filled with large stones. After the *Kava* ceremony, in which we drank from half coconut shells, the old Chief, who spoke excellent English, sat between Joan and me, and explained to us in a low voice about the fire-walking.

Every young man on Beque had to do it at least once as an act of faith in the protection of God. Those who refused

I

were expelled from the island. He had done it many times, but had recently been ill so was not conducting the ceremony that day. A log fire had been lit in the pit at 7.30 that morning and the stones then piled on to it. There were, too, many burning logs on top of the stones. The first proceeding was to clear these off. This was done by groups of natives on either side of the pit, throwing long ropes of *liana* across and with them dragging the burning wood out over the sides. Next, several natives used long poles to prod the stones so that they should lie flat and there be no risk of a protruding stone tripping a fire-walker. One of the poles snapped off about two feet from its far end and the piece immediately burst into flames, which proved that the stones were terrifically hot. Not far from the pit there was a hut. In it eight men had been shut up, fasting and praying for the past twenty-four hours. They now emerged from it in single file, wearing cotton shirts and leather shorts. Running to the pit they stepped down into it and walked slowly round it with expressionless faces. They afterwards showed us the soles of their feet. There was not a blemish or a blister on them. . . .

Work

Readers may well wonder how, with my brick-laying, gardening, jollifications with neighbours, weekends with friends in the country and travels abroad, I ever had time to write my books. But work I did, and put in more than the hours of a normal factory hand.

At nine-thirty my secretary arrived and I spent an hour or so dictating replies to the many letters I received. From about ten-thirty I worked on the book that I was writing. At one o'clock a short break for lunch; afterwards another hour's work until, say, half-past two. Then a nap on my sofa for, as Churchill had discovered long before me, work in the afternoon has almost invariably to be done again. Four o'clock and a cup of tea was brought to me. Then work until dinner time and, after dinner, till midnight or sometimes two o'clock in the morning. I had been brought up to work on Saturdays so – unless we were staying away, travelling, or had friends staying with us – I stuck to this routine six days a week.

On average we were travelling abroad about two months in every year and as I am not a quick writer I did not usually cover more than four sheets of foolscap a day; so it took me, with research, about seven months to produce a book.

My books were, on average, about 160,000 words, which is over twice the length of the ordinary thriller. But in the fact that my books were not ordinary thrillers lies the secret of their success. Actually to create each book I wrote and combined two. One of these would consist of a history of Ceylon or Mexico, or of a period in the Napoleonic or Hitler wars. Into these factual accounts I wove a spy story, desperate situations and boy jumping into bed with girl.

This blend proved amazingly successful as many people who normally never read thrillers would read a 'Wheatley' for the pleasure of recalling the country described, if they had visited it, or to learn about it or about some interesting historical events.

Of course it was hard work because the research had to be thorough. Innumerable young people read thrillers and I regard it as a crime for any author to distort the facts of history for the sake of his story. Many crises last for ten days or more. In that event my hero must be laid up with a sprained ankle, or something of that sort, until the genuine date arrives when he can play his part again.

I have tried most ways of getting my thoughts on paper, and from long experience have found that the method which gives the best results is pencil and india-rubber. If an author dictates, his mind goes too fast to get the best out of situations. When the typescript comes to him he must write additions on the top of the typed sheet, or even on the back of the page. He then tends to make his additions as short as possible, so fails to get the best out of a thrilling episode. By writing in longhand, too, he can see at a glance what he has put down and, if he has used a multi-syllable word twice in one paragraph, change one for another expression. And, of course, rubbing out pencilled words, instead of scratching out writing in ink, makes the draft much easier for one's secretary to type.

I have also found that it never pays to correct work a day or so after writing it. Somehow one does not spot the faults. The thing to do is to write about five chapters – say a month's work – and only then read and revise them before having them typed. After that one should leave it until the whole story has been typed; then read it through to make certain that a minor character who appears in an early chapter with blue eyes is not said in a much later one to have brown; and those kinds of details.

Months later the galley proofs come along. The publisher's proof-reader rarely spots more than a third of the printer's errors or mis-spellings. I naturally read a set myself, and I also get four other people to read sets. Each of them spots some error that the others have missed; and even when the page proofs arrive one finds in them a few oversights that must be corrected.

While at Lymington I wrote thirty out of my seventy-odd books. In addition to many in the Gregory Sallust and Roger Brook series I naturally wrote others about the Duke de Richleau and his companions 'Those Modern Musketeers', who featured in my first book (1933) *The Forbidden Territory*. One of them, about the Duke before he met the others, was *The Second Seal*. It covered the months of April to September 1914, describing the events which led up to the First World War and the first great clashes of the armies on both the Russian and Western Fronts. I consider it my best book.

When in Bavaria I stayed for some nights with that most distinguished teacher, Dr Kurt Hahn, who had formerly been headmaster of Gordonstoun and Prince Philip's tutor. I gave Kurt a copy of *The Second Seal*, and when he had finished it he said, 'Dennis, this book is remarkable. It gives the true facts about what happened and is just as fair to Germany and Austria as it is to Serbia, Russia, France and England. I intend to buy two hundred copies of it for my students. They loathe learning history from their school

books; but they will simply lap this up, and it will fix in
their minds what really happened.'

The Launching of Roger Brook

When I was in the Cabinet Offices I used to give little lunch
parties about once every ten days for a few of my colleagues
and senior officers with whom my work brought me into
contact. At one of them Air Commodore Kenneth Collier,
who was then Director of Plans, asked me:

'When the war is over, Dennis, and you can write another
novel, what will it be about?'

'I hardly know, sir,' I replied. 'As a writer of "thrillers",
by becoming a member of the JPS I've landed myself in a
pretty mess. Before I went into uniform, wide reading and a
knowledge of international affairs enabled me to write
interestingly on all sorts of matters as a background for my
spy stories. But, during the past two years, I have been given
access to every sort of secret and the way in which our intelligence systems really work. The war provides scores of plots
I could have used, but now I daren't or I'll find myself in the
Tower for having infringed the Official Secrets Act.'

He smiled at me, 'I think I can suggest a way out. All
you have to do is to create a hero who lived in Napoleonic
times. Then you can use any exciting episodes you learned
about in this war and nobody will be able to lay a finger on
you.'

The Napoleonic Wars were so very different from the war
we were then waging that, at the time, I was inclined to
laugh at the idea. But Collier was right, of course, that
personalities, loves and perils do not really alter with the
centuries – only methods of communication and weapons.
So, although the germ of the idea lay dormant for a long
time, in 1946 I decided to begin an historical series, and
wrote the first volume of it: *The Launching of Roger Brook*.
It eventually ran to a series of twelve volumes covering the
period 1785–1815 – the French Revolution, the rise and fall
of Napoleon, his Egyptian and Syrian campaigns, and
Roger's missions to Turkey, Persia, India, Brazil, the

Caribbean, the United States, Canada, St Petersburg and every other principal city in Europe.

Democracy

On our first post-war visit to Athens we were given a corner room on an upper floor of the Palace Athenée Hotel, from which we could see the Acropolis; and now it was floodlit every night, looking like a fairy palace.

It was on the slope of the mountain which it crowns that the first democratic government was established; but it was a very different form of democracy from that implied by the word today. Previously, the numerous States of Greece were ruled by Kings – or Tyrants as they were termed. The leading citizens of Athens decided to end that system. Two hundred or so of the most important merchants, philosophers, property owners, priests and shipping magnates constituted themselves into an assembly to debate the state of the nation and decide on measures which should be taken. They negotiated trade pacts with their neighbours, decreed such taxes as were to be imposed from time to time and whether there should be peace or war. The tens of thousands of other inhabitants of Athens had no say whatsoever in such matters.

This very sensible form of government has now degenerated into something very different from the original. Every male and female over the age of eighteen now has the right to vote in favour of the party which he or she *thinks* would govern the country best. But what are their qualifications for this? The standard of education of the vast majority is distressingly low. They do not read the serious papers, have little knowledge of what is happening in other countries, no knowledge at all of economics and have few interests outside local problems. How can it possibly be maintained that young fellows who tear up the seats of railway carriages or girls whose only thought is to have as much fun as possible without getting put in the family way should be allowed to have an equal right in electing a government as, let us say, a university Professor?

The solution was put forward by Nevil Shute in one of his novels. Everybody should have one vote, but the following qualifications should entitle anyone to extra votes – a university degree, a commission in one of the Services, having lived for five years or more in some other country, contributing to the nation in taxes more than a definite sum; so that it would be possible for exceptional people to have up to six votes. This system would ensure a continuance of democracy, but give greater weight to the opinions of people really qualified to judge the issues.

Bill and Poo

Early in 1961 we lost Joan's eldest son, Bill. I was more distressed by the news of his death than by any other event in my life and I actually shed tears, a thing I had not done since my infancy.

The signs of his budding brilliance appeared early. In 1935, when only seventeen, he wrote a book of verse called *Madonna and Other Poems*. Poetry, like pipe-smoking and ball games, is one of the things I have missed out on. I can enjoy what one might term narrative poetry, such as much of Kipling, Macaulay's *Lays of Ancient Rome* and so on, but the finer flights of fancy mean positively nothing to me. However, when Bill brought me his manuscript, seeing how much it meant to him, I took it to Hutchinson and had his poems published at my expense. They met with a very kind reception from the critics, and it can be imagined how delighted I was to have backed the boy when Howard Spring wrote of it, 'William Younger is writing better poetry than Byron did at his age'.

When he was twelve he had been stricken with poliomyelitis. It had the effect of checking his growth, so his height never exceeded more than about five feet five and, although not apparent when he was dressed, one of his arms was withered though still capable of use. In consequence he would not have been accepted in any of the Services. But immediately on the outbreak of war he became officially a member of MI5.

He was so secretive about his activities in MI5 that we nicknamed him 'the bearded oyster'; but from friends of mine under whom he worked I learned that he was very brave. Although he was so small he wangled his way into many Communist meetings armed only with a pair of knuckle dusters in his pocket.

After the war he continued as a permanent member of MI5 and soon after we had moved down to Lymington he married Nancy Leslie (*née* Brassey) – always known as Poo. She was the widow of Wing Commander Reginald Leslie, DSC, DFC, AFC, a distinguished pilot in the Royal Naval Air Service during the First World War. He rejoined in 1939 but was lost in 1943 when flying over the Mediterranean. During the war she had worked in the Air Ministry as PA to Sir William Teeling and also in one of our women's corps in Italy. I can hardly describe dear Poo better than quoting the dedication of one of my books to her: 'For Poo. The Life and Soul of the Party'.

William wrote three more books of poetry, then turned to detective fiction, published under the pseudonym of William Mole. They were good stories and the best of them, *The Hammersmith Maggot*, was quite outstanding. Poo also took to writing novels, good stories some of which were set in Central Europe, which she knew well from travels between the wars with her first husband. Bill and Poo then combined to write *Blue Moon in Portugal*, and it was hailed as the best book about interesting places in that country that had ever been written.

For the first years of their marriage they lived just off Knightsbridge, then they bought a house called 'Pelling', not far from Windsor. By that time a Trust created by Bill's grandmother had been broken, which had resulted in their becoming very well off. I always remember how I laughed when Poo told me what the woman who owned the fish shop in Windsor that she patronized said to her one day, 'It's only you, mum, and them up at the Castle wot really appreciates a bit of good fish.'

Unfortunately in the late fifties the owner of the fields adjacent to their garden sold them to be turned into a building estate. This would have destroyed the charm of 'Pelling', so they sold it and bought a house in London.

It was about this time that Bill decided to resign from MI5. Now he wished to devote himself entirely to writing, and he set about a work that required many months of conscientious research.

Early in 1961 Bill and Poo went for a holiday to Sicily. While staying in Taormina he caught Asiatic 'flu and had to go to bed. He did not appear to be in any danger and after a short spell the doctor told him that he could get up and would be fully recovered if he did not leave the hotel for the next few days. Those who have known the lovely sunshine in Taormina, high on its ledge above the sea, will appreciate the temptation to go out and enjoy it. Feeling that no harm could come to him, Bill did go out for an hour or so's stroll. That night he had a relapse. A specialist was telephoned for. Before he arrived Bill was dead.

After many months' labour he had just finished the big book he had been working on. It was called *Gods, Men and Wine* and was an account of man's cultivation of the vine from the earliest ages up to the great wines of France and Germany that we enjoy today.

It was published posthumously by George Rainbird in a beautiful edition with many coloured illustrations. It won a prize at the International Book Fair at Frankfurt and is now regarded as a classic on its subject. When I read the dedication I was touched beyond words. It was 'For Dennis, who taught me to love fine wine.'

Cadogan Square

For the first sixteen years that we lived in Lymington whenever we came up to London we stayed, at first, at the United Hunts Club, then at Brown's Hotel. Then in 1961 we acquired a flat of our own.

The Marquess of Donegall had long been a friend of mine. He was a great *raconteur* and over the years we had many a jolly meal together.

Although he and his first wife were not living together,

she was adamant in her refusal to divorce him when he fell in love with the charming Maureen Mackenzie. Maureen had the first floor flat at No. 60, Cadogan Square, and he lived round the corner in Clabon Mews.

In 1961 he was informed by his advisers that he could obtain a divorce which would be valid in England if he lived for a certain period in Switzerland. It was decided that they should both go there and, while he retained his house in Clabon Mews, she should sell her flat. Having learned this one night at dinner, and the price asked for the lease, I telephoned next day and said I would like to buy it. Don was most generous and said that as I had saved him commission he would not take a penny for the heaters, fittings, curtains and so on, which saved me several hundred pounds.

We had ample surplus furniture at 'Grove' so, apart from redecorating No. 60, it did not cost us much to move in, a month or two later; and from then on enjoy this well-situated flat with its large and lofty rooms whenever we came to London.

A very different book

Colonel Sheridan, a cloak-and-dagger chap with whom I had numerous friendly dealings during the war, wrote and asked me if I would come to see him in his office.

It emerged that he was now associated with the Foreign Office and was one of the top boys concerning Propaganda. He wanted me to write a romance for publication in the Near East. Under cover of an exciting love story it was to back up the old Muhammedan faith and reveal the evils resulting from Communism.

This was a tricky business because it had to be of the highest morality; not even kissing permitted until a couple were married; but I took it on. The bones of the story I wrote were a fine, young businessman in love with a lovely girl who sold scent in the bazaar. A Russian diplomat falls for her and lures her into the garden of the Soviet Embassy where, in a summer house, he tries to rape her. She pulls a knife from under her clothes and kills him. She is then arrested and charged with murder.

It was many years since I had read the Koran but I vaguely recalled a passage in it which I managed to find. After hearing the case the *Kadi* (magistrate) declared: 'It is written by the Prophet, blessed be his name, [*verse so and so*] that every woman, even a slave, has the right to defend her honour by any means she is able to do so.'

I called the book *Of Vice and Virtue*. Sheridan and his colleagues were delighted with it and particularly my use of the Koran to save my heroine. No English version, other than my typescript, exists. It was printed in Arabic and, I believe, Persian; but I have only a copy of the former. Anyhow, I was told that it became a bestseller in the Near East.

Early on, the question arose of how much I should be paid for this little effort. By that time each new book of mine was earning thousands. But it was then suggested that for such an operation the use of Secret Funds was fully justified, and these would be tax free; so I readily agreed that I would be happy to settle for a very much smaller sum in cash. When the time came my only problem was how to convey several hundred pounds in notes from Sheridan's office to my bank without risking one of my pockets being picked, or an accident enabling someone to relieve me of a good wad of notes by just putting a hand in my pocket. I solved this by bringing with me a dozen or more large safety pins. Sheridan stuffed all the notes into my two hip pockets then cross-pinned them so that it would take a good ten minutes to get them out.

Hammer Films

Towards the end of 1968 I at last received an offer for the film rights on two of my books. Christopher Lee, unknown to me, had long been a fan of mine and was pressing Colonel Carreras of Hammer Films to make *The Devil Rides Out*.

Christopher took the part of the Duke de Richleau and

played the role magnificently. Another factor which led to the great success of the film was that the script-writer stuck, as far as film technique permitted, to the story. I wrote to him at Hollywood to thank him for that. His reply was, 'I have written several novels myself and had their film versions murdered by script-writers; so when I became a script-writer myself, I swore that I would never mess up another author's story.'

Hammer also made my *Uncharted Seas*, re-christening it *Lost Continent*. But the story was entirely altered, with the result that it was less successful.

Characters in my books

I have often been asked how many of my characters have been taken from real life. The answer is very few.

Simon Aron, the generous, kindly, little Jew who appeared in my first book, *The Forbidden Territory*, and several others featuring my four Modern Musketeers, was a deliberate portrait of my friend Mervyn Baron.

Lady Veronica Wensleydale, who featured in *Black August*, was also a portrait. In real life she was Betty Jopling and married first Sir Lionel Earle, for twenty years permanent Secretary of State at the Office of Works. To him we owe most of the beauty of our parks and the handsome neo-Georgian designs of many public buildings erected in his time. Later Betty became the Marquise de Chasseloup Laubat. She was one of the gayest people I have ever known, and Joan's best friend.

Rudd, who appeared in a number of Gregory Sallust stories as his cockney manservant, was taken from Lewis, my second cellarman when I was a wine merchant, of whom I was very fond.

Gregory Sallust was, physically at least, copied from my great friend of the First World War, Gordon Eric Gordon-Tombe, to whom I owe so much of my general knowledge and literary education. But, apart from ruthlessness, the characters of Gordon Eric and Gregory as he developed had little in common.

Canon Copley Syle, in *To the Devil – a Daughter*, is often
taken for a portrait of Aleister Crowley, but this is not so.
Copley Syle was modelled on the Reverend Montague
Summers. Mocata in *The Devil Rides Out* was much more like
Crowley, although that was not a conscious attempt at a
portrait. I can think of no others based on real people.

I often get letters from readers suggesting that the Duke
de Richleau is a copy of myself. That is very flattering. I
would like it to be, and the ideas he expresses are often my
own, but I fear I lack his nobility of character. He rivals
Roger Brook as my favourite character. Had I lived in his
age I would like to have been Roger, but, alas, I would have
lacked his courage. I have a very soft spot, too, for Sir
Pelinore Gwaine-Cust.

We leave 'Grove'

1969 was a year of upheaval for us. It started smoothly enough
by our having a winter holiday in Nice. We were met at the
airport by our old friends, the Donegalls, who had been
living in Vevey for several years. We were very happy
to see a lot of them and on one occasion Don took me to
Adrian Conan Doyle's castle, where he showed me over his
museum and the special room which is a replica of that of
Sherlock Holmes's in Baker Street.

It was on our return that the upset started. For several
years a Captain Georges and Mrs Betty Pigache had occupied the servants' wing at 'Grove'. He was an unusual
character who had lived rich as a young man. His family
had owned the Café Royale and he had had a set in Albany.
I believe there was nothing about cooking that he did
not know; but he never cooked for us, nor, having still
a small private income, would he ever be employed by me
in any way. He was a jovial chap, had received a Mention
in Despatches in the First World War, and spent a great part
of his time simply yarning in pubs up in the town with
other old soldiers. It was, I suspect, his generosity that had
brought him low financially. For some years he and Betty
had run a small hotel, and I'm sure all the profits went in

free drinks to people he liked. Betty, who cooked for us very well indeed, made an excellent housekeeper.

Georges suddenly decided that they should retire and live in a council house. Why, when they had complete privacy in a fine, roomy flat, goodness alone knows. True, they were getting on in years but Betty had no wish to leave us – she still comes to see us when she is up in London – and one of our 'women in' cleaned the kitchen quarters for her. But their son, young Georges, a charming youth who had spent his boyhood at 'Grove' and qualified as a teacher for handicapped children, was just about to marry and emigrate to Canada. That perhaps influenced old Georges's decision.

To secure a British couple whom we liked to replace the Pigaches proved impossible. The situation was aggravated by the approaching retirement of my good, old-fashioned gardener, Bob. And what is the fun in having a sizeable country house if you cannot have members of your family and friends to stay in comfort?

Our problem was solved for us quite unexpectedly. The tenants of the second-floor flat at 60 Cadogan Square were Australians. They wished to dispose of the remainder of their lease and return to their own country. I at once made an offer for it which was accepted. But when I saw a Mr Murray, who had the lease of the whole house from the Cadogan Estate, he objected to certain alterations I proposed to make. Then, after a while he said: 'Let me retain the third-floor flat at a token rent and for £1000 I'll sell you the leases for the whole house.' It was a good deal for him, and it suited me.

From then on Joan and I spent many hectic weeks, changing all the rooms round, putting in a private lift between the two floors and having both redecorated. Added to which, we had to take innumerable decisions about 'Grove'. In selling the house I had very bad luck; in disposing of a large part of its contents very good luck.

My solicitors thought the freehold of the house and grounds should fetch £40,000. To be on the safe side we put a reserve of only £30,000 on it; but it did not even fetch that. The Auction was on the 30 September and it was bought in for £28,000. The trouble was that it was too big for a private house, unless one could be certain of getting satisfactory servants and gardeners, and it was not large enough for a school, hotel or nursing home. Some days later when I went to London to spend my first night in my new home, my solicitors telephoned me that they had received a firm offer of £29,000. I accepted it rather than run to the expense and trouble of a second auction on the off-chance of getting a bigger price.

I sold 'Grove Place' in the hope that it would continue to be protected as a perfect example of a small Georgian Manor House. But this was not to be, and sadly this beautifull house was eventually demolished and about a score of terrace houses were built in its garden. All that survives is the serpentine wall which I built.

What to take and what to leave behind to be auctioned at 'Grove' was an appalling problem. At No. 60 we had eight main rooms of a fair size, but they were already furnished, and accommodation had to be alloted for me to write in, for my secretary, and for literally tons of files and papers and my 4000 books.

We sent nearly everything with which we had furnished our first-floor flat at No. 60 down to the country, and brought most of our more precious possessions to London. But certain things we were fond of just had to be left behind because they would have occupied too much space in the flat. And, of course, there were lots of beds, bedding, wardrobes, kitchen and garden utensils that we no longer required.

Southern Television, on which I had appeared a number of times, sent a team over from Southampton to interview me and take shots of both the interior of the house and the gardens.

The showing of this film undoubtedly had the effect of enormously increasing the number of people who came to look over the house. On the two view days, 27 and 28 September, the place was a seething mass from nine in the morning until nine at night.

The sale was on 1 and 2 October, in a big marquee on the lawn. The auctioneer said, 'What am I bid?' Someone started off at perhaps £2 – then £3, £4, £6, £8, £10, £12,

£16, £18. Auctioneer: 'It's against you; the lady in the front there.' £20. '£20, £20; going at £20. Sold.' It went on like that for hour after hour. Someone even paid £50 for a garden seat I had made out of three curved and four straight kerbstones cemented together. Joan and I netted over £11,000 for things very few of which we regretted parting with. And so to London as our permanent home.

Religion

Forty-minute-long sermons on Sundays when I was at my preparatory school made me antagonistic to the Christian Church at an early age, and as I grew older my reason confirmed this dislike.

Yet reason also told me that a non-corporeal power, which we call 'spirit', must exist to account for many happenings. Through the ages there have been too many well-vouched-for supernatural manifestations for them all to be dismissed as dreams, fantasies, hallucinations, and since so great a proportion of them emanate from human beings, it is reasonable to believe that every living person has a spirit within them.

If this is so what happens to the spirit when the body dies? The Christian religion teaches that the spirit is brought before the judgement seat of God and on its performance in the body it has left it is elevated to enjoy eternal bliss or condemned to suffer everlasting torment.

Could any belief be more implausible than that a spirit's timeless future depends upon its behaviour during a single life on earth? What of children who die before they can be made fully aware by their elders of what we consider right and what wrong? What of children made bitter and resentful from having been born with some incurable disease or physical handicap? What of children born to criminal parents and taught from youth that success in life depends on the ability to lie and cheat successfully? What of the person of blameless life until a moment arrives when, driven to uncontrollable exasperation, he commits murder?

Other religions have taught that the spirit in each person

has inhabited many bodies; that the body is only an envelope and when it ceases to function, in due course, its spirit is reincarnated in another, chosen by the powers that control all things, as most suitable for it. This progression of the spirit through many ages is based upon the belief that it is a growing thing; that in each life it has some lesson to learn. At times it may slip backward, but in due course it conquers greed, impulses to violence, meanness, injustice and other evil tendencies until it achieves complete serenity and happiness in helping other spirits that are still bound to the flesh to progress.

Where I first heard of these beliefs and whether from a person or a book I cannot recall, but I certainly accepted them as the only logical and just explanation of life on earth and of life after death, while still in my teens. I am a convinced believer in Reincarnation.

Old age creeps on

By 1974 both Joan and I were beginning to feel our age. In spite of my tendencies to cirrhosis, diabetes and chest trouble, I kept fairly fit and people were always saying how young I looked for my age, but Joan's condition became very poor. All her vital organs are perfectly sound, she still keeps up with events and enjoys reading five or six books every week; but the strength of her legs has sadly decreased, so that she has to keep them up nearly all the time, and she tires very easily.

In August Hutchinson published *Desperate Measures*, the final novel in my Roger Brook series. I then decided that I would write no more fiction, but endeavour to complete my Memoirs, a part of which I had already written.

I lunched out at my Club, or by invitation elsewhere, two or three times a week. But home entertaining had to be cut down to asking just a couple of old friends to come in for a drink between six o'clock and seven-thirty, as a greater number at one time tired Joan too much.

Looking back

From the beginning I have been incredibly lucky. Yet it is
not luck alone that has enabled me to fly year after year to
beauty spots all over the world, enjoy the most expensive
food and knock back bumpers of Champagne.

It has meant countless hours of very hard work. Except
when on holiday or having friends to stay I have always
treated Saturday as a full working day. Allowing eight weeks
a year for travel and other times taken off, during my forty-
five years as a writer I have worked thirteen hours a day
for six days a week, often until two o'clock in the morning.

The result has been seventy-four fiction and non-fiction
books. My first, *The Forbidden Territory*, was reprinted seven
times in seven weeks; and every one that followed it has also
proved a bestseller. My work has been published in thirty-one
languages and by now nearly fifty million copies of my books
will have been sold.

As a high proportion of these books have gone to lending
libraries, where each copy of a book is read by a hundred
or more people, the number of hours of enjoyment I have been
privileged to provide must be astronomical.

Among the many thousands of letters I have received
from readers, a considerable number have been from patients
in hospital who say that while reading my stories they have
been able to forget their pain. That is a wonderful thing
and for the gift which has enabled me to do this I am
truly grateful. I have enjoyed my life to the full and it
makes me happy to think that it has not been altogether
wasted.

Joan and I have decided to go abroad no more. We have
travelled in sixty-one countries but every year cities and
holiday resorts now become less attactive, and packing to
go away a more laborious chore.

I have also decided to write no more. My last fiction book
having been published in 1974, I then started these memoirs.
The first volume was published in January 1977, but I
doubt if I shall be here to see the last one on sale. That is

why I am finishing them now, the day before Queen Elizabeth's II's Jubilee Day 1977, which is rather appropriate as I was born in 1897, the year of Queen Victoria's Diamond Jubilee.

The families of my wife and myself now number forty, including four great-grandchildren. The older ones have done much to contribute to our happiness; so we have been greatly blessed.

My life both in private and public has been one of extraordinary good fortune and I am deeply grateful to all those who have shared my joys and wished me well. But 'The Party's Over Now'.

EPILOGUE

DENNIS Wheatley died on 10 November 1977. Some days earlier, he was visited by his old friend, Cyril 'Bobby' Eastaugh, retired Lord Bishop of Peterborough. During the whole of their long friendship, going back more than fifty years, the Bishop had never ministered to him pastorally; but at this final meeting he did so and gave him conditional absolution. It is clear that this was not merely a courteous gesture to the religious susceptibilities of his old friend; because he subsequently wrote to another dear friend, Derrick Morley, saying how much he had appreciated Bobby's visit and that he felt at peace having received conditional absolution. It would therefore seem that he died a Christian.

The funeral service was conducted by the Bishop at Putney Crematorium; and, in accordance with his express wish, his ashes were buried at Brookwood Cemetery. The place is marked by a small tombstone, simply inscribed: 'Dennis Wheatley 8.1.97–10.11.77 "Prince of Thriller Writers" RIP.'

ANTHONY WHEATLEY

INDEX

Compiled by Gordon Robinson

Dennis Wheatley's work has been published in:

Belgium	Switzerland
Brazil	Turkey
Czechoslovakia	The Unitd States
Denmark	Yugoslavia
Finland	
France	
Germany	
Holland	*also in*
Hungary	Arabic
Italy	Armenian
Mexico	Flemish
Norway	Hindi
Poland	Maltese
Portugal	Russian
Rumania	Serbian
Spain	Slovene
Sweden	Thulu